THE SOUTHEAST ASIA CONNECTION

The Southeast Asia Connection

Trade and Polities
in the Eurasian World Economy
500 BC–AD 500

Sing C. Chew

berghahn
NEW YORK · OXFORD
www.berghahnbooks.com

First published in 2018 by

Berghahn Books

www.berghahnbooks.com

© 2018 Sing C. Chew

Library of Congress Cataloging-in-Publication Data

A C.I.P. cataloging record is available from the Library of Congress

British Library Cataloguing in Publication Data

A catalogue record for this book is available from the British Library

ISBN 978-1-78533-788-8 hardback
ISBN 978-1-78533-789-5 ebook

For my mother
(1923–2015)
Place of Birth: Medan, Sumatra, Dutch East Indies

Contents

Figures and Tables

Figures

Tables

Preface

This book had its origin almost fifteen years ago. In the course of writing my trilogy on world ecological degradation over world history, I came across literature on the Nanhai Trade that discussed the trading relations of China with Southeast Asia. What struck me was the volume of trade, the vast number of kingdoms, and the level of urbanization that existed in early Southeast Asia. It seems to me then that the writings of Southeast Asia, and even now, painted an image of the "peripherality" of the region, and did not fully account for what has been presented empirically in some of the studies I have read, and especially during the period between 200 BC and AD 500. Unfortunately, at that point in time, other obligations prevented me from pursuing further this issue. The passage of time and the many opportunities extended to me to visit Southeast Asia for lectures, workshops, and colloquia have given me the opportunity to complete this book, which attempts to address this discrepancy, and thus my attempt for a reconstructed historical account of Southeast Asia's place in the world economy from 200 BC to AD 500.

Many scholars, colleagues, and students have contributed to the research and the writing of this book. My initial collection of Southeast Asian literature was facilitated by the prompt and generous email responses of Charles Higham and Miriam Stark. Tom Hoogervorst kindly sent me a copy of his doctoral dissertation on Southeast Asia before its publication. Philippe Beaujard provided me with useful comments and critique on the manuscript, and additional literature sources. Tom Hall, Bill Thompson, Wang Gung-wu, Dan Sarabia, Matthias Gross, Alvin So, Bob Denemark, and Mitch Allen read chapters of the manuscript and provided remarks and useful comments. Any errors or omissions are solely mine.

I wish to note the various invitations extended to me to present the themes of this book in various colloquia, conferences, and public lectures in the United States, Hong Kong, Australia, and Singapore. Wang Gung-wu generously made arrangements for me to be a visiting fellow at the National University of Singapore so that I could conduct the research for this book and present some of the themes of this book to the university. I benefited from a brief stay at the Hong Kong University of Science and Technology through an invitation from Alvin So. I also had the opportunity to visit the Sungai Batu excavations in Malaysia, kindly arranged by Mokhtar Saidin of the Universiti Sains Malaysia during one of my regional trips. Invitations from Youngho Chang to give public lectures at Nanyang Technological University on environmental issues provided further opportunity to conduct research for this book.

Alex Melinkoff was a wonderful research assistant, and Kathy Corridan (interlibrary loan coordinator) provided excellent searches for obscure books and articles, and permissions for late returns. Annie Thomsen, who has been responsible for drawing all the maps in my previous books, deserves my thanks as well for this one. I would like to thank my former editor/publisher Mitch Allen, who not only provided editorial comments but also helped to place this manuscript with Berghahn Books. At Berghahn, I wish to thank my editor, Caryn Berg, for her assistance and prompt responses to my queries. I would also like to thank Rebecca Rom-Frank and Lizzie Martinez for their efforts in the production process of this book, and Lynn Otto for her careful copyediting.

The writing of this book was made more relaxing by my dear late friend, Cooper (2010–2015), who passed away unexpectedly and prematurely. While he was alive, his bark, along with Elsa's, reminded me of the need to go for our daily walks along the banks of the Mad River and Clam Beach. Finally, as always, my wife, Elizabeth, encouraged profusely my completion of this project.

Sing C. Chew
McKinleyville, California

Southeast Asia in World History
Macrohistorical Considerations and World System History

Southeast Asia in World History

Southeast Asia's place and contribution to the world economy prior to the 1500s, especially in the early millennia of the current era (first century AD),[1] have been much overlooked by scholars.[2] Sandwiched between India and China, Southeast Asia has often been viewed as a region of just peripheral entrepôts, especially in the early centuries of the current era. Its geographic location and most of the type of products it exported from its mainland and islands further reinforced the perceived peripherality of the region. From the perspectives of most scholars analyzing and comparing the Indian, Arab, Chinese, and later European civilizations, Southeast Asia has been viewed mostly as a way station on the vast Maritime Silk Roads of the world trading system. The region's trade ties have been understood and viewed historically as being connected to the two (then) core centers (China and India) of the world economy that it has geographic proximity to, and thus further underscoring its assumed peripheral status. In world historical analyses, even by those like the late Abu Lughod (1989) whose work has shown sensitivity to the rise and fall of world system hegemonic dominance dating back to the twelfth century, Southeast Asia is not given its due.[3] For Abu-Lughod, following others, Southeast Asia is also viewed as a peripheral region that is no more than a set of trade entrepôts. However, such widespread perceptions do not mesh with recent archaeological evidence and assemblages that show established and productive polities existing in Southeast Asia in the early parts of the current era and long before. In order to reorient these commonly shared views of Southeast Asia's peripheral socioeconomic and political status, a recalibration of the interactions of Southeast Asia with other parts of the Eurasian world economy is required. To do this, it is necessary to place Southeast Asia in the dynamics of a world history of an evolving world economy (economy of the world). For the period between 200 BC to AD 500, it was a time of large volumes of trade exchanges occurring via land and sea in an increasingly connected Eurasian world. In Southeast Asia's case, the region was connected by land and sea routes crisscrossing its mainland land mass and its archipelago and islands. Southeast Asian goods thus were shipped mainly on the Maritime Silk Roads for exchanges between the East and West of the Eurasian world, and such exchanges rose and fell following the rhythms of expansion and contraction of the Eurasian world system.

To reset the commonly accepted position and status of Southeast Asia in the world economy then, this book proposes to reexamine the past. The object is to offer a revisionist interpretation of Southeast Asia's place in world history. From recent archaeological findings and historical literary accounts, a world system of trade connections involving Southeast Asia has existed by perhaps 200 BC or earlier. Such findings on trading goods being exchanged between the Mediterranean and South Asia and eastward to Southeast Asia and China have revealed a set of trading contacts between ports of these regions. Such a system connected Europe, the Mediterranean, the Arabian Peninsula, East Africa, the Persian Gulf, central Asia, South Asia, Ceylon, Southeast Asia, and China through a series of both land and sea trading routes, commonly known as the Silk Roads. Trade exchanges via land and sea, along with the movement of peoples, defined this system. China was at one end, with the Roman Empire at the other end, and central Eurasia, South Asia, and Southeast Asia geographically somewhat in the middle of the system.

In view of the above, we can define the extent and coverage of this world system of trading connections in operation from mid-prehistory onward as extending across seven regions: Europe/Mediterranean, East Africa, Arabian Peninsula and the Gulf, South Asia, Southeast Asia, central Asia, and China/East Asia. Given the scope of these trade connections extending over seven regions of the world, excluding the Americas that were not part of the system at this point in time, this historical economic linkage can be viewed as the "first Eurasian world economy" in terms of geographic extent. Thus, this book will highlight Southeast Asia's participation in this world trading system and the importance of its trading goods as commodities for consumption in the first Eurasian world economy. For by then, the Southeast Asian region was an important node of this world trading system.

By no means can an in-depth examination of Southeast Asia's participation in the Eurasian world economy be attempted without considering the rhythmic socioeconomic trends of expansion and contraction that underlie the dynamics of a world economy, and their influences on the socioeconomic and political structures and the economic trends of Southeast Asia. Pari passu, the expansion of Southeast Asian socioeconomic activities exporting commodities to a growing Eurasian world economy also further transformed the volume of consumption and habits of the other parts of the system, especially in the core areas. Such expansion of commodities consumption, in certain ways, turned what was previously elite luxury consumption to the level of mass consumption with the expansion of the world economy, and the concomitant rise in urbanization and population levels throughout the system. The consumption of Southeast Asian incenses, spices, medicinal plant products, etc., for example, before considered commodities only for the elites, increasingly became mass consumption items utilized in religious practices and health prescriptions. This transformation was reflected in the volume of exports to meet the needs of China, India, and other parts of the Eurasian world economy, such as the Roman Empire.

Besides the above, Southeast Asia's dynamic economies and polities led to technological innovations in the area of seafaring. These technologies were transferred to the neighboring regions of the Indian Ocean and the South China Sea. Furthermore, some of Southeast Asia's crops were transplanted, though much earlier than my period of study, to the Indian Ocean region, as recent studies have shown.[4] At the regional level, Southeast Asia's coastal trading ports, its riverine communities, and its agrarian kingdoms located on the mainland were always interconnected, even much earlier to my period of investigation as evident by the distribution of the bronze Dong Son drums, for example, throughout the mainland and islands of Southeast Asia. Such connections fostered a regional trade network stretching from Burma to the Philippine Islands whereby varied commodities were exchanged throughout the region.

Macrohistorical Considerations and World System History

Macro Structure and Duration

Prehistoric socioeconomic and political connections between regions that are separated by rivers, mountains, seas, and oceans spanning from Europe, central Asia, South Asia, Southeast Asia, and China have long been identified and pinpointed by archaeologists, historians, historical geographers, sociologists, and ethnographers (see for example, Kristiansen 1998, 2005; Algaze 1993; Beaujard 2005, 2010; Chase-Dunn and Hall 1997; Chew 2001, 2007, 2015; Earle and Kristiansen 2010; Frank 1993; Higham 2002, 2006, 2011; Higham and Higham et al. 2011; Higham and Kijngam 2010; Ratnagar 1981, 2004; Rowlands et al. 1987; A. Sherratt 1997; Wilkinson 2000). Rather than viewing the social evolution of these social communities in the above regions as transforming within their ecological and natural environments apart from other social systems, the identification of such prehistoric linkages and connections suggest a social evolutionary process that is not only interactive within the specific particular locale's natural and ecological environments, but also between different locales/regions. The uncovering of such connectivity occurring during prehistory further suggests that these linkages are not necessarily time dependent whereby the connections only emerged later in the historic period, as exemplified by the European voyages of discovery or as a result of advances in technology and knowledge that enables such linkages. Instead, these structural connections have existed in certain regions of the world—depending on the state of social evolutionary capacities of the social systems—for at least five thousand years.

Given such identifications and evidence, the theoretical and methodological arguments for an overarching structural framework that circumscribes and conditions the social evolutionary process of these socially connected human systems not only provides an explanatory dimension but also offers a more holistic understanding of the evolutionary trajectory of world history. If, however, only an isolated locale–dependent methodological approach was pursued, certain dynamics and tendencies would otherwise have not been mapped and captured for our overall understanding of the social evolutionary processes at the world historical level. Increasingly therefore, we need to address the flows and connections that link human systems over world history so that we can explain the historical patterns that determine the trajectory and forces that conduce the human enterprise, in other words, a world system history.

With the increasing efforts to explore and understand the dynamics and character of the social evolution of human communities along such lines of connectivity and interactions within and between regions over the course of world history, a careful articulation of the theoretical and methodological framework(s) will place my presentation of historical information and dynamics of Southeast Asia in a clearer light. Therefore, using a historically informed theoretical perspective to decipher the historical patterns and dynamics will give us a theoretically informed account of Southeast Asia in world history. It will enable us to recast our interpretation and understanding of the received history of Southeast Asia.

The positing of macrohistorical structures such as a world system/economy can be found in the writings of the French Annales School of historians, for example. Their approach covers several levels of analysis, stretching from deep structures to specific *conjonctures* and events. Such a methodological approach honors the role of time or duration and the specific concatenation of events and structures (such as climate and geography) in the explanation of historical outcomes. One of the Annalistes, Fernand Braudel (1972, 2001), in trying to understand the dynamics of the trajectories of the societies and civilizations surrounding the Mediterranean Sea, revealed how this region's transformations were shaped by its structural dynamics, which were physical, socioeconomic, political, and temporal in character. This structural whole underlies the material basis of the reproduction of the socioeconomic and political aspects of an area which the structural unit encompasses geographically and temporally.[5] For Braudel, this structural whole has its dynamic histories of *la longue durée, conjonctures, et événements*. This historical structural whole for Fernand Braudel (1981, 1982, 1984) became categorized as a "world-economy" with a set of dynamics and trends when his studies moved beyond the Mediterranean Sea to document the history of world transformations, capital accumulation, and the rise of capitalism.

Braudel's macrostructural framework for explaining world historical transformation was embraced by Immanuel Wallerstein (1974, 1980, 1988, 2011), who adopted the Braudelian structural whole (with its trends and dynamics) as an analytical concept and a tool to account for the course of world history from AD 1500 onward, and to explain how world transformations occurred within the dynamics of this world-system/economy, which had its origins in western Europe. With his choice of the temporal starting point (sixteenth century AD) for the rise of the European world-economy, and that this system was capitalistic in nature, the assumption for Wallerstein was that this world-system existed only from the sixteenth century onward and not before. This belief fits well with most contemporary scholars at that time, especially when the system is assumed to be capitalistic, and that capitalism as a "mode of production" is not supposed to exist prior to this period as feudalism is supposed to hold sway in western Europe then. That is the standard understanding of most Marxist and non-Marxist scholarship then and now, and this also included contemporary economic historians' interpretation of the making of the modern world. However, this time bracketing and the pinpointing of the nature of the mode of accumulation (capitalism), if it stays unchanged, pose a methodological conundrum for historical materialist studies in the social and historical sciences that adopt a macrohistorical structural approach but wish to focus on the prehistoric economic and political relations in world history.

How then to proceed? The late Abu-Lughod's work (1989) mapping an earlier world-system of global trade connections stretching from Asia to Europe and developing by the mid-thirteenth century prompted a reconsideration of the timing issue for the emergence of the world-economy. If there was an earlier system, as Abu-Lughod (1989) has insisted, it expands our understanding of the evolution of the world economy.[6] It opens up the possibility of considering that a macrohistorical structure was evolving through time, encompassing and connecting geographic space and human communities. Of course, like any academic finding and debate, such an articulation of a/the world economic structure existing three hundred years earlier than that posited by Wallerstein (1974) further prompted questioning of the emergence, evolution, and formation of the world system by a number of scholars (see, e.g., Denemark et al. 2000; Frank and Gills 1993). Questions—such as has there been only one world-system or were there several successive world-systems, or has there been only a single world system that has been evolving for the past five thousand years—were raised (Abu-Lughod 1993; Beaujard 2005, 2010; Chase-Dunn and Hall 1997; Frank and Gills 1993; Modelski and Thompson 2000; Wilkinson 2000).

Notwithstanding the deliberations over the existence of the number of world systems existing at a given time, another dimension of the intellectual discourse—besides the accusation of Eurocentrism because of the AD 1500 dating of the emergence of the world-system by Wallerstein—covers the debate on the nature of capitalism and its timing of emergence and transition to the capitalist mode of production. Basically, there were two main strains in the debate, one by Gunder Frank and Barry Gills (1996, 2002), who argue that capital accumulation (in this context, capitalism) has existed for thousands of years, and the other expounded by Wallerstein, who suggests otherwise (1991, 1999). In the latter's case, capitalism has been in operation only for the last five hundred years. This debate has implications for my present study as the debate attempts to clarify the specific characteristics and nature of the concept of capitalism and the period of its emergence. Over the last three decades, these latter questions and debates were addressed by various scholarly treatises that have been published on these issues concerning the formation and evolution of a/the world system(s) and the nature of capitalism (see, e.g., Wallerstein 1974, 1991, 1999; Abu-Lughod 1989; Amin 1974, 1991, 1999; Arrighi 1994, 1999, 2007; Beaujard 2005, 2010; Chase-Dunn and Hall 1997; Chew 2001, 2007; Denemark et al. 2000; Ekholm and Friedman 1982; Frank and Gills 1993; Modelski and Thompson 2000; Wilkinson 2000).

In the context of this book, with my interest in locating Southeast Asia in world history, it is very clear that the encompassing process or incorporation of regions via trade exchanges structure the linkages of the world economy. Trade by no means is only an exchange of goods; along with it comes an exchange of knowledge and belief systems (religion, for example) as well. In other words, in a broad sense, as Habermas (1981, 1989) puts it, production occurs conjointly with communication. If this is the case, the different regions of the world that are connected by trade have exhibited a synchronized developmental pattern, perhaps even cultural hybridization, therefore underlining the systemic nature of their relations. This means that we are witnessing the outlines of a world system with a structure and trends.

Looking for global trade connections as an indicator of the formation of a world economy can perhaps be the first indicator of world system formation in a historical materialist sense. This by no means is the only evidence of the formation of a world system. It would be the minimal indicator that a system is in operation whereby global exchanges are taking place between and within regions of the world (see also Frank and Gills 2000). With the existence of trade relations, it also means that a (global) division of labor exists. My earlier studies (2001, 2007, 2008) along with others (see, e.g., Chase-Dunn and Hall 1997; Frank and Gills 2000; Kristiansen 1998; Kristiansen and Larsson 2005; Modelski and Thompson 2000) have shown this international division of labor existing as early as 3000 BC.

If we examine world history in terms of trade connections, we can trace the contours of a regional world economy encompassing the Eurasian region of Mesopotamia, the Arabian Peninsula, Levant, Anatolia, Iran, the Indus Valley, and Egypt by 3000 BC (Chew 2001, 2007). Beaujard (2005, 2010) has identified three possible regional world systems from 1000 BC onward. For him, there was the Western world system, the Eastern world system, and the Indian world system during the Iron Age, with growing interactions between these systems from 350 BC onward. Regardless of whether it is a single world system that started in the Fertile Crescent and over time encompassed other regions of the world, as postulated by Frank and Gills (2000), or Beaujard's (2010) three regional world systems coalescing into one world system, what is clear is that by the turn of the first century of the current era, we find a world system encompassing Europe, East Africa, and Asia (South, Southeast, and East) (Beaujard 2010; Chew 2001, 2007). In world history, we can conceive of it as the first Eurasian world economy as the only major region that has not been connected at this point in world history is the Americas.

This Eurasian world economy during the time period of examination also experienced crisis and restructuring, the result of the various trends and tendencies of the nature of the world system. I have argued in earlier writings (see, e.g., Chew 2000, 2001, 2007), along with others such as Thompson (2006) and Beaujard (2010), that climate, scarcity of natural environmental resources, ecological degradation, and diseases should be added to the usual socioeconomic and political causes for this restructuring.

The Nature of the Structure

I use the term world economy instead of world-economy because the latter has been used by world-systems specialists for a historical structure that has a certain set of socioeconomic and political attributes and trends, "capitalistic" in nature, that do not necessarily cover a wide geographic space. To world-system specialists, this historical structure of a world-economy is a world in itself, hence the hyphenation between world and economy (Wallerstein, 1991). In our case, a world economy is not distinguished necessarily by a mode of production other than it covers a global geographic space with multiple cores/regions linked at a minimum by a trading system. It is an evolving global economy "of the world." Depending on the temporal sequence, an economy of the world encompassing different chiefdoms, kingdoms, civilizations, empires, and states in a global division of labor, technology, and knowledge circumscribed by different cultural patterns.

Along this vein, in European archaeology, a number of prehistoric studies such as those by Kristian Kristiansen (1998, 2005), Michael Rowlands (1987), and the late Andrew Sheratt (1997) utilizing a theoretical-methodological framework that we have described above have arrived at some revealing patterns, trends and tendencies of prehistoric European Bronze Age that a specific processual site investigation would have missed. These studies reveal the exchange of knowledge, information, and technologies through migratory processes following climate changes, environmental transformations, wars, trade, diseases, and accumulation processes. Similar studies of the Fertile Crescent and South Asia's prehistoric connections with the Arabian Peninsula by, for example, Guillermo Algaze (1993), Shereen Ratnagar (1981), and my work (2001, 2007) have also uncovered patterns and tendencies of social, climatological, and ecological interactions between these regions and the eastern Mediterranean and central Europe. Similarly, trade, wars, accumulation processes also underline the trajectory of social system transformations, expansions and contractions.

For Southeast Asia and China, Glover (1991) has made reference to how Southeast Asia's exchange systems became linked to a vast network of trade connections to a Wallersteinian world-system at the dawn of the Christian era, and the significance of this to the socioeconomic development of Southeast Asian societies. Other than this fleeting theoretical-methodological reference of Glover on early Southeast Asia in a world economic context, the archaeological studies of the prehistoric and early historic periods undertaken were focused mainly on processual studies of mainland and island Southeast Asia. Here, the rich seminal studies of Charles (C. F. W.) Higham (1996, 1998, 2006, 2011) on Bronze Age Mainland Southeast Asia and its relationships in terms of technological transfer between China and mainland Southeast Asia needs to be noted.

Archaeological and historical studies of the prehistoric period of these regions (China and Southeast Asia) tend to be more regionally focused with the exception of studies examining the relationships and connections between South Asia and Southeast Asia, and also the latter with China. Guided by art history and excavated finds, the thesis of the Indianization of Southeast Asia has been pursued, underlining the connections between these two regions without any reference to the dynamics of the world economy. The early work of G. Coedes (1966, 1968) is an example that comes to mind, and it has influenced studies on the socioeconomic and evolutionary transformations of Southeast Asia. There are others as well, perhaps with a more emphatic stress on autonomous Southeast Asian development, such as Van Leur (1967),

Wheatley (1961), and Wolters (1967), that fall within this genre of regional studies of Southeast Asia that will be covered in the following chapters.

China's linkages with Southeast Asia have also been subjected to numerous studies, though in this case, besides cultural artifacts and archaeological finds, Chinese texts and accounts have also been used to reveal the Sinicization of Southeast Asia. Wang Gung-Wu's seminal work (1958) remains the key reference point for my understanding of the prehistoric trade connections and exchange. Reid's (1988, 1993) two-volume work on Southeast Asia and its relations to the maritime world, though focusing on a later period (AD 1450–1680), follows the Braudelian framework of a Mediterranean world, and views Southeast Asia within the context of a connected region, with its varied landscapes of mainland and islands determining its socioeconomic transformations.[7] Somewhat along similar lines is the work of Lieberman (2003, 2009). Veering away from the early studies of Coedes (1966, 1968) and proposing a framework that incorporates Reid's Braudelian model and extends it to account for local interactions with global trends and forces, Lieberman has tried to show some of the linkages of the region and world systemic trends especially in Europe at similar points in time. Unfortunately, his work focuses mostly on Southeast Asia around AD 800 onward, and does not cover my period of investigation, which is the formative time period in which Southeast Asia socioeconomically developed as a connected region participating in the Eurasian world economy.

Do the socioeconomic and political structures that formed then determine the arc of socioeconomic and political transformations that Lieberman has delineated for the later periods of Southeast Asian socioeconomic and political landscapes? Of consideration also would be the need to assess systematically the weighting in which world systemic forces and trends play in the dynamics of socioeconomic changes of Southeast Asia within the long periods of global expansion and contraction of the Eurasian world economy between 200 BC and AD 500. Rather than viewing the transformations between Europe and Southeast Asia as "strange parallels" when we use a comparative historical approach, we need to consider the socioeconomic evolution of Southeast Asia as occurring within the trends and dynamics of world economy depending on the state of its linkages within the system. Can we find the synchronous development of socioeconomic and political patterns that result from such interactions between Southeast Asia and the other core regions of the Eurasian world system? Undoubtedly, strong linkages of a region like Southeast Asia with the core regions at a specific time period will undoubtedly reveal the synchronicity of such "parallel" transformations and vice versa. If such is the case, we need to be careful how we explain so-called parallel development, and consider the position that it is not just local regional transformations that determine the arc of the regional political and socioeconomic landscapes, and that the world-systemic and world-historical events and trends also shape the Southeast Asian landscapes. This will help us to navigate between the Scylla of externalist historical interpretations and the Charybdis of autonomous historical explanations.[8]

Given the above, what follows is my attempt to trace Southeast Asia's place in the patterns of history, a place that has been generated from a world economy circumscribed by trade, climate, and other socioeconomic activities.

Notes

1. Some of the sources used in this book have indicated dates only in the form of BC or AD without any clarifications of whether these dates are carbon dated. I have used BC and AD datings for the whole of this paper so that they reflect the original sources from which the citations were taken.
2. There are exceptions, such as Lieberman (2003, 2009). Even Lieberman starts his analysis from AD 800. For the period post-1500 this has not been the case. See, e.g., Reid (1988, 1993).
3. Abu-Lughod's dating of the emergence of a world economy is different from that of Wallerstein (1974). Wallerstein (1974) perceived the emergence of a world economy in the fifteenth century.
4. See the publications of the Sealinks Project led by Nicole Boivin at the University of Oxford. Some of project members' publications have been cited in the chapters of this book (Fuller 2006, 2009, 2010, 2011).
5. Wang Gung-Wu (2008, n.d.) has assessed such a model of Braudel for Asia and Southeast Asia. See also Sutherland (2003).
6. The use of the hyphenated "world-economy" conforms to the practice of some world-system analysis scholars who view the structure of the world-economy as a world in itself, hence the hyphen. Such a use is based on the belief by these scholars that the world-economy is distinguished by a singular mode of production (Wallerstein 1991). Whereas others also examining the evolution of this world economy do not utilize the hyphen. The latter scholars do not assume that there is a singular mode of production that depicts the nature of the world economy. See the next section of this chapter for a fuller explanation on the use of the hyphen. The reader should note that the use of hyphenated "world-economy" or non-hyphenated "world economy" in this book is intentional to reflect the scholarly beliefs and understanding of the practitioners of the world-economy or world economy approach.
7. Wang Gung-Wu (n.d.) has also framed Southeast Asia within a Mediterranean complex but termed it as a semiterranean one in view of its historical development. See also Sutherland (2003).
8. For an explanation of these two different interpretations and approaches to writing and explaining Southeast Asian historical development, see Lieberman (2003).

CHAPTER 1

Early Southeast Asia

Southeast Asian populations during the Neolithic and early metal periods also contributed much to human achievements in agriculture, art, metallurgy, boat construction and ocean navigation.
—Ian Glover and Peter Bellwood,
Southeast Asia: From Prehistory to History

As a region, Southeast Asia is diverse in its physical landscape. Comprised of a mainland, a peninsula, and an archipelago, the mainland terrain is traversed by five major rivers: the Mekong, the Red, the Irrawaddy, the Salween, and the Chao Phraya. Throughout history, these rivers with their respective tributaries have provided the major river valleys and deltas suitable for agriculture and fishing, especially for human communities that were transitioning from hunting and gathering to sedentary systems. Beyond the lowlands, the Southeast Asian mainland landscape is also lined with extensive mountain chains connected to the mountains in Yunnan to the northeast and to the Himalayas in the north and northwest.

From archaeological evidence unearthed to date, human habitation of the Southeast Asian terrain has occurred in the mountainous highlands, river valleys, and the coastal plains. Climate and sea level changes have also conditioned human adaptation to this landscape. Besides the weather, rises in sea level have reduced the coastal areas and, over time, have led to acreage losses of the coastal plains in Vietnam, Thailand, Cambodia, the Malayan peninsula, and some areas of the archipelago. With the socioecological processes at work, the temporal spatio-social orderings may change in a manner that could undermine and erode the particular supposed permanences that we often conceived as givens. Because of this, the spatial pattern of human occupation of the deltas and coastal lowlands is quite different six thousand to eight thousand years ago than what it is now. Within the ambit of these natural parameters, starting from the mountainous highlands, we find human habitation on mainland Southeast Asia occurring primarily in caves, especially for those communities involved in hunting and gathering. According to archaeological and anthro-pological reasoning, these caves provided protection and shelter from adverse climatic and other environmental conditions. Over time, with the spread of the use and fabrication of metals such as bronze and iron, and the acquisition of knowledge of rice cultivation in the river valleys and coastal plains of Southeast Asia through interactions and exchange with other social groups, the demo-graphic contour became populated with various communities.

As with other regions of the world, these human innovations and inter-actions thus naturally led to population increases and, as well, increases in complexity in the area of social organization and structure. Conventionally, according to most archaeologists and historians, a developmental sequence of this nature leads to the emergence of a hierarchical order in the form of chiefdoms—the next "universal" stage in the transformation of human social organization, structure, and governance—without delving into the discourses and debates on the evolution of human societies, and stages of socioeconomic and political transformations. State formation and more complex political systems of governance usually follow chiefdoms or "Big Man" systems. There is less attention, however, paid to the networks of trade relationships and in-teractions within and between the Southeast Asian trading complexes with other regions of the world during late prehistory. Nevertheless, it is within such historical, social, and environmental parameters that the land use typology of Southeast Asia has been analyzed and explained by archaeologists, anthropol-ogists, and historians. They have sketched out the contours of the history of human socio-organizational practices in Southeast Asia—keeping in mind the geological and natural environmental factors as described above—by utiliz-ing the sociohistorical organization transformation models that have framed the examination of civilizational studies in other parts of the world, such as the Fertile Crescent, China, India, and Europe, looking for parallels or dif-ferences in the timing of social evolution (see, e.g., Bellwood 1997; Coedes 1966, 1968; Glover and Syme 1993; K. R. Hall 2011; Higham 1989, 1996, 2002, 2014; O'Reilly 2007; Van Leur 1967; Wheatley 1983; Wolters 1982). Furthermore, these studies have adjusted their analyses accordingly, adapting their conceptualizations to the local environmental variables that have had an impact on the cultural assemblages that have been unearthed. In this light, even though the studies framed their analyses vis-à-vis the local environment, they also continue to follow the arc of a socioeconomic developmental trajectory by mirroring their analyses in relation to frameworks adopted elsewhere by archaeologists and anthropologists on the socioevolutionary trajectory of long-term social change in the river valleys of the Euphrates/Tigris, the Nile, the Indus, and the Hwang Ho.

Given such directions, our understanding and appreciation of Southeast Asia are organized around this optic of viewing the socioeconomic development of Southeast Asia in relation to what archaeological and/or historical/ literary evidence exists to account for the historical timing and developmental trajectory of the formation of chiefdoms, mandalas, and urbanization patterns compared to other parts of the world system, such as India, China, the Fertile Crescent, and Europe. On such a basis, if there is an absence in the social organizational features of kin relations or governance within a given historical time frame in comparison to what has occurred in other parts of the world—and notwithstanding a lower level of archaeological excavation initiatives for Southeast Asia in contrast to other parts of the world (Stark and Allen 1998)—the region would therefore be viewed as less transformed politically, socially, and economically, or its developmental trajectory would be seen as having been determined by external powers/regions that were more developed by then (see, e.g., Christie 1990). Evaluations based on this supposedly universalistic modernization scale have resulted, for example, in the categorization of Southeast Asia's role and function in the world economy by some—such as Abu-Lughod (1989), K. R. Hall (1982), Leong (1990), etc.—as a marginal region fulfilling the function of an entrepôt in global trade connections, or one playing a peripheral role in world trade. To this extent, studies such as that of Coedes (1968) and others (e.g., Wheatley 1983) have refined further the typology of the socio-organizational pattern of the Southeast Asian landscape with social and political analyses categorizing and summarizing Southeast Asia's developmental trajectory as being infused or conditioned by Indian or Chinese influences—thus determining the arc of socioeconomic transformation of Southeast Asia within the context of the Indianization of Southeast Asia motif. This acceptance of social evolution or development along a "universalistic" (Eurocentric) modernity approach thus frames most of the past analyses, and has even added a modernocentric bias to the Indocentricity that has already existed in various accounts of the long-term development of Southeast Asia. The results have been that they have limited our understanding of long-term change, and have precluded alternative visions of our global past,[1] and Southeast Asian histories' place within a world history of human civilizations.

Should this be the case for our understanding and perception of Southeast Asia's place in world history? Or should we apply a different optic that will recalibrate our knowledge and understanding of Southeast Asia's role in world history and its overall developmental trajectory compared to other regions of the world economy? What can be done to reorient such established accepted understanding and conception? Rather than engaging in a debate on "centrisms," a more appropriate and fruitful engagement will be to provide a revisionist, world historical, materialist account (empirical study) of Southeast Asia's long-term historical transformations, and to identify the global trade linkages that Southeast Asia had with other regions of the world during its prehistory and early history. Coupled with this will also be an attempt to trace the networks of communication and interactions that occurred. An intensive sweep of recent archaeological and historical literary accounts of early Southeast Asia can give us a different view of what we have been informed about it to date. Furthermore, we need to trace the evolution of a Eurasian world economy during late prehistory and Southeast Asia's part in this global formation and transformation. The mapping of the evolution of this global historical trade system will allow us to move away from regional or localized analyses that most often result in privileging the country, empire, or civilization under study, leading most often to criticisms of the many labels of "centrisms" that have been applied to the many studies done to date.[2]

Prehistoric Southeast Asia

The landscape contours of mainland Southeast Asia are formed by the river basins of the five major rivers (Irrawaddy, Salween, Chao Phraya, Mekong, and Red) and their tributaries, with high relief in the north intervened by alluvial plateaus trending southward to low-lying river plains and deltas. Out of this topographical landscape, we find human habitation of highland regions and coastal/riverine areas. This pattern of human habitation also occurred for the peninsula and archipelago parts of Southeast Asia. Climate-wise, Southeast Asia lies within the tropical and subtropical zones, with almost uniformly high temperatures except in the highlands of the region. The peninsula part and the archipelago have a nonseasonal weather pattern, with rainfall and high temperatures occurring throughout the year. On mainland Southeast Asia, outside of the equatorial zone of the region, the rainfall tends to occur during certain months, with the winter season being much drier.

Ecologically, within such a climatic zonation, species diversity predominates in the tropical rainforests. The cultivation of crops following forest removal requires constant human attention due to the hot humid conditions that foster weed growth that would compete with the sown crops. The topsoil of the forest floor is thin in terms of fertility, and hence most agricultural cultivation in the prehistoric period was undertaken in the low-lying fertile river plains and deltas. Besides the tropical rainforest being a source of food in terms of animal biomass, the coastal areas provided bountiful amounts of bivalves and aquatic life for protein. Within this natural environment, the availability of food was abundant for hunting and gathering systems. These ecological parameters conditioned the socioeconomic development of human communities in Southeast Asia. Human habitations tended to cluster in the river valleys and lowland areas, and in certain cases were grouped in the highland plateaus of mainland Southeast Asia.

Environmental parameters do change over time, as we have also observed elsewhere, and do not maintain a "natural" permanence. In Southeast Asia's case, rising sea levels resulted in the loss of the coastal land mass. This loss is contingent on the different periods of glaciation when there is a rise and fall. The last glacial maximum eighteen thousand years ago produced a sea level of about 100 to 130 meters below the present (Chapell and Thom 1997). Eight thousand years later, the sea level was between forty and sixty meters below

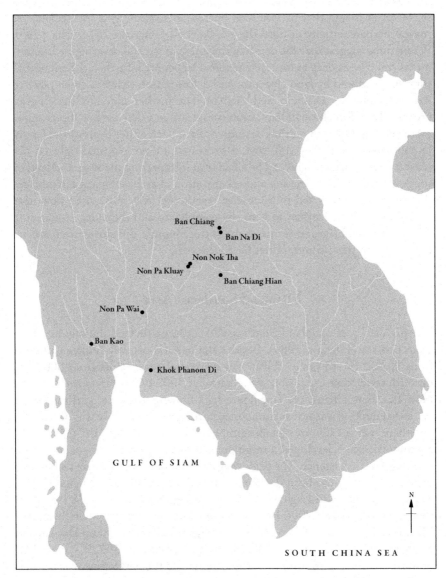

Figure 1.1. Mainland Southeast Asia: Bronze Age Sites. Courtesy of Annie Thomsen, Cartographer.

its current level. Between eight thousand and six thousand years ago, the sea level rose from −12.8 meters to +1.2 meters on the Southeast Asian mainland. The sea level rose even further by 2.5 and 5.8 meters higher to the present level between five thousand and six thousand years ago (Geyh, Kudrass, and Streif 1979; Higham 2002, 2014). What this means is that in the lowland areas of the coasts of Southeast Asia, a significant amount of land was lost to rising sea levels. It is said that the sea level fluctuations submerged any evidence of coastal human settlement onto the Sunda shelf (Higham 2014; Tjia 1980). Estimations suggest that the depth of thickness of the soil covering such settlements could be as deep as fourteen meters. Deepening it further, the amount of siltation produced by land clearance and deforestation that has taken place to date in Cambodia, Thailand, and Vietnam have further added to this siltation process. Therefore, human habitation complexes in existence five thousand or more years ago located on the coast might have been either been washed away or submerged or, if they still exist, if excavated are now located right on the coastal areas. Such changes can be a factor in interpreting the state and level of socioeconomic transformation and urbanization of archaeological assemblages that have been excavated in Southeast Asia, especially those sited now near coastal areas. This further adds to the complexity and difficulty in assessing excavated assemblages in terms of the socioeconomic transformation and attainment that these communities have achieved.

Mainland Southeast Asia

The prehistory of mainland Southeast Asia can be divided initially into four main periods (Higham 1989). Besides the periods of early hunter gatherers from 10,000 BC to the establishment of coastal settlements from 5000 BC onward, settlement expansion started around 3000 BC in places such as Non Nok Tha, Ban Chiang, etc. (see figure 1.1). During this latter period (Period A), social ranking was not as pronounced; the agricultural base was developed, but there was no sign of metallurgical production. By 2000 BC (Period B), communities had developed a more defined hierarchical ranking, and bronze working was in existence. The beginning of the adoption of Bronze technology in Southeast Asia has been determined based on two models (Higham 2015; Higham, Douka, and Higham 2015). The long chronology model has dated this adoption around 2000 BC while the short chronology model has identified it as around 1200 BC–1000 BC (Higham 2015; Higham, Douka, and Higham 2015; White and Hamilton 2009, 2014). From 500 BC (Period C) onward, we find the transition to iron making and the development of centralized systems. From AD 200 (Period D) onward, we find the rise of states or mandalas. Such was the periodization of the prehistoric period of mainland

Southeast Asia that Higham (1989) proposed almost three decades ago. With recent radiocarbon dating, Higham (2014) has periodized Neolithic settlements at Ban Non Wat starting from the seventeenth to fifteenth centuries BC, and Ban Chiang on the Korat Plateau from 1600 to 1450 BC (Rispoli et al. 2013).

The early prehistoric assemblages in Southeast Asia were human foraging groups developing flake stone technology. Examples of such communities have been discovered as early as thirteen thousand years ago, ranging geographically from mainland Southeast Asia to the Malayan peninsula, Sumatra, Sabah, Sulawesi, Timor, Moluccas, and the Philippines (Bellwood 1978, 1997; Higham 1989, 2014; Tan 1980). One of the earliest was the Hoabinhian material culture, with origins from eighteen thousand years ago, and the Bacsonian, dating back to ten thousand years, discovered in Vietnam. Other cultural groupings were comprised of the Nguom, Dieu, and the Son Vi, with even earlier chronologies. These earlier groupings in some cases, such as the Son Vi, later developed into the Hoabinhian in some regions of Vietnam (Tan 1997).

Madeleine Colani (1927) described the Hoabinhian communities as hunting and gathering systems living in northern Vietnam and fashioning stone tools from river stones. Mostly living in cave and rock shelters, the Hoabinhians' diet was comprised of animals, fish, bivalves, and wild rice. The work of Colani (1927, 1930) has revealed the widespread hunting and gathering of local food sources from both the forested inland as well as from the rivers and coastal zones. Contact with coastal groups is also evident with the finding of marine shells in these Hoabinhian sites. Burial remains are rare for the earlier periods according to Higham (2002, 2014) other than a find at Lang Cao, where two hundred skulls were unearthed within an area of twenty-five square meters, buried with stone tools. Besides the technological advancement achieved in the grinding and polishing of the surfaces (edge grinding) of the stone flake tools, the making of fired pottery vessels was also undertaken by the Hoabinhians. Other hunting and gathering communities excavated in the province of Bac Son have yielded ground and polished stone implements. Such discoveries led to the postulation of a different type of grouping, which has been designated as Bac Sonian, with its origin ten thousand years ago. It has been suggested that the Bac Sonian had Hoabinhian roots, based on the archaeological discovery of common material practices. The fact that Hoabinhian and Bac Sonian sites have yielded tools and pottery that share both cultural origins and have been uncovered in different parts of Vietnam suggests that there were trading exchanges of goods as well as cultural and material practices between these two hunting and gathering communities. Other excavated sites on the coasts of Vietnam have yielded finds that can be traced to the Hoabinhians. Four other cultural types that resided on the coastal areas have been identified: Bau Tro,

Hoa Loc, Ha Lang, and Cai Beo (Higham 1989; Tan 1980). Chronologically, these sites date back to 4500 BC.

West of Vietnam in the highlands of Thailand, excavation of caves in the uplands has shown human habitation sharing similar material patterns with the Hoabinhians. Stone flake tools have been unearthed. These early human sites exhibit hunting and gathering patterns between 9000–5500 BC (Spirit Cave) and 5500–3500 BC (Steep Cliff Cave), with some in continuous habitation from 3500 BC to even AD 900 (Higham 2014). The diet of these cave dwellers was comprised of marine life such as shellfish, and animals such as otters, langurs, badgers, porcupines, macaques and even leopard cats. In addition, plants were consumed (the remains of twenty-two genera were discovered). The plants were either utilized as food or as condiments and stimulants. The fact that hunting and gathering systems existed until AD 900 attests to the long-lasting survival of this socioeconomic system in Thailand. Other archaeological excavations at Tham Lod and Ban Rai further confirmed the long-lasting practice of this socioeconomic system (Shoocondej 2006; Treerayapeewat 2005).

There were also hunting and gathering groups located from peninsula Thailand to the Chao Phraya plains. Groups with Hobinhian lineages have been identified at Pak Om, Khao Khi Chan, Buang Baeb, and Khao Thao Ha on the Thai peninsula (Shoocondej 1996). These hunting and gathering communities might be located further inland instead of the coastal areas of the peninsula when they are unearthed. With the submersion of the coastal areas and the rise in sea levels as discussed in the previous pages, these excavated sites are now located nearer to the coast of the peninsula.

On the Korat plateau in northeast Thailand, evidence of human settlement at Ban Non Wat has been excavated. Located in northeast Thailand, it consisted of moated prehistoric settlements with initial settlement established at the mid-seventeenth century BC. Higham, an archaeologist, has suggested that at this site, the hunters and the gatherers came into contact with Neolithic groups who were already cultivating rice (Higham and Higham et al. 2011). Evidence of pig bones and chickens suggests they were reared at these sites, with Storey et al. (2012) confirming evidence of chickens via mitochondrial DNA signatures on Mainland Southeast Asia. It is also evident that besides domesticated animals as sources of food, the Neolithic settlements also exploited marine resources: abundant catfish and shellfish remains were found. The raw material for the making of adzes was not available within the vicinity of these settlements, and their presence indicates that these communities must have undertaken exchanges. Spindle whorls were also excavated, thus suggesting a weaving industry was in place. Burial remains were found within lidded pottery coffins. The refined motifs of these pots resembled those also found in other parts of Thailand and in Cambodia and Vietnam. There was very little evidence of jewelry, indicating perhaps that hierarchical structures had not evolved as yet. By the thirteenth century BC (and this phase, according to Higham [2014], lasted from 1050 to 1000 BC), transformations had occurred in the social structure; one can witness the change in the burial mortuary traditions. Instead of the refined painted pots, pots were placed beyond the head. The late Neolithic settlement ended about 1280 BC (Higham and Thosarat 2006). The Bronze Age sequence for this site is between 1280 and 400 BC, and Iron Age is from 400 BC to AD 300.

In the Chao Phraya River valley, with rock shelters located on the upland areas, site occupations by hunting and gathering groups have been uncovered. Stone beads, polished adzes, pottery sherds, and wildlife bones have been discovered. Occupation dates in these rock shelters have ranged from the earliest around 5580 BC to 1470 BC, with initial occupation at around 7000 BC. Shoreline settlement along the Gulf of Siam occurred between 4710 and 3960 BC. The coastal zone of the Gulf of Siam has yielded two settlements: one at Nong Nor and the other at Khok Phanom Di. For the latter, carbon dating of the occupation of this site is between 2000 and 1500 BC and was settled continuously for up to five centuries (Higham and Higham et al. 2011). The first three phases of occupation according to Higham and Kijngam (2010) appear to be peoples descended from Nong Nor. Located about twenty-two kilometers from the present day coast, the assemblage revealed items related to fishing (fish bone awls, bone harpoons, and clay net weights), the manufacture of pottery and jewelry, and wood working, as well as adzes (D. M. Hall 1993; Moore 1993). Wildlife hunting was also practiced, with the existence of animal bones such as the macaque and pig unearthed along with the other cultural economic objects. Consumption of grain such as rice and the harvesting of it are also evident. Participation in a regional exchange network can also be seen in the different stone adzes found. The varieties of stones that made up the stone adzes indicate that they came from different multiple sources of origin.

The excavation of Khok Phanom Di also involved the examination of burial patterns, grave goods, and interred skeletons. Higham (2002), summarizing the socioeconomic conditions and patterns of the human habitation at Khok Phanom Di, suggested a high mortality rate of almost 41 percent dying at or soon after birth, with over 50 percent failing to reach adulthood. According to his calculation, only 7 percent lived beyond the age of forty years old. Heightwise, females averaged about 1.54 meters and males an average of 1.62 meters. Analysis of the grave remains indicated the inhabitants suffered from joint degenerations, anemia, and tooth decay (Tayles 1999). There were differences between males and females in these health afflictions, with a higher number of males suffering from shoulder joint degenerations, while females had more caries in their teeth. The difference in shoulder joint degenerations can be attributed to the division of labor, with males perhaps doing more strenuous tasks such as canoeing, etc., and the difference in the frequency of tooth decay can be a result of nutrition differences.

Over time, these coastal settlements, such as Khok Phanom Di, located in an environment that is rich with marine resources and wild life, had population increases and started to develop a mixed economy of hunting, gathering, stock raising, and the cultivation of rice. The latter activity came about in the interaction with rice farmers who were establishing their settlements further inland (Higham and Higham et al. 2011). Rice cultivation was established after the eighteenth century BC (Higham and Higham et al. 2011). A recent study by Castillo et al. (2015) on the archaeogenetics of prehistoric rice remains from Thailand and India has suggested a dating from circa 1050 to 420 BC. Environmental impacts on food sources and rice cultivation were also affected by sea level rise. After 1700 BC, with the rise in sea level, the community reverted to sourcing its food supply from the sea and the hunting of wild life.

Because of the sedentary nature of these communities, over time they were much more different from the more mobile upland groups in the Bac Bo region of Vietnam and Northern Thailand. With sedentism, there is much more opportunity to accumulate surplus and wealth, leading to a hierarchical structure of social ranking. The display of status and the existence of elite groups can be seen very clearly in the graves and in the amount and type of items buried with the dead. Exquisite manufactured pottery, turtle breastplates, and shell beads were buried with the male and female dead. As the millennium proceeded, the dichotomy between rich and poor became more and more pronounced. Burials displays were very different, with the rich being buried with elegant pottery, beads, and port wines. By the end of the third and fourth millennia BC, such expansionary trajectory of these coastal communities was well on its way in northeast Thailand and central Cambodia. Population increases in these communities over time led to the fission of these communities, with groups breaking apart, moving, and expanding elsewhere.

Neolithic burial sites in Thailand, especially at Ban Non Wat, have yielded pottery sherds. These finds are similar to those discovered at other sites such as Ta Kae, Khok Charoen, and Khok Phanom Di. The pottery was well made with fine designs. Along with the sherds were bones of pigs, cowrie-shell earrings, and bivalve shells. Included in these internments were also rice grains. At Ban Non Wat, the excavations of grave sites have yielded a large amount of pottery, pots, shells, bangles, cooper axes, and bronze items. A chronological assemblage of these finds spanning from the Neolithic through the Bronze Age have been categorized (Higham 2011). With the amount of Bronze Age grave goods surpassing the Neolithic era, it seems that there were periods of wealth at Ban Non Wat during the Bronze Age between 1000–850 BC and between 850–800 BC. What is also distinct is that the wealth expansion ended at around 800 BC. Higham's (2011, 2012) explanation suggests that such a burst of accumulation is a consequence of the development of a social hierarchy, but it does not explain why there is a decline of accumulation after 800 BC. This decline at Ban Non Wat continued until the early Iron Age, around 200 BC (Higham 2012). Can the decline be connected to Thailand's trading links and the regional collapses that were occurring in the eastern part of the Mediterranean, the Arabian peninsula, and northwestern India starting in phases from 2200 BC onward, with the final collapse of the Bronze Age world system from 1200 BC until 500 BC with the emergence of the Iron Age world system (Chew 2001, 2007)? Notwithstanding these socioeconomic decline factors, climatological changes such as reduced rainfall, increasing temperatures, and the shifting of the monsoon winds that powered the trading ships should also be considered. We know that there was a warm period that prevailed over the ancient Near East between 1200 and 900 BC, and arid conditions were reported for the southern Levant from 1300 to 600 BC (Dubowski et al. 2003; Neumann and Porpola 1987). The changing climatological conditions could also have had an impact on the communities in Thailand. Unfortunately, the lack of temperature time series and dendochronological studies have limited our understanding of the factors that caused the decline in wealth and accumulation beyond what archaeological grave burials have been able to reveal.

The Peninsula and the Islands

The early Holocene period on the Malay Peninsula showed multiple occupations of Hoabinhians similar to what has been discovered in southern Thailand. The Hoanbinhian site at Kota Tampan in the state of Perak has revealed the manufacture of pebble and flake tools (Zuraina 1990, 1991; Zuraina and Tjia 1988). Hoabinhian sites on the Malay Peninsula extend back to 13,000 years and were mostly located in rock shelters similar to mainland Southeast Asia. Tools discovered were mainly unifacially or bifacially flaked flat river pebbles with cutting edges. The bifacial ones were found mostly in southern Thailand adjacent to the Malay Peninsula, whereas the unifacial ones were mostly discovered on mainland Southeast Asia.

Habitations in caves predominate on the Malay Peninsula, and excavated sites were located mainly in the northern states of Malaya, such as Perlis, Perak, Pahang, Trengganu, and Kelantan. On these sites, numerous bifacially flaked river pebble tools dating back to ten thousand years ago have been unearthed. The excavated site at Gua Cha, in the state of Kelantan, has revealed a diet of fruits and honey. One can assume that this was the diet according to the tooth caries found in the skeletons unearthed. No plant remains were found, indicating that no cereal cultivation was undertaken. A protein diet of animals, such as pigs, deer, bear, monkeys, rats, squirrels, foxes, etc., was also established. The consumption of freshwater shellfish was also noted on inland sites, and with the absence of marine shells leads me to conclude that foraging was undertaken within the vicinity of the habitation complexes.

On the island of Sumatra, Hoabinhian sites bear similarities with those in northern Malaya, though they were not found in caves, but on the coastal areas and the interior inland terraces, and on limestone rises that are about 150 meters above sea level. Shell middens dating back to about 7500 BC have also been unearthed. Similar to Malaya, pebble stone tools were used, though they were mostly unifacially flaked oval or elongated pebbles, unlike those found in Malaya, which were mostly bifacially flaked pebbles. Bifacial ones seem to be rare in Sumatra. These finds also included grindstones and mortars, suggesting a production-type complex. As on the Malay Peninsula, freshwater shells were also consumed, and a protein diet comprised of animals such as elephants, bears, deer, monkeys, wild pigs, etc. was also part of the dietary habits of these early Hoabinhians.

In other parts of Southeast Asia, such as Sarawak (now part of Malaysia) and eastern Borneo (Sabah, now part of Malaysia), Hoabinhian settlements have also been unearthed revealing pebble-stone tool technology such as edge-grinding of pebble axes instead of flake axes. Habitation continued to be in cave structures in Sarawak. That hunting was also quite predominant was shown by the discovery of various animal species' bones found in the caves (Harrison 1996; Medway 1977). Wild pigs, monkeys, porcupines, deer, bovids, rhinos, tapirs, and bears were the most common. In eastern Borneo, bifacial tools were found that are made up from locally quarried tabular cherts. The bifacial tools were also turned into knives. The excavations also revealed similar type animal bones to those found in Sarawak. Shellfish was also part of the diet, as shown by the discovery of shell middens.

Such assemblages were also unearthed in southwestern Sulawesi, eastern Java, and eastern Timor. Flaked tools found seemed to indicate that they were used to cut leaves and other parts of the foliage for the making of baskets and mats (Sinha and Glover 1984). Marine shells were not as prevalent, indicating that the area of settlement was quite far from the seas. Bone spatulae have also been excavated. In other parts of Sulawesi, such as the north, shell middens have been uncovered. These have been radiocarbon dated around 6500 BC (Bellwood 1997). Other occupation levels have indicated similar flake tools, red ochre, and other faunal remains. The dietary habits of the people of the Malay Peninsula, Sarawak, and Borneo are repeated here: monkeys, rodents, pigs, etc.

The Philippine Islands' assemblages share similar characteristics to the rest of the peninsula and islands of Southeast Asia. Blade-like flake tools have been discovered in marine middens on Palawan and Cebu. Cave dwellings have also been located in the islands.

Rice Cultivation and Metals Fabrication

Rice Cultivation

Transition from hunting and gathering to sedentarism in world history comes pari passu with cultivation of crops and the domestication of animals. In Southeast Asia, the cultivation of rice signaled the arrival of the Neolithic phase. According to Higham (1989, 1996, 2002, 2006), Neolithic societies appeared at least on mainland Southeast Asia between 2500 and 2000 BC. The consumption of rice did not just start during this period in Southeast Asia, as wild rice was consumed by the existing hunting and gathering systems much earlier, as indicated in the previous pages. Whether this transition to rice cultivation was prompted by climate changes, local population increases and urbanization—which has so often been used as an explanation for the transition to agricultural practices in prehistory—or was a result of diffusion of agricultural knowledge as a consequence of trading and migratory movements of people from one region to another (for example in this case, from southern China to mainland Southeast Asia or from Taiwan to island Southeast Asia [Fuller et al. 2010]) is dependent on how social evolution, diffusionism, climate changes, and historical transformations are interpreted. As well, it need not be an either/or interpretation; it could be both, in an interactional and interconnective manner.

If one follows the processual archaeology approach, we would interpret the development of the knowledge of rice cultivation and that of metallurgical fabrication to be transformations that are derived from more of a local origin. Bending away from this approach to that of another that includes both regional and world systemic processes in its interpretation, unlike the more localized analysis of a processual archaeology approach, Kohl (2008: 503), explains the spread of the diffusion of technologies in prehistory of Eurasia through a consideration that cultures "continuously imbricate and get caught up in shared historical processes that extend far beyond the areas they occupy, and cultural evolution does not proceed typically through internal developments and local adaptations to restricted environmental settings but occurs as a product of these shared interconnections and experiences." In doing this, he connects these interactions beyond the local and the regional contexts to the macro level that is world systemic. The late Andrew Sheratt (2006: 53), sharing Kohl's view, refines the process further: "The theme of this essay has been contact and the transmission of techniques . . . . This has revealed a more intricate reticulation of give and take [between cultures], and especially the creation of novelty out of new combinations or reinterpretations of things received: not so much diffusion as dialectic." Within this dialectic, Sheratt (1997, 2006) extends such exchange and interactions to the regional and prehistoric world systemic levels.

Besides diffusion processes, the other factor that might have also conditioned the development of agriculture is climate change. This, along with the other socioeconomic factors discussed above, could also have led in an interactive manner to the emergence of agriculture in Asia. For example, we know that significant changes about fourteen thousand years ago gave rise to a wetter winter season in Southwest Asia, which led to the development of agriculture in that region. Along with the shift back to a cooler and drier climate during the Younger Dryas, the wetter winter season further reinforced the changed climate condition that would enhance the cultivation of cereals. If this could be a likely model that can account for agricultural development in Southwest Asia, then, transposing it to central China, we find the cultivation of rice and millets eight thousand years ago. In China, temperature increases started about thirteen thousand years ago, followed by the development of a stronger summer monsoon. Between ten thousand to four thousand years ago, the climate in China was almost similar to that of present conditions.

Rice Cultivation on Mainland Southeast Asia

For mainland Southeast Asia, the emergence of rice cultivation and the fabrication of bronze have been attributed to group migrations, travels, and knowledge transmission from outside the region. Initially though, there was the assertion of indigenous development of bronze metallurgy with the unearthing of bronze artifacts at Non Nok Tha in Thailand, where initial radiocarbon determination suggested a date of the fourth millennium BC, thus placing this find as one of the earliest evidence of bronze metallurgical fabrication in the prehistoric world. Coupled with the bronze wares of Non Nok Tha, the excavation of bronze finds at Ban Chiang has also claimed a similar dating period (Gorman and Charoenwongsa 1976; Solheim 1968). Subsequent datings, however, have revealed that the bronzes were cast later, thus undermining the earlier date that had been established (Higham 2002; Higham, Higham, and Kijngam 2010).

Rice cultivation in mainland Southeast Asia and the fabrication of bronze have engendered discussion about timing and origin(s). Let us proceed to discuss the historical processes of the emergence and origin(s) of these consumptive material products that have occurred to date in Southeast Asian archaeology. Numerous attempts to discover whether the cultivation of rice was developed indigenously have been attempted in various early archaeological excavations. Those undertaken at Spirit Cave and the caves in Banyan Valley by Gorman (1972, 1977) showed rice husks in the upper layers of the excavated sites. It suggested that there was perhaps early domestication of plants by the hunters and gatherers living in these caves. Yen's (1977, 1982) analysis of the rice husks, however, has suggested otherwise—they probably came from wild sources.

Khok Phanom Di, another site excavated in the coastal zone of the Gulf of Siam in addition to the hunter and gatherer site of Nong Nor (with site habitation around 2450 BC), showed occupation levels between 2000 and 1500 BC. Rice husk fragments and chaff impressions on broken potsherds were found.

Whether their origin(s) was/were from wild species or domestic is not evident (Higham 1989, 2002). Instead, according to archaeologists Charles Higham and Tracey Lu (1998), the origin of rice cultivation on mainland Southeast Asia is more likely to have been diffused from China. This follows Sorensen's (1972) earlier claim of the Chinese origin of rice cultivation, which was dropped when rice husks were discovered in the excavations of Spirit Cave and the caves in Banyan Valley, suggesting perhaps an indigenous origin. Because the origins were not resolved in these earlier excavations, more recent work attempting to trace the dispersal of rice cultivation by Crawford and Shen (1998), Higham and Lu (1998), and Fuller et al. (2010) have mapped the likely origins of rice cultivation in East Asia and mainland Southeast Asia to the Yangtze river valley. Other analyses on the origin of rice cultivation in East Asia have further supported it to be in the river valley of the Yangtze, where pigs and cattle were also domesticated (Bellwood 2005; Fuller et al. 2009). Fuller et al. (2010) have also suggested that this migration occurred in waves out of the Yangtze valley, and that the migration to Southeast Asia probably occurred in the fifth wave around 2000 BC. In view of this geospatial location and the archaeological evidence to date (Higham, Higham, and Kijngam 2010; Higham and Lu 1998; Rispoli 2008; Zhang and Hung 2010), it has been suggested that cultivation of rice was a result of the movement of rice farmers from southern China to northern Vietnam and northeastern and central Thailand, and their interactions with the existing hunting and gathering systems. Exchange relationships were forged between these migrants and the local hunting and gathering groups and could have involved men and women moving permanently from one group to another. The timing of such intrusion and social exchanges was around 2000 BC. Given such social evolutionary transformation, cultivated rice grains have been found in hunting and gathering communities and sedentary ones in Vietnam and the highlands and lowlands of Thailand. A recent study of the archaeogenetics of rice remains from Thailand and India has indicated that the Thai rice remains were cultivated and consumed from c. 1050 to 420 BC, and that the rice was of the Japonica subspecies and not the Indica subspecies (Castillo et al. 2015). What this indicates is that the cultural exchange processes, at least for Thailand (northeastern and southern), were between the region and China, and not with India. The southern Thai sites that had the earliest contact with India, such as Khao Sam Khao and Phu Khao Thong, did not yield Japonica subspecies rice remains in the Bronze Age strata. The Indica subspecies was only introduced to Southeast Asia, including Thailand, during the first centuries of the historic period (Castillo et al. 2015).

Rice Cultivation on Island Southeast Asia

For peninsula and island Southeast Asia, after 3000 BC, there was an influx into the region of people (speaking an Austronesian language) with farming knowledge and practices, along with hunting and gathering skills. The Austronesian Dispersal Hypothesis, according to Bellwood (2004), occurred between five thousand and one thousand years ago. The dispersal started from southern China and the island of Taiwan. Interactions with the local ecologies led to the cereal cultivation replacing tubers and fruit trees—for example, in Indonesia—while some managed to move away from agricultural cultivation to hunting and collecting terrestrial and maritime food sources. Rice cultivation spread from Taiwan to island Southeast Asia around 2000 BC, similar in temporal sequence with mainland Southeast Asia (Fuller et al. 2010). From 500 BC to AD 500, through various interactions, metallurgical development took place in island and peninsula Southeast Asia along with wide-scale cultivation rice in the Philippines, Java, and Bali. It is also suggested by Fuller et al. (2010) that rice from island Southeast Asia was also transported by Austronesian ancestors from Malagasy to Madagascar on the East African coast.

Neolithic practices in island Southeast Asia, such as the Philippines, are also associated with pottery fabrication. The northern Luzon Island of the Philippines shows settlement occupation from 2500 BC to 1500 BC where pottery has been unearthed. Mainly of the red-slipped type typical of the region, pottery sherds have been excavated along with shells, stone beads, stone jade earrings, spindle whorls, and stone adzes. Design and type seem to parallel those excavated on the island of Taiwan (Bellwood 1997). In the southern Philippines, shell midden deposits have been discovered, containing rice grains and pottery sherds. In these Neolithic settlements, animal bones have been found, indicating hunting practices had been retained. Indonesia and Borneo also exhibited similar Neolithic development tendencies. Between approximately 2000 BC and 500 BC, pottery sherds were found mostly between a layer dated between 1000 BC and 300 BC. Other objects, such as adzes, beads, bracelets, agate blades, and obsidian materials, were also unearthed. Some parts of Borneo produced finds of pottery that were decorated, and also pottery stoves and pedestals. Agate blades were also evident, which might have been produced locally or traded for in Guandong, China, as it was a production center during this period (Bellwood 1997). In Sarawak, Neolithic assemblages start around 1400 BC, with non-paddle-impressed pottery making its appearance around 1000 BC. Double-spouted vessels were also discovered in the grave goods. The pottery sherds discovered in the cave of Lubang Angin had carbon dates of between 700 BC and AD 500. On the now Indonesian island of Sulawesi, small amounts of pottery have been discovered dating back to 2500 BC. The pottery sherds are mostly from cooking pots. Red-slipped pottery similar to those found in the Philippines and Taiwan has been unearthed in the northern Moluccas as well. Besides pottery sherds, there were also shell beads, bracelets, and spoons. Animal bones of pig and domesticated dog were also included in the finds. These finds were repeated in the caves of eastern Timor, with dates between 2500 and 2000 BC, and pottery sherds dating to AD 500 were excavated in the upper layers of the assemblages. Plant remains such as chestnut, bamboo, gourd, and millet were also uncovered (Glover 1977).

Burial practices during the Neolithic phase are represented by the burial finds in Sarawak. Graves were dug very shallow and marked with stakes. Bodies were buried in log coffins or in cigar-shaped caskets of bamboo strips, and some were partially burnt. Later sequences also included textiles with the burials. Earlier sequences also contained pottery and bone rings, while later ones had glass beads and metal items. Carbon dating places them from 1750 to 500 BC (Bellwood 1997).

My discussion above of the Neolithic phase of island Southeast Asia has been based on the model articulated by archaeologist Peter Bellwood (1979, 1997, 2004). Basically, Bellwood's explanation (1979, 1997, 2004) has suggested that agricultural practices, initiated in China, were transmitted via migrations of Austronesians from China/Taiwan to island Southeast Asia from the Philippines onward. This migration and transmission was based on the similarity of pottery assemblages (red-slipped), polished stones, adzes, and bracelets found in Taiwan with those assemblages found in the Philippines and other parts of island Southeast Asia. The works of Spriggs (2003) and Paz (2002, 2004) over dating issues, and the lack of systematic evidence of agriculture, have complicated our understanding of migration and transmission of the Neolithic phase of island Southeast Asia. Using archaeobotanical analysis, Paz (2002, 2004) has reported the invisibility of macro rice remains, with the exception of two finds—at Gua Sireh in Sarawak, and at Ulu Leang in south Sulawesi. Carbon dating of rice finds at Gua Sireh was about 2334 cal. BC. This date corresponded to the Austronesian dispersal period, whereas other rice finds associated with pottery in other parts of island Southeast Asia were dated much later, around 500 BC. The lack of overall evidence on the regional level of agricultural activity that is inferred by the existence of pottery sherds found in various sites of island Southeast Asia further muddies our understanding of this Neolithic phase.

Without abandoning the Austronesian China/Taiwan model completely, Anderson (2005) has suggested that perhaps there were two Neolithic population dispersal phases to address the variance in archaeological chronology. The two dispersal phases were from Southern China via mainland Southeast Asia to Sarawak, and from Sulawesi to the Philippines. These dispersal phases were prompted by the improvements in sailing and the climate changes during an El Nino (2250–2050 BC) that would change the trade wind patterns of the Southern Oscillation. These climatic changes caused massive drought in the Near East, which led to societal collapse (Chew 2007). As well, the impact of these climatic changes had catastrophic consequences in China, with massive drought in the north and severe flooding in the south (Wu and Liu 2004).

Such floodings could have led to out migrations in southern China and Taiwan that correspond to the Austronesian dispersals. Clearly, from the various assemblages of pottery and other items found in various sites in peninsula and island Southeast Asia, a more complex model can be developed based on further dating exercises and excavations of Neolithic sites. That there were various avenues of transmissions, maritime technological innovations, and migrations over the long term and in various phases should not be overlooked.

Metals Fabrication

The shift to bronze fabrication for Southeast Asia parallels the timing of the emergence of rice cultivation. Between 2000 and 1500 BC bronze working was occurring in the Mekong and Red River delta and some parts of the coast of Vietnam (Pigott and Ciarla 2007). By 1500 BC, a distinct Bronze Age can be distinguished, with sites for bronze metallurgical works in Vietnam, Cambodia, Thailand, and Burma. By the second millennium BC, bronze was widespread in the northern part of mainland Southeast Asia, and especially by the second half of the second millennium, when communities began to cast axes, chisels, arrowheads, fish hooks, awls, ornaments, bells, and bangles from bronze. In neighboring Burma, excavations in 1998 in Nayunggan have yielded socketed bronze spearhead, adzes, and arrowheads from around 1000 BC, before pre-urban settlements arose. Along with these finds, bracelets were also unearthed similar to the ones found in Thailand and China (Gutman and Hudson 2004). For the archipelago and the island parts of Southeast Asia, by the end of the first millennium BC, bronze working was in place. According to Bellwood (2004), bronze and iron metallurgy seems to have arrived together in island Southeast Asia. Throughout Southeast Asia, widespread fabrication of tools, household items, jewelry, and adornments for production and individual consumption was evident.

There is no consensus among archaeologists for the arrival time of the Bronze Age in Southeast Asia. The much earlier dating of fourth millennium BC for bronze fabrication derived from artifacts discovered at Non Nok Tha and at Ban Chiang in Thailand by Solheim (1968) and Gorman and Charoenwongsa (1976) has not been confirmed. Instead, 1500 BC has been acknowledged as the more reliable timing, derived from Accelerator Mass Spectrometry (AMS) dating of rice chaff. Archaeologists Joyce White and Elizabeth Hamilton (2009) noted that, in the excavation of Ban Chiang in northeastern Thailand, the appearance of bronze artifacts spanned from the late third millennium BC to the first millennium AD. This has led to the dating of the bronze artifacts to AMS dates around 2000 BC. On the other hand, Higham (2013, 2015) and Higham, Douka, and Higham (2015) proposed the date of 1000 BC following their analysis of burial sites at Ban Non Wat to be between 1259 and 1056 cal. BC. The issue of timing of the Bronze Age is also complicated by the lack of agreement about the origin for the development of metallurgical fabrication in mainland Southeast Asia. There is accord that the knowledge to make bronze wares had its origin outside of Southeast Asia. Where this knowledge was transmitted from has been debated (Higham and Higham et al. 2011; White and Hamilton 2009).

The knowledge of fabricating bronze was discovered in the Near East, and over time it was diffused to the rest of Eurasia. This knowledge to transform ores requires highly skilled metallurgists and is considered to have spread through migrations and movement of skilled craftsmen from the Near East (Chernykh 1992; Childe 1939; Muhly 1988; Wertime 1964). Others have questioned this single-origin explanation and have argued that different parts of the globe could have also developed the process of metal cupellation, and that there were different trajectories for transmission (see, e.g., Barnard 1993; Lechtmann 1979, 1980; Renfrew 1969, 1973, 1986; Trigger 1969). The latter argument would imply a more indigenous approach instead of a diffusionist/migrationist one. For Southeast Asia however, the question is where this knowledge of bronze fabrication came from. Archaeologists Joyce White and Elizabeth Hamilton (2009) noted the appearance of bronze artifacts from an excavation of Ban Chiang in northeastern Thailand. Chronologically, the deposits spanned from the late third millennium BC to the first millennium AD. This chronologization has led to the dating of the bronze artifacts to AMS dates around 2000 BC. According to White and Hamilton (2009), bronze appeared in Ban Chiang around the early second millennium BC and the technology was fully developed, suggesting further that it came from other regions of the world, and that it was a process of diffusion that lead to the transmission. For northern Vietnam, the dating was the early second millennium BC.

For the choice of copper-based metallurgy in mainland Southeast Asia, the preferred type was tin-bronze. Likely, local sources for the copper in Thailand were located at Phu-Lon and the Khao Wong Prachan valley in central Thailand (Pigott and Natapintu 1988; Pigott and Weisberger 1998), though there was no evidence of prehistoric mining in these places until several centuries later, following the time period of discovery of bronze artifacts in Southeast Asia. According to White and Hamilton (2009) the earliest sign of the ore processing at Phu Lon has been dated around the mid-second millennium BC. As for sources of tin, it is known that northern Laos has alluvial tin along the Mekong river. The other locations in central Thailand that had ore processing were at Non Pa Wai and Nil Kham Haeng, located in the Kao Wong Prachan valley. Slag remains at one of the sites, Non Pa Wai, are known to weigh over hundreds of thousands of tons (Pigott 1999). This processing also began around 1500 BC. Shaping the smelted and alloyed metal into the final product required object fabrication techniques such as lost-wax casting and bivalve mold casting. These casting techniques were used to produce items such as bangles (lost-wax casting) and blind socket implements such as spears and axes (bivalve mold casting).

Production of bronze items in Thailand involved social relations of production organized around decentralized systems based on kin groups located in separate communities. The discovery of crucibles in various places indicates that the knowledge for bronze production was not exclusive, or it could mean that there was easy movement of metallurgists from one community to another. The discovery and distribution of the molds and crucibles suggest that production of the alloyed metals happened close to the ore sources, whereas final fabrication of the alloyed metal to consumer items happened near the consumers (White and Hamilton 2009). There must have been distribution networks and exchange between producers and consumers over some distance and perhaps also the movement of metallurgical experts along these networks. In sum, such an array of activities, the consistency and uniformity of the products produced (White and Hamilton 2009), and the technological style could mean that there might have been a Southeast Asian metallurgical province along the lines discussed by Chernykh (1992) in the early metal age of the former USSR.

Returning to the source for this knowledge of bronze making, the conventional understanding of this follows Higham's (1996) and Higham, Douka, and Higham's (2015) tracing of exchange relationships that occurred in China's Central Plain with communities located in the Yangtze river valley, which then went through exchanges and networks with communities in southern China located in Lingnan, and finally to northern Vietnam following the Red River, Mekong, and Chao Phraya watersheds. White and Hamilton (2009) have countered with another possible source for the bronze technology transfer. The route they offered is one from eastern Eurasia. To support their contention of a more likely origin than that of the northern Central Plain of China, a detailed critical appraisal of the basis of Higham's (1996) and Pigott and Ciarla's (2007) Sinocentric model is proffered. The critique of the northern China Plain as the source of origin ranges from selective use of chronological data and selective use of technological evidence to the use of models that have an inherent bias, according to White and Hamilton (2009: 372–379). Relying on literature on Eurasia's metallurgical communities with its history starting east of the Urals from the late fourth millennium to the third millennium BC, the indication is that there was movement of metal workers in the various cultural networks of exchange. One such community is that of the Okunevo and Seima Turbino groups of the late third millennium, who were utilizing tin-bronze. Pertinent to this argument is the Seima Turbino community's existence from the third millennium to the second millennium BC, who were using tin-bronze items that closely resembled the earliest bronze artifacts in Thailand; their technological system was also an important source for the third millennium bronze technology of the Qijia culture of Gansu. The Seima Turbino's technological system employs lost-wax casting and bivalve molds that are similar to those used in prehistoric Thailand.

The route of transmission proposed is not from the Central Plain of China, as the Erlitou culture inhabiting the plain at this time (1900 BC) had different metallurgical technology. Instead, a southern route from Eurasia is proposed. Such a transmission route implies that metal workers from upper Eurasia would follow river courses in the forested areas east of the Altai mountains, using the Jialing River, for example, to the Sichuan Basin and the Chengdu Plain, and entering the Yangtze at Chonqing. From the Yangtze, the travel goes south to Lake Erhai, which provided easy access both to the Mekong and Red River, and to northeast Thailand and the Bac Bo region of northern Vietnam (see figure 1.2). These latter two areas are ones that have the earliest copper artifacts of mainland Southeast Asia. As a transmission model, White and Hamilton (2009: 388) propose the following:

> For the purposes of developing a transmission model consistent with the technological and chronological evidence, we therefore hypothesize that metal workers trained in the Seima-Turbino metallurgical system traveled along this western route c. 2000 BC, bypassing the Huanghe Central Plain. This model sees extremely rapid dispersal of metal workers with Seima-Turbino training, not only to the west from the Altai to Finland, as long been recognized, but to the south as well. These metalworkers presumably actively sought metal resources, so metal-rich Southeast Asia would be attractive. As their social ethos apparently facilitated long distance travel and their assimilation with other societies, they presumably trained locals in the fundamentals of their technology, and those locals may have carried it forward and possibly further afield.

Responding to this new proposed routing for the possible origin of bronze metallurgical technology used in Southeast Asia, and hence the timing of the start of the Bronze Age of Southeast Asia, some of the proposers (Higham and Higham et al. 2011) of the original northern Central Plain model have offered some substantive critiques. The main critique of the White and Hamilton (2009) model was of the dating (seven radio-carbon determinations) method of the Ban Chiang bronzes at 2000 BC, and also the dating of the artifacts of the Seima-Turbino culture, which the White and Hamilton model relies on as the possible source of Southeast Asian bronze technology. Besides the dating issue, the paucity of evidence of the Seima-Turbino artifacts in mainland Southeast Asia and the issue of bioturbation at the Ban Chiang site were also raised. To maintain their original proposal that the Bronze Age of Southeast Asia started much later than the 2000 BC timing suggested by White and Hamilton (2009), Higham and his colleagues (Higham 2015; Higham and Higham et al. 2011) provided further data from new radio-carbon determinations for

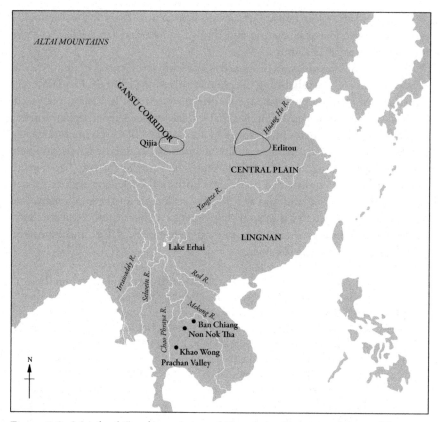

Figure 1.2. Mainland Southeast Asia and East Asia. Courtesy of Annie Thomsen, Cartographer.

their dating of the bronze artifacts with a new series of dates.[3] This new series ranged from 1600 BC to 540 BC. To further counter the proposal of White and Hamilton (2009) in terms of the lack of evidence of bronze fabrication in northern China, Higham and Higham et al. (2011: 251–252) specified centers in northern China and in the Yellow and Yangtze river valleys, especially in Shang sites that by the late third to the beginning of the second millennium BC were engaged actively in copper and bronze. Included in these items were socketed bronze tools and weapons, and also remains of bivalve molds. Besides presenting the counter evidence, Higham and his colleagues also addressed other nonmaterial issues that White and Hamilton (2009) raised in questioning their framework, such as the use of models that have an inherent bias.

Higham and his colleagues elaborated further on the spatial dimension of the spread of Bronze Age technology in world history for Asia. For them, the transmission process was an outcome of the Central Plain populations of

China interacting with the Steppe populations in Siberia and central Asia, and the knowledge then being exchanged with Neolithic communities in the mid-low Yangtze valley including the Lignan area and Yunnan-Guizhou Plateau and the Guangxi-Guandong region. The migration of the Neolithic farmers to northern Vietnam and northeastern Thailand brought the bronze technology to mainland Southeast Asia. The dating of such transmission is most likely to be the second half of the second millennium BC. There is also the likelihood that besides the Neolithic farmers, metal workers might be responsible for the transmission of the Bronze Age technology. These workers were either internal aggrandizers who had learned the technology or external aggrandizers who had moved into the region and provided the technology in order to seek a special status in the receiving communities.

How does one make sense of these two different contentions about the origin and the timing of the emergence of Bronze Age technology adopted in mainland Southeast Asia? In later articles on utilizing human bone collagen, Higham (2013, 2015) and Higham, Douka, and Higham (2015) continued to press forth his position by suggesting that the dating techniques used to determine the timing of Bronze fabrication in mainland Southeast Asia should be done with "greatest care," especially in the case of pottery, to ensure that it is properly done. The late Andrew Sherratt (2006), in his attempt to address the issue of transmission of Bronze Age technology over world history as first proposed by Gordon Childe in the earlier parts of the last century, and even before White and Hamilton (2009) proposed their model, offered a framework that reinforces the response by Higham and his colleagues discussed in the previous paragraph. Sherratt proposed that the Seima-Turbino metallurgical system was one that was transmitted both westward and eastward from Eurasia. In the case of the eastward transfer, it was adopted by the Shang and the communities in the Central Plain; of course the adoption, as he puts it, was a process of give and take in terms of reinterpretations, more like a dialectic instead of just straight diffusion. Which model will hold will depend on future excavations and reinterpretations or as Higham and Higham et al. (2011: 265) have stated, "Models will of necessity remain in flux as they adjust to the data emerging across the vast expanse of the Eurasian Steppe, China, and Southeast Asia. Such data, more than ever, reinforce the relatively new concept that these regions, at least from the Bronze Age onwards, were participants in the same interaction sphere."

Beyond mainland Southeast Asia, island Southeast Asia's Bronze Age period evolved in interaction with mainland Southeast Asia and eastern India. With respect to the latter region, bronze metal working started around the second half of the second millennium BC and lasted until 800–700 BC, when iron fabrication replaced it. This by no means was the start date for the appearance of knowledge to fabricate bronze for early bronze metalworking in India.

In this context, it began much earlier in the valleys of the Indus by way of the Harappan civilization as early as the third millennium BC (see, e.g., Allchin and Allchin 1982; Chew 2001, 2007; Ratnagar 1981, 2002, 2004). By the end of the third millennium, knowledge of bronze metal-working can be seen in the regional cultures of India. The appearance of Munda languages in the groups inhabiting eastern India by the second half of the second millennium, and this presence of Austroasiatic languages with a shared cognate for copper-bronze, would suggest to Higham (1996) a linkage between the metal traditions of the two regions. Bellwood (1997) has also noted these interactions of India with island Southeast Asia from about 200 BC onward.

For island Southeast Asia, copper is found quite abundant in the Philippines, Indonesia, Malaysia, and Borneo (see figure 1.3). Tin is found in some of the Indonesian islands, such as Bangka and Bleitung, in the Malayan peninsula, and in central Thailand. Among archaeologists, the common assumption is that bronze production and casting were undertaken on mainland Southeast Asia, and the bronze items that were found widespread over island Southeast Asia, such as Heger 1 type drums, were obtained through trade exchanges between communities of island and mainland Southeast Asia. From the distribution of these drums in Java, Sumatra, Malaya, Irian Jaya, and Sulawesi, it is clear that there was a sophisticated trade exchange occurring between island Southeast Asia and mainland Southeast Asia and other regions. In this context, the assumption would be that through trade, travels, and migration, there were considerable maritime exchange links between island Southeast Asia and the mainland by the end of the first millennium BC.

On the Malay Peninsula, Heger I drums, as well as fragments of them, have been excavated in Selangor. These types of drums have also been found in Java, Sumatra, and the Moluccas. Sources for such drums have been attributed to Vietnam, where they were cast. They were distributed either through trade or through migrations of peoples escaping from Chinese rule of or conflicts with Vietnam. Besides drums, other bronze items, such as statues and figurines, were discovered in Java. The trade exchanges also introduced the knowledge of bronze casting to the island region. Several sites found on the island of Bali have indications of local bronze casting, with molds discovered that have similar patterns to those found on the Pejeng drums. A range of local bronzes, such as bracelets, armlets, belts, ear rings, and axes, revealed the extent of local casting taking place. The preference for local bronzes is intriguing in view of the opportunity for control for local elites with imported bronze wares. Could it be that that the culture in question is less socially stratified, or that bronze items were readily available because of unlimited supply of copper and tin, or that the Eurasian world economy was during a phase of expansion? Unfortunately, there has been little reflection on this from the archaeologists and anthropologists and other specialists researching Southeast Asia.

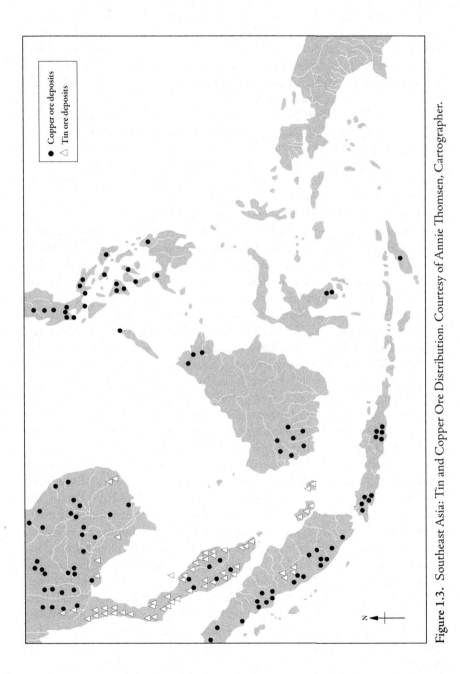

Figure 1.3. Southeast Asia: Tin and Copper Ore Distribution. Courtesy of Annie Thomsen, Cartographer.

The availability of bronze items in the Philippines is evident by 200 BC with the wide availability of copper in the islands of the Philippines. Bronze axes have been unearthed in cave dwellings, and the presence of molds further confirmed bronze production. The absence and scarcity of tin in the Philippines further suggests that there must be a sophisticated maritime exchange trade between the products of the Philippines and other parts of mainland and island Southeast Asia and beyond.

Calò's work (2009) on the widespread distribution of Dong Son and other types of bronze drums throughout Southeast Asia from the mainland during the first millennium BC reveals the ancient trade networks, exchanges, and routes covering eastern India, mainland Southeast Asia, peninsula and island Southeast Asia, and Yunnan in southern China (see figure 1.4). With the exchange of these drums from Vietnam, the interactions that ensued spurred on local innovations and adaptations in bronze making as evident in the other types of drums that were produced that have been discovered. For example, the arrival of the Dong Son drum in western Indonesia led to the casting of the Pejeng drums that are found in Bali and Java in the first half of the first millennium AD. The Pejeng drum does not show the vertical casting seams that are seen in the Dong Son drum. Instead, it has horizontal seams, suggesting that the mode of casting was modified, though still using the lost wax technique that was used for the Dong Son drum. The local bronze artisans also modified the shape and decorated it with local motifs that were not present in the Don Son drum.

North Vietnam has the highest concentrations of drums of various kinds of the pre-Heger, or Wanjiaba, type. Uncalibrated radiocarbon datings suggest the earliest production date of fourth century BC. These types have also been uncovered in Yunnan and Guangxi. Following the course of the Red River, Dong Son, Dian, and Wanjiaba types have also been excavated. Three hundred early Dong Son bronze drums have been found in Vietnam with over two hundred found in the north, especially in the river valleys of the Red, Ma, and Ca rivers (Calò 2009). Along with this concentration of bronze drums, there are also settlement sites of the Dong Son culture in the Red River flood plain. Moated settlements, such as Co Loa, had a citadel and three manmade moated walls. One of the outer walls of Co Loa was about eight kilometers in length. Pottery remains, as well as over two hundred bronze tools, ploughshares, and axes, have also been unearthed. This site, Co Loa, has been dated between the second or first century BC to the first century AD. Higham (1996) noted interactions of this site with Ban Chiang Hian in northeast Thailand. We can trace the trade from the Red river valley by the distribution of drums in northeast Thailand and the existence of a bronze-making industry from the second to the early first millennium BC. Dong Son culture casting reached its peak from the third to the first century BC. Other bronze materials and objects were also uncovered, including spears, ornaments, axes, daggers in the area.

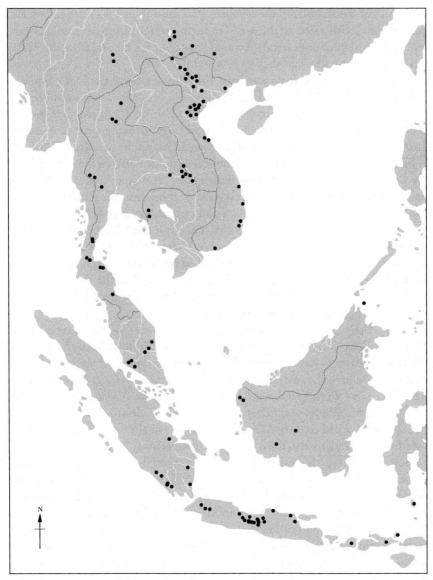

Figure 1.4. Southeast Asia: Distribution of Excavated Dong Son Bronze Drums. Courtesy of Annie Thomsen, Cartographer.

The production of these drums, especially in Vietnam, promoted a network of trading centers on the mainland covering Vietnam, Laos, Thailand, and the Malay Peninsula. Over time, trading centers grew in these places that not only included exchanges of these drums, but also necessary goods for social reproduction. For the mainland, these routes were land routes via river valleys and coastal zones with access to the seas. Trade connections from peninsula Southeast Asia to island Southeast Asia would have to be via the sea, from the Malay Peninsula to Sumatra, and then to Java and Bali.

These routes started from northern Vietnam in sites of the Dong Son culture and went south to the Sa Hunyh culture in the central and southern part of Vietnam approximately between the fifth century BC to the first century AD. From north-central Vietnam, the route would swing west to southern Laos and the Korat Plateau in northeastern Thailand. In mainland Southeast Asia, there are trade routes from Cambodia and southern Vietnam to the Malay Peninsula. As early as the first millennium AD, these routes were established. From the south and southeast coast of the peninsula, a maritime route existed to southern Sumatra and west and central Java supporting a sea trade. Central Java has the largest concentration of drums in island Southeast Asia. River routes on the Malay Peninsula and southern Thailand also were conduits of trade besides the sea routes that were taken from Cambodia and the eastern Malay Peninsula (Jacq-Hergoualc'h 2002; Leong 1990). The Pattani River in southern Thailand and the Perak and Kelantan rivers of the Malay Peninsula were also part of the trade network system.

Calò (2009) has argued that the drums found in the western part of island Southeast Asia and their distribution and type could have been the result of the trade exchanges that occurred along the routes described above, but those that were found in the eastern part of island Southeast Asia in Indonesia were ones that were from production centers in northern Vietnam and traveled along the sea route from northern Vietnam. These drums were dated to the late second to third century AD, unlike the ones in the western part of island Southeast Asia that were dated third to second century BC.

Southeast Asia, like other regions of the world, had widespread bronze production throughout its mainland and islands. As part of a regional trading network, the region was transforming in the type of materialistic practices that were undertaken: agriculture (cultivation of rice) and metallurgical fabrication (bronze and later iron production). Similar to other parts of the prehistoric global world, Southeast Asia's socioeconomic and political transformations followed quite similar trajectories—albeit not within the same time horizon as civilizations such as the Mesopotamian, the Indus, and the Hwang Ho—in the form and character of long-term change in the fundamental areas of food production and material production. As such, this region on the crossroads of the ocean trade routes connecting the East with the West developed and transformed with the dynamics of a Eurasian world system that was emerging from the third millennium BC onward. Given such connections and flows of trade, culture, and peoples, the Southeast Asian region developed and participated actively in the emerging Eurasian system.

Notes

1. See Bentley (2006) for an exposition of modernocentrism in our understanding of prehistoric times. Modernocentrism to Bentley (2006: 17) is an "enchantment with the modern world that has blinded scholars and the general public alike to continuities between premodern and modern times."
2. See, for example, Frank's (1991) critique of Wallerstein's (1974) conception of world transformations.
3. Bacus (2006: 107) has categorized the Bronze Age of Mainland Southeast Asia in the following manner: Early Bronze Age (c. 2000–1500 BC), Middle Bronze Age (c. 1500–1000 BC) and Late Bronze Age (c. 1000–500 BC).

The Networks

CHAPTER 2

Global Linkages
The First Eurasian World System

Introduction

Exchange of goods and services has been one of the main forms of interactions between human communities located in different regions of the world. With the advent of the Neolithic Revolution and the production of surplus, such trade exchanges ensued within specific regions and between different regions of the world. Occurring as early as eight thousand years ago, signs of these trading activities between civilizations were evident in the Fertile Crescent as early as five thousand years ago. Trading expansion and coverage during the Bronze Age in Europe, Eurasia, and Asia has become increasingly documented (Higham 1996; Kohl 2007; Kristiansen and Larsson 2005; Liu 2012; Parker 2012; Ratnagar 2004).

Not only did these trading exchanges foster accumulation processes, they also facilitated and intensified the dynamics between the different social systems' relations with Nature. The interactive process also engendered the transmissions of ideas, cultural traits, and technological knowledge, such as the fabrication of metals. These trading circuits increasingly joined different regions closer together, increasing flows of connectivity in the socioeconomic spheres, and in some ways introduced the sense of duration and space through the categorization of time that is necessary to transport goods from one place to another. Along with this is the awareness of the changing seasons and Nature's rhythms when the transportation of goods and services required the seasonal monsoon or coastal winds to power the sea vessels that carried the goods and peoples to various shores. With time, the trade linkages encompassed different regions with dense networks of trade routes within a region, and also extended these networks between regions.

Toward the end of the prehistoric period, these trading exchanges were extensive, connecting Europe, the Mediterranean, the Arabian Peninsula, East Africa, the Persian Gulf, Central Asia, South Asia, Ceylon, Southeast Asia, and China through a series of both land and sea trading routes. Movement of peoples and trade exchanges via land and sea defined this increasingly global system. The Roman Empire was at one end, with China at the other, and Central Eurasia, South Asia, and Southeast Asia geographically somewhat in the middle of the system. From approximately 200 BC onward, the emergence of a Eurasian world system of trade connections extended from the Roman Empire in the West to China in the East. Such was the scope of the trading system at the dawn of the new millennium.

Land and Maritime Trading Routes of the First Eurasian World Economy: An Overview

The dawn of the first century of the historic period witnessed a world economic exchange system that extended from China through Central Asia, Southeast Asia, South Asia, the Arabian Peninsula, and the Gulf Region, East Africa to the Mediterranean and Roman Europe. This world system of trading relations was via land and sea connections whereby goods and peoples were transported and exchanged. Thus the trading world was quite globalized at this point in time, with economic exchange—between kingdoms, empires and other polities—of manufactured goods, bullion, animals, and slaves in the various ports, markets, and trading centers of these regions.

Starting from the western part of this world economy, with its terminus ending in the eastern portion of the Roman Empire, the trade routes geographically fanned out in three general directions (see, e.g., Begley and De Puma 1991; Charlesworth [1926] 1970; Thapar 1997; Tomber 2008; Sidebotham 2011; Warmington 1928; Young 2001). The northernmost circuit traversed the Black Sea through Byzantium and Central Asia to China. The central route went via Syria through Antioch and the Euphrates to the Persian Gulf, South Asia, Southeast Asia, and beyond. The southern circuit was through Alexandria, northern Africa, the Red Sea and the Nile, East Africa, Arabia, and through to South Asia and beyond. The complexity of these trade routes are distinguished further by trade circuits that radiated from these main routes at the local and regional levels. Each region had its own local densities of trade routes, and the different items traded and exchanged (see figure 2.1).

The central and southern routes mainly used the river systems of the Euphrates and the Nile as conduits funneling through the Persian Gulf and the Arabian Peninsula and then onward to South Asia. The Red Sea was also one of the branches of these trade routes, with ports and entrepôt centers located around it. Its ports were also connected via land routes to the Nile, which was then a trade conduit downstream to the towns/cities of Egypt. Initiated by the Ptolemies, this trading route with its beginning in Alexandria provided

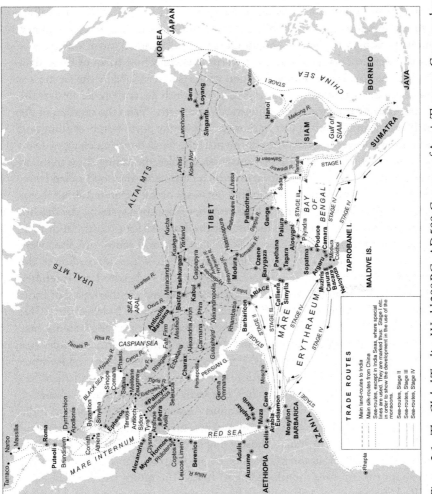

Figure 2.1. The Global Trading World 200 BC–AD 500. Courtesy of Annie Thomsen, Cartographer.

a centralized mart in which traders from the Mediterranean, North Africa, East Africa, and Arabia could exchange goods from South Asia, Taprobanê, and beyond. Departure times to these regions were different. The annual monsoons determined the sailing times and, as well, connected Africa, Saudi Arabia, and India for trading and exchanges (McLaughlin 2010; Mitchell 2005; Sheriff 2010; Sidebotham 2011). The monsoons, discovered in the later part of the second century BC, reduced sailing times (Hourani 1995). The alternate cooling and heating of the Eurasian land mass in winter and summer, and its proximity to the vast Indian Ocean with its annual warm waters, gave rise to a seasonal reversal of wind patterns over the whole basin of the Indian Ocean. The circulation of the monsoon winds is determined by the air masses of Eurasia during the winter months that cool much faster than the air over the oceans, thus shifting the air south toward the equator. With the rotation of the earth, the air in the Indian Ocean thus blew from the northeast, propelling and facilitating voyages between the continents. The wind direction changes again in the summer, blowing from the southwest, enabled the sailing ships to sail in the opposite direction, depending on which continents they had sailed from. In this respect, sailing times for trading purposes usually spanned about a year for outward and return journeys. Based on these monsoon systems, the rhythm of trading patterns and economic life on the East African coast, Saudi Arabia, South Asia, and even as far as Southeast Asia and southern China were determined by annual changes in directions of these winds. According to the *Periplus Maris Erythraei*, merchants heading for Arabia departed in September, whereas those intending to head for the west coast and southern part of India would leave between June and September (Casson 1989; Sidebotham 2011; Young 2001; see figure 2.1). Such timing was contingent on the frankincense harvest in Arabia in the case of those merchants involved in this trade, and the timing of the monsoon winds. For those ships leaving from the Red Sea ports to East Africa, departure times were between November and April, returning between May and September. For India, vessels would take advantage of the southwest monsoon blowing around August taking the vessels to India across the Indian Ocean; a distance of over seventeen hundred kilometers from Arabia to northwestern India. Those going to southwestern India would have traversed over five thousand kilometers. Even using the monsoons, sailing time was about two to three months going to India. The return trip from India to the Red Sea would take place only when the northeast monsoon was blowing, and usually this does not take place until November. In total, a year's duration—including the wait for the change in the monsoon winds for the return journey—was usually the norm. An estimated 120 ships left for the East each year, visiting Somalia and India from Egyptian entrepôts such as Alexandria (McLaughlin 2010; Warmington 1928). Barbaricon on the River Indus and Barygaza in Gujerat were the main ports of call for these ships. At Barbaricon, Indian, Tibetan, Arabian, and Chinese goods could be exchanged. By no means was Barbaricon the only place of exchange. Further south, there were other marts under the control of local Indian kingdoms. These kingdoms had control of the trading centers on the eastern and western coasts of South India.

Besides the sea routes, there were also land routes that connected the western part of the world economy to the central and eastern parts. Land routes for the western portion of the world system radiated from the shores of the eastern Mediterranean (see figure 2.2). Starting perhaps from Antioch, located in northern modern-day Lebanon, traders would travel eastward, most often having to cross the river systems of the Euphrates and Tigris, and then move southeastward toward Seleucia or eastward to Echbatana. From Seleucia, it was onward to Ctesiphon and beyond to the Iranian plateau comprising modern-day Iran, Afghanistan, and Baluchistan. Eastward from Ctesiphon, Roman traders would travel to Antiochia Margiane (Merv) via Jah Jirm. At Merv, the land route was divided into two branches that formed the famous silk roads to Central Asia. East of Merv, the silk routes had branches going south to India through Bactra, where it connected with routes that converged from India in the valley of the River Oxus. Further eastward, along the silk route to Maracanda (east of Merv), were a set of routes where marts such as Kashgar, Khotan, and Yarkand were located. These trading marts were places where the Indians, Kushans, Parthians, Romans, and Chinese traders met for the exchange of products from the western, eastern, and central parts of the world economy. For those western traders who were interested in Indian products, the routes they would take would be southward after Merv or Bactra. Indian goods destined for Russia and the Scythian lands would move northward on the River Oxus and either cross or round the Caspian Sea to the Black Sea. The land routes ended at Loyang, China.

From South Asia eastward, the timing of the monsoons was also used to travel to Southeast Asia, China, and other parts of East Asia. Like the pattern of sailing from the Red Sea to northwestern India, the ships from the Indian Ocean sailing to Southeast Asia would also take advantage of the northeast or southwest monsoon, depending on what directions they were sailing: outbound eastward or the return journey westward. Periods of sojourn would be taken by the merchants and sailors in different parts of Southeast Asia—in particular, the landfall on the Malayan Peninsula—and Southern China, depending on the sailing direction, while waiting for the wind directions to change.

The maritime routes from South Asia to Southeast Asia and China were along the east coast of South Asia and Ceylon, across the Bay of Bengal to the Malay Peninsula. Initially in the first century AD, specific trade contacts were on the western and eastern coasts of the Malay Peninsula (Hall 1985). There was also a land route from South Asia to the western edge of the Mekong Delta. Within Southeast Asia, the maritime trading routes connected south-

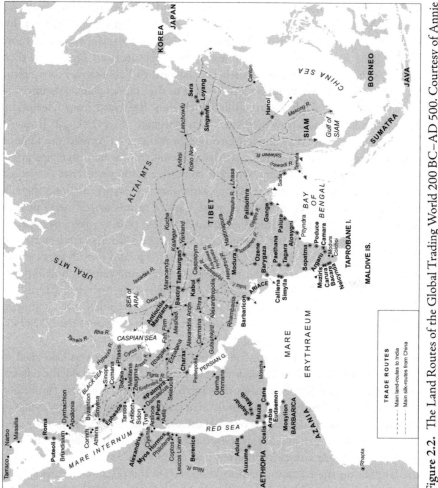

Figure 2.2. The Land Routes of the Global Trading World 200 BC–AD 500. Courtesy of Annie Thomsen, Cartographer.

ern Sumatra and western Java to the ongoing trade routes in the northern part of the Malay Peninsula. By the fifth century AD, the Straits of Malacca became the direct trade route that connected the northwestern Java Sea region with the major trade routes involved in the global trade exchanges between China, South Asia, Southeast Asia, and the eastern Mediterranean (Wolters 1967). This Java Sea region consisted of, in addition to Java, the Sunda Islands, the Moluccas, Borneo, and Southern Sumatra. The trade routes even extended as far as Sulawesi and New Guinea in search of feathers and other products of the sea.

From Southeast Asia there were also land routes to southern China, mostly traversing mainland Southeast Asia and ending up, via Vietnam and the Red River Delta, in southern China. Archipelago Southeast Asia was covered with maritime routes linking the Malay Peninsula and the Java Sea region with the ports of southern China.

The First Eurasian World Economy

From Europe and the Mediterranean to the Red Sea

Trade exchanges between Europe, the Mediterranean, Central Asia, the Gulf Region, and South Asia were not initiated by the Romans at the end of the first millennium BC. If one examines third millennium BC world history for trading connections within a region and between regions of the world, one notices an evolving economic exchange network within the Afro-Eurasian geographic context that included Egypt, Mesopotamia, the Arabian Peninsula, the Levant, Anatolia, Iran, and the Indus Valley (Chew 2001, 2007; Frank and Gills 2000; Kohl 1987; Possehl 2002; Ratnagar 2004; Wright 2010). Such systemic connections via trade were an outcome of a division of labor whereby social systems, especially those located in river valleys and watersheds, sought natural resources such as copper, precious stones, pearl, ivory, gypsum, marble, and wood, for their production activities and the reproduction of their socioeconomic lifestyles from the peripheries. In turn, they exported to the peripheries manufactured items and cultivated agricultural products: bronze wares, textiles, wheat, etc. Mostly, such exchanges occurred because the immediate environments of these social systems were either devoid or depleted of these resources (such as wood) as a result of the intensification of extraction of these products that had occurred historically to satisfy the urbanization process, population growth, and hierarchical reproductive needs and surplus generation of these systems.

In the third millennium BC, there were trade connections between the civilizations of Egypt, southern Mesopotamia, and their geographic vicinities, and between Mesopotamia, the communities of Anatolia, the Arabian Peninsula, the Persian Gulf, Iran, the Harappan civilization of northwestern India, central Asia, and their peripheries—either directly or through merchant middlemen (e.g., see Algaze 1993; Allchin 1982; Ashthana 1993; Chew 2001; Edens 1992; Kohl 1987; Lamberg-Karlovsky 1975; Moorey 1994; Oppenheim 1979; Possehl 1982; Ratnagar 1981, 1991, 1994, 2001, 2004; Tibetts 1956; Tosi 1982; Wright 2010). Further west of this system, in Europe during the third millennium BC there were widespread travel and migrations as well (Earle and Kristiansen 2010; Kristiansen 1998; Kristiansen and Larsson 2005). By the middle of the third millennium BC, strong connections between Greece, the Adriatic, and the Carpathians were forged. The later period of the third millennium BC saw trade connections established between the eastern Mediterranean and central Europe (Kristiansen 1997; Kristiansen and Larsson 2005). These linkages were the result of migrating parties from central Europe interacting, and through raids with communities in Anatolia and the Near East.

Trading networks were disrupted beginning around 2200 BC following the demise of the economy of southern Mesopotamia and Northwestern India, which was coupled with the socioeconomic and political upheavals in the Levant and their associated peripheries. This contraction (Dark Age) initiated a restructuring of the trade networks (Chew 2007). Various conditions have been attributed to these trade realignments from wars, invasions, and human-induced ecological degradation, besides climate changes and natural disturbances, which were also part of the mixture that contributed to the stress (Chew 2001, 2007). The demise of the economies of Egypt, southern Mesopotamia, and northwestern India, and the concomitant deurbanization, meant also the collapse of the Persian Gulf trade, which was a major corridor of the trading system at that time.

With recovery occurring around 1700 BC, the other parts of the system such as the eastern Mediterranean littoral (centered around Crete and mainland Greece), along with central Europe and Anatolia, increasingly began to take advantage of the vacuum generated by the collapse of the southern portion (the Gulf region) of the system (Chew 2007). With Mesopotamian traders changing their orientation "from the East (Indus valley, Magan and Meluhha) to the West (with Syro-Palestine, Egypt and Cyprus)," trade in the eastern Mediterranean littoral boomed (Cline 1994: 9). Thus, trade orientation that in the past was directed to the East now shifted to the West. Egypt, Syria-Levant (such as Ugarit, Mari, Byblos, and Ras Shamra), Crete, Cyprus, and mainland Greece expanded their trading volumes utilizing the peripheral areas, such as central and eastern Europe, Nubia, and, in the later period, northern Europe, for their resource needs (Chew 2001; Knapp 1993; Kristiansen 1998).

With the above developments, we find increasingly the evolution of an integrated system of trade linking Europe's dispersed and distant communities

(Kristiansen 1998). The need of urbanized centers for various raw materials and their peripheries exchanging these materials for manufactured preciosities produced by the urbanized centers, led to the development of peripheral central Europe and the western Mediterranean following an expansion of bronze production and trade. England was drawn into the orbit of trading linkages with its tin mines in Cornwall, and so was Erzgebirge, Germany. These raw materials, including amber, were transshipped to the eastern Mediterranean, including Mycenaean Greece.

At the start of the early second millennium BC, communities throughout Europe, including Northern Europe, became more dependent on the distribution of metals (tin, gold, silver, and copper) that their surroundings were devoid of. Suppliers to these communities were from the Near East, with Assur, located in northern Mesopotamia, as a center of distribution. Tin, most likely from Afghanistan or Elam, was redistributed by Assyrian traders from central Anatolia (Larsen 1976, 1987). Assur was the center of regional trade in the eastern Mediterranean until 1600 BC (Larsen 1987). Northern Mesopotamia continued to supply agricultural products and textiles to the region, including those from southern Mesopotamia, through Assur, and the raw materials from this region, such as copper, wood, wine, silver, gold and tin, were also redistributed to the other urban centers. Copper was from eastern Anatolia and Cyprus, and, within this trading zone, Syria provided the wood, wine, purple-dyed textiles, and other aromatic products (Liverani 1987). The eastern Mediterranean, with Mari as one of its centers, also hosted numerous land and sea trade routes that connected to Egypt, Crete, and mainland Greece. Egyptian trade flowed through the Syro-Palestinian zone. In the eastern Mediterranean region, the land and sea trade routes were also connected to the land routes with central Asia, and from Egypt, Lebanon, and Syria they were connected via land and sea to the Arabian Peninsula, the Red Sea, the Persian Gulf, South Asia, and East Africa.

During this period also, there was the beginning of an intensive trading arrangement between western Europe, central Europe, and the eastern Mediterranean. After 1600 BC, exchange networks were established between southern Scandinavia and northern Italy for the amber produced in northern Europe (Kristiansen and Larsson 2005). Trade routes were also connected to Hungary and eastern central Europe and the eastern Mediterranean.

The globalizing trajectory was extended starting from the second millennium BC onward when the cores in the Near East, as Kristiansen and Larsson (2005: 17) put it, "turned their interest towards the barbarian peripheries in central and western Europe" for their natural resources and livestock such as horses. In the Caucasus, the mines supplied the copper, and there was the development of a Circum-Pontic metallurgical province that included Anatolia, which received its metal ores from the Caucasian region (Chernykh 1992;

Kristiansen and Larsson 2005; Sheratt and Sheratt 1993). Serbia, the Slovakian Ore Mountains, southeast Spain, Cornwall, Brittany, Erzgebirge, and Tuscany were possible areas that provided sources of tin for the peripheral areas of Europe and the eastern Mediterranean (Pare 2000). Anatolia became an important eastern node of the trading system, especially with the demise of the southern Mesopotamian trade, thus shifting the trade loss northward (Chew 2001; Larsen 1987; A. Sheratt 1997). Such transformations revealed the increasing nature of the globalizing process of the system of trade exchanges as early as the second millennium BC. What flowed through this system were natural resources, manufactured products, and agricultural produce, as well as preciosities. The cores had production activities controlled by the palace, temples, and the merchants, and the peripheral areas supplied the natural resources, as well as agricultural products. Colonization of distant lands in the eastern Mediterranean, Sicily, and southern Italy for agricultural production and natural resource extraction were also undertaken by the core centers, such as Crete and Greece, during this time period (Immerwahr 1960; Vermeule 1960). Increasingly, Europe was being incorporated into the trading orbit via the establishment of trading outposts, similar to what the southern Mesopotamians were undertaking toward the end of the third millennium BC with northern Mesopotamia and Iran (Algaze 1989, 1993a, 1993b).

The eastern Mediterranean in the second millennium BC reveals a trading network that ranged from Crete, the Cyclades, and the Greek mainland on one side of the Aegean Sea, with Troy, Cyprus, and Anatolia located across from it. Anatolia exchanged its metallic resources, such as gold and silver, for textiles, lapis lazuli, olive oil, horses, tin, and so forth (Bryce 2002). Utilizing trade routes that were in the control of the Assyrians, the trade proceeded using the Assyrian-established merchant colonies. From this geographic position, further south we find the communities of Syria and Palestine, and to the southwest the Kingdom of Egypt. To the southeast, we have northern Mesopotamia. This trading network of socioeconomic exchanges of the eastern Mediterranean region was also linked to communities of western, central, and eastern Europe and central Asia. The Aegean and the Carpathians became the nodal points for these trading networks.

Intermediary centers of the past, such as Crete, increasingly played a part in the eastern Mediterranean within this trading network (Chew 2001). From 1750 BC to 1450 BC, the boom in trade—as a result of economic disruptions in southern Mesopotamia, the Gulf, and northwestern India—engendered a period of palace construction (that followed an earlier phase between 1950 BC and 1700 BC).[1] On the trading backbone that benefited Crete, Mycenaean Greece later in the period also began to establish its economic dominance within the Aegean. Trade relations were also established with southern Italy and the Syro-Palestinian coastal areas (Chandler 1974). The establishment of Greek outposts in Sicily and southern Italy further connected the trading routes to communities in western Europe and, in turn, to Scandinavia.

The trade routes in the eastern Mediterranean ran counterclockwise in sailing direction, from the Greek mainland to Crete and south to Egypt, up the Syro-Palestinian coast to Cyprus, and then west to the Aegean via the coast of Anatolia, Rhodes, and the Cyclades. According to Cline (1994), there was also a clockwise routing that went from Egypt, along the Libyan coast to Crete and to the Greek mainland, then to the Cyclades, Rhodes, the southern coast of Anatolia, and Cyprus, down the Syro-Palestinian coast, and back to Egypt.

Given the mostly synchronic mapping of the trading connections of the centers of the ancient Near East outlined above, it should not be assumed that these trading networks were stable structures over time.[2] The mapping of these connections is to reveal the interlinked patterns of commercial activities that were in existence, and thus underline the development of a globalized system of regions and polities. Their vitality and concentration changed over time and were conditioned by the pulsations of socioeconomic, political, ecological, and climatic changes. Thus, when the Dark Age returned in 1200 BC, the collapse was system wide.

The date 1200 BC marks the beginning of a social system transformation, and the final phase of the crisis which started in 2200 BC, leading to the end of the Bronze Age. Disruptions in trade, along with socioeconomic and political collapses, occurred throughout the region—with the exception of northern, central, and eastern Europe—and were the conditions of the times (Chew 2007). The latter parts (northern, central, and eastern Europe) experienced these crisis conditions much later. With the collapse of the Near Eastern–Mediterranean trade networks and the shortage of metals there, metal production boomed in central and eastern Europe. As a result of the Mediterranean collapse, the eastern and western European trade exchanges were strengthened. Such exchanges led to the development of a regional (Urnfield) trading and production system (Kristiansen 1998). Crisis appeared much later, around 750 BC, for this area.

According to Drews (1993), the crisis in the Near East and the eastern Mediterranean emerged in sporadic upheavals in the last quarter of the thirteenth century BC. Stretching from Greece, the Cyclades, and Crete to Anatolia, Cyprus, Egypt, Syria and the southern Levant, the catastrophe was widespread. With the exception of the periphery noted above, the core centers of the system were in crisis. Economic recovery returned around 700 BC for the Mediterranean region, and what followed was a series of colonization and expansion of trade networks under the control of Greece and Phoenicia (Chew 2007).[3] For the Greeks, it came in two phases. The first, between 775 and 675 BC, was the colonization of western Asia and southern Italy, Sicily, and southern France. The second, between 675 and 600 BC, was focused not only on colonization but also on commerce. The latter led to the strengthening and fixing of the trade routes already in existence. Besides Greece, other centers, such as Phoenicia, Egypt, and Persia, were also establishing trading networks, and as Braudel (2001: 225) puts it, the Mediterranean never became a "Greek Lake." With these different polities, no core center ever gained control of the Mediterranean; it is only with the arrival of Rome toward the end of the first millennium BC, that the Mediterranean became a Roman Sea. The emergence of Rome as a major core center of the world system by the end of the first millennium—there are others as well during this time period in the East, such as China—also led to the expansion of the trade connections between East and West. It is at this point in world history that we have the development of the first Eurasian world economy connecting the West with the East.

Beginning from the early Roman period (first century BC to third century AD), this increasingly globalized trade network covered at least seven regions of the world economy. In a world historical context, the scale and volume of trade had a globalized orientation stretching from West to East. In contrast, during the earlier Bronze Age, the trading activity was more regional in orientation as the trading connections from the eastern Mediterranean across the regions (Red Sea, Persian Gulf, and Indian Ocean) to Southeast Asia and East Asia were not that developed.

The trading networks encompassing Europe and the Eastern Mediterranean under Roman rule were established over a period of time in line with the pace of Roman conquest. Up to the second century BC, the Roman trading networks focusing on land routes were centered around Italy, North Africa, Sicily, Sardinia, Carthage, and the Aegean. The more remote areas, such as northern Gaul, northwestern Spain, eastern Anatolia, northern Mesopotamia, Egypt, Britain, and Dacia, were connected later, following Roman conquest. Total control of the Eastern Mediterranean region was achieved by the Romans after 31 BC, when Egypt came under the Roman Empire. By AD 200, the western portion of the globalized world economy—stretching from Britain in northwestern Europe south to the Mediterranean and North Africa and eastward to the Near East—were set with Roman-built roads over mountain passes and along valleys, as well as maritime routes (including the river systems) crisscrossing the Mediterranean, the Baltic, and the Black seas (Drummond and Nelson 1994; Garnsey and Saller 1987; Millar 1981).

During the Roman period in the western part of the Eurasian world system, the goods and peoples that traversed these trading networks reflected the economic, social, and political interests of the core areas. With Rome being the major core center, transportation of goods and peoples were shaped by the political and economic needs of Rome. Between 200 BC to AD 400, the Roman world in the West can be divided into three spheres (Hopkins 1980). Basically, the inner sphere was comprised of Rome and Italy, where the surplus generated throughout the empire was mostly sent. Surrounding this inner sphere was a ring of resource provinces such as Spain, Syria, Greece, Gaul, North Africa, and west Asia. This group was a net exporter of surplus, and its exports were consumed in the inner sphere. The second sphere paid their taxes in money form (silver coinage), and in order to generate the income for payment, agricultural produce (grain, wine, oil), natural resources, wool, hides, and other manufactured items (cloth, dyes, ropes, etc.) had to be produced for commercial exchange. Thus, across the two outer spheres of the empire, slaves, goods, agricultural products, and silver and gold bullion were transported on Roman roads and the river systems of western and central Europe. Free commerce was established in the provincial towns of the second sphere, and trading networks were also developed. Furthermore, appropriate manufacturing to meet local needs of the provinces was also encouraged, and extractive industries of natural resources also followed mainly in the second sphere. Production of leather, wool, and pottery emerged as the towns connected by a network of roads enhanced the trading exchanges facilitated by the river systems that were intertwined with the provincial urban centers (Haselgrove 1980; Hedeager 1980; Hopkins 1980). Provincial centers like Narbo and Tolosa in Gaul and Aquilea on the Adriatic became large commercial places, and they even served trade beyond the empire (Nash 1987).

The eastern portion of the Roman Empire had several urban centers, such as Carthage, Alexandria, Constantinople, and Antioch, which were the large metropolises that were connected by the land and maritime routes to central Asia, the Arabian Peninsula, the Persian Gulf, East Africa, India, Ceylon, Southeast Asia, and China. Notable among these urban centers within the empire and beyond were Byzantium/Constantinople, Alexandria, Antioch, and Ctesiphon. Byzantium, founded by Greek colonists from Megara in 657 BC, was one the gateways to the East via the Black Sea. The city was attacked by Roman legions during the reign of Roman Emperor Septimius Severus in AD 196 and lay in ruins until the ascendance of Roman Emperor Constantine, when the city was rebuilt, reinaugurated, and renamed Constantinople after the emperor in AD 330. It was also made the center of the Roman Empire in the east by Emperor Constantine. With its natural harbor and location, Byzantium could control the sea routes between Asia and Europe of this portion of the Eurasian world system. Its port handled amber, furs, metal, and wood from the north; oil, grain, flax, and papyrus from the Mediterranean; and mainly spices from the East. Byzantium also handled the overland trade routes between the West and the East of this region of the Eurasian world system (see figure 2.2).

Byzantium by no means was the only urban center that participated in the Eurasian world system land trade network. Other centers radiated from the shores of the Eastern Mediterranean such as Antioch, Tyre, etc. The northern route of this land trade network started from Byzantium/Constantinople, traversed the Black Sea, and traveled eastward to Bactria, where there were trade routes along the Oxus River and the Caspian Sea. Further east of Bactria, the caravans would join on to the northern silk route traversing central Asia and across northern Tibet to China. Along this route flowed the goods from the Roman Empire eastward to China, Indian products northward, and Chinese silk and other items westward.

The central portion of the trade routes that radiated from the Eastern Mediterranean started from Antioch, Palmyra, or Petra. Here the caravans would move southeastward along the Euphrates and Tigris river systems to Seleucia, Ctesiphon, and Charax. From these urban centers, the goods would either be shipped via the Persian Gulf or by land routes toward India. At Seleucia, the goods could also be transferred to the silk route that radiated toward Antiochia and onward to central Asia and beyond. After Antiochia, the routes would be part of the major silk route system spanning central Asia, Afghanistan, Tibet, India, China, and mainland Southeast Asia. Although the silk route network is normally understood as one mainly stretching east and west between the Mediterranean and the South China and East China seas, the silk routes also radiated southward to northern India (Indus and Ganges river systems and the Bay of Bengal) and the mainland Southeast Asia coastal zones of Burma, Thailand, and Vietnam (see figures 2.1 and 2.2). Given such a geographic span of trade network linkages, the increasing globalization trajectory of a Eurasian world system should be noted. One can assume that by the first century AD such a globalizing network of trade linkages was firmly in place, if not earlier.

From the Red Sea to East Africa and the Gulf

The Eurasian world system from the eastern part of the Mediterranean spans to the East via land, river systems, and seas. The maritime routes in the north were via the Black Sea, with Byzantium/Constantinople as the gateway; in the south the trade routes were via the Red Sea and the Persian Gulf. For the western part of Red Sea region, the sea routings started from Alexandria and went on to Clysma, Myos Hormos, Philoteras, Leukos Limen, Nechesia, and Berenike, via ports such as Adulis, Mundu, Damo, Opone, and along the east African coast to Rhapta (Casson 1989; Ptolemy [AD 150] 1991; Strabo [7 BC–AD 23] 1917–1935; see figure 2.1).

The port of Berenike, the southernmost port of Roman Egypt located on the western part of the Red Sea south of Myos Hormos, was a port that had a long history of being a trading center even during the time of the Ptolemies. Ivory and elephants were sought after by the Ptolemies, in addition to gold and amethysts from mines in the eastern desert. Roman Berenike flourished up to the first century AD. It was part of the maritime trading route involved primarily in the lucrative spice trade. Besides spices, imports from Southeast Asia were thought to have been transshipped on their way to the Mediterranean. Sidebotham (2011), in his team's excavations, uncovered a bead supposedly from East Java dated to no earlier than the fifth century AD. The excavations also yielded many botanicals and artifacts from South Asia and from the northwestern region of the Indian Ocean. Visitors from sub-Saharan Africa, southern Arabia, Nabataea, and Palmyra and Indian sailors and merchants mingled with the local population. There is a sharp decrease in the quantity of coins, pottery, and datable finds from the second century AD (Sidebotham 2011) through to the fourth century AD, with a decrease in shipping and a reduction of harbor facilities. Population levels went down, as it did in a number of places in the Eurasian world for this time period of decline. Local wars also erupted among the states of Saba, Himyar, and Hadramat. Such conditions reflect the global systemic third Dark Ages occurring from AD 300 onward (Chew 2007).

Berenike's trading contacts with South Asia were mostly with Muziris and Arikamedu on the southern coast of India and Sri Lanka. Sri Lanka exported honey, ginger, emeralds, amethysts, gold, silver, and other metals to the Red Sea ports, including Berenike. Large quantities of Bronze Roman coins (circa fourth century AD) have been discovered on the island. Instead of gold *solidi*, bronzes have replaced gold and silver as the base metals, indicating perhaps of an economic downturn that dovetailed with the period of global collapse that has been widely reported—the Dark Ages of antiquity (Chew 2007).

The peak of trade for Roman Berenike was the first century and through to the first part of the second century. The third century experienced upheavals in both the political and economic arenas. Upturns returned in the middle of the fourth century and continued until the fifth century, after which it went into decline (Sidebotham 2011). It experienced ups and downs in its trading activities, reflecting the rhythms of the global economic system at the time (Chew 2007). The material culture began to utilize local materials instead of those imported from India or from the Mediterranean. Such shifts clearly indicate the demise of the ongoing global trade dynamics during the period of the third Dark Ages (Chew 2007). Local production of materials for consumption was the predominant theme. Berenike's fate was eventually sealed by the middle of the sixth century and the city was abandoned by this period.

On the East African coast, south of Egypt, was the centralized inland kingdom of Aksum. It is a region that has not had many archaeological explorations. Our sources come mostly from the *Periplus*. The kingdom of Aksum was at its height between the late third to the seventh centuries AD. At its port in Adulis, products from the region were exchanged, similar to other Red Sea trading marts. Goods from northwestern India were available, such as iron, dyes, and textiles. Adulis also exported ivory, turtle shell, rhinoceros horns, and hippopotamus hides from the interior of the African continent (McLaughlin 2014; Seland 2010). Besides these items, African slaves from the interior were also available for trading exchanges (Charlesworth [1026] 1970; Chew 2001; Horton and Middleton 2000; Wheatley 1959). Historical sources indicate African slaves were being exported to the Mediterranean, South Asia, and China from the ports on the East African coast. The dominance of the Roman trade is reflected in the discovery of Roman currency, a medium of payment for these trade exchanges.

There were other parts of the East African coast that formed part of this Indian Ocean trading system. Long-distance trade for this region perhaps started around 100 BC when the region became part of the trading system of the Eurasian global system (see, e.g., Horton and Middleton 2000). Unlike archaeological sites in India, the sites that have been excavated on the East African coast have yielded lesser finds of coins and ceramics. Primarily, the trade was mostly conducted by Arabian and Roman traders and sailors, along with Indian and perhaps Southeast Asian ones. In exchange for the African products, Roman traders provided Egyptian cloth, colored glass, and brass and copper pans and drinking vessels. Because of the scarcity of good quality iron, Roman traders also provided this metallic substance for the making of knives and other weapons. Indian products secured were also part of the trading range of goods.

After the ports on the Red Sea come the ports of the northern coast of Somalia, such as Avalites, Malao, and Mundu. Ports on the eastern coast of Somalia included Opone. These ports of Somalia were also trading marts offering East African products, such as ivory, tortoise shell, rhinoceros horn, etc. Besides these products, there were also incenses and other goods, including frankincense, myrrh, and cassia. Besides exporting to Roman Egypt, these Somali marts also exchanged with the ports located in southern Arabia on the southeastern portion of the Red Sea. In this manner, East Africa formed a component of the incense trade network that stretched from Southeast Asia, South Asia, and Southern Arabia to the Red Sea. Incenses were in high demand in the Mediterranean region and Europe. These products, used for religious purposes and for certain lifestyles, made the incense trade a lucrative trading commodity, similar to the spice trade. East African incenses were also shipped from Ethiopia to Roman Egypt via the Nile River.

Sailing south on the east African coast, one would come to the port of Rhapta, located on the modern-day Tanzanian coast. According to the *Periplus*, this was the last port of the East African trading system. It had trade contacts with Muza, located in southwestern Arabia across the Indian Ocean. Similar types of products available in Adulis were also traded here between Arab, Roman, and Indian merchants. Ivory, rhinoceros horn, and tortoise shell were the main exports from this region. Rhapta's importance stretched from the mid-first to the mid-second century AD, and the ports on the Red Sea, such as Hafun Main, were active from the first to the fifth century AD. They had strongest trading relations with India during the second/third century AD and ceased after the fifth century AD. Such decline in trading activity can be explained by the third Dark Age collapse of the system starting from the third century AD, with its peak of decline around the fourth–fifth century AD (Chew 2001, 2007).

Alexandria and Qana were the entrepôts of this part of the trading system. Trading communities surrounded this maritime route. Another port, Leuke Kome, located on the eastern portion of the Red Sea in Arabia at the mouth of the Gulf of Aqaba, served the aromatics (such as frankincense) trade and as a port for the seaborne and overland routes to Gaza. The Arabian Peninsula borders both the Red Sea and the Persian Gulf. As such, its coastal areas were dotted with trading areas and towns that for centuries before the formation of this first global trading system had partaken in the regional trade handled by Greek and Arab merchants from Alexandria southward, and with Indian merchants, who also arrived from northwestern and western India.

The Arabian Peninsula (Arabia Felix to the Romans, and Arabia Eudaimôn to the Greeks) had close ties to East Africa, with control of Azania under the kingdoms of Himyar and Saba. These, along with two other kingdoms, Qataban and Hadramawt, both located in the southern part of the peninsula, shared control of the southern seaborne routes of the Red Sea and East Africa. The ports of Muza, Okelis, al-Madhariba, and Qana, located in the southern portion of the southern Arabian Peninsula and in the territories of these kingdoms, were part of the overall trading systems of the Red Sea and the East African coast. Qana, especially, acted as the entrepôt for the southern part of the Red Sea region, East Africa, and south Arabia. Goods from the northern part of the Red Sea and Alexandria and beyond were transshipped to East Africa and India, and those from these latter regions were shipped northward either via maritime or overland routes. Excavations have revealed settlement patterns from the first century AD or earlier. For example, in the sixth century AD, the kingdom of Himyar was acting as the intermediary for the Romans in this region of the trading system (Mango 1996; Tomber 2008). The main products shipped within this region were aromatics, such as myrrh and frankincense. Myrrh was used as an ingredient in perfume, as an incense that was burnt during funerals and religious offerings, and as an ingredient in medicines. Such trade was established by the eight century BC. Seaborne routes and land routes across the Arabian Peninsula were used, and for goods destined for Gaza, the overland route was popular, with Qana and Timna funneling the goods overland to Gaza and beyond. Qana can be seen to have been established between the mid-first century BC and the late first century AD, with the most intense expansion between the second and the fifth centuries AD (Seland 2010; Tomber 2008). At Qana, textiles, metals, such as copper and tin, coral, and storax—besides frankincense—were exchanged. Moscha Limen or Khor Rori, located east of Qana in south Arabia and founded in almost the same period, was also an incense center that supplied Qana with frankincense. Indian merchants and sailors would land at Khor Rori to spend the winter before sailing home to India (Sedov 2007). Qana also served as a port for ships going to north and south India. The island of Socotra on the Indian Ocean also had Arabs, Indians, and Greeks living on the island, and it was a stop for ships on their way to India and from east Africa (Hourani 1995).

Further east of Khor Rori is the Persian Gulf, and according to the *Periplus*, there were two main towns/ports. Apologos, situated at the mouth of the Gulf, and Omana, located on the Arabian Peninsula, were the main trading ports. Occupied between the second half of the first century BC to the second century AD, Apologos is the site where large quantities of Roman wares (such as glass) and Indian products have been excavated. Associated with Omana and located inland is Mleiha. Goods such as Roman glass wares, Indian pottery, and Egyptian and Hellenistic amphorae have been found there. Their relationships to each other have been hypothesized, but the relations have not been confirmed. The role the Persian Gulf played in the overall trading system of the eastern portion of this Eurasian world system has not been fully established by the few excavations attempted to date, especially on the Iranian part of the Gulf. Was it a transshipment point between the eastern Mediterranean and India? From what has been excavated so far, we can say that, most likely, ports such as Apologos handled the products from southern Mesopotamia or from the eastern Mediterranean, exported from Palmyra, and from the caravan routes traversing the Arabian Peninsula, and perhaps even the incense trade from Khor Rori.

From the Gulf to the Indian Ocean

The trade exchanges between the western with the eastern portions of the Eurasian world system were conducted via land and sea. The maritime routes primarily witnessed ships leaving the ports of the Red Sea in July to take advantage of the monsoon winds, with the first landfall of the trading ships on the western coast of India (Casson 1989: 75, 81, 85). Pliny ([AD 77–79] 1961–68) indicated that the return voyage would then take advantage of the northeast monsoon in December or January. According to the *Periplus*, usually such voyages took approximately twenty days (Casson 1989: 289), though others have suggested a much longer duration lasting around two to three months because of the rough seas (Sidebotham 2011). Sailing south from the Red Sea ports, Muza, Okélis, and Eudaimôn Arabia are the first ports that appeared on the sailing horizon on the south Arabian coast. Okélis was the first stop on the way to the western coast of India, and a place to wait for the monsoon wind to facilitate the sailing into the Gulf of Aden and across the Indian Ocean. Eudaimôn Arabia, located further east, was a mart where the ships sailing from India and Egypt rendezvoused, though its importance receded after the conquest of Egypt by the Romans. Muza was noted to be busy in the *Periplus*, as it had a trade linkage with the Indian port of Barygaza, and also with the northeastern African coast. Textiles, wine, and grain such as wheat were actively traded in this southern Arabian mart.

On the northwestern coast of India, two ports, according to the *Periplus*, Barbaricon and Barygaza, were trade marts where wine, glass, metals textiles, gold coins, and frankincense from western parts of the Eurasian world system, in particular from Egypt and the Arabian Peninsula, were exchanged for precious stones, ivory, cotton cloth, perfumes, and silk from India, central Asia, Southeast Asia, and China (Casson 1989: 75, 81). At Barbaricon, the goods from central Asia and China, transported via caravans from Afghanistan, and ship-borne products from Southeast Asia and China were exchanged for items from the West. Another center of trade after the port of Barbaricon was Barygaza, one of the most important ports of the monsoon trade.

Further down the western coast of India lay the port of Muziris, which, according to the *Periplus*, presumably had a Roman merchant colony (Casson 1989: 85). Besides Muziris, another port was Nelkynda, where Roman ships would pick up the goods shipped from the eastern coast of India, primarily from Arikamedu, located on the southeastern coast of India. The latter port, Arikamedu, had contacts with the Mediterranean from the first century BC onward, and the peak period of activity lasted until the first century AD (Will 1991). Besides shipping goods via sea routes from the southeastern coast of India to the southwestern and western coast of India, traders also used land transportation from the southeastern part to the western ports of India. Finds of Roman coins along these land routes attest to the use of this form of transportation.

Politically, the Andhra rulers controlled much of the western and eastern parts of India during this time period, starting from Barbaricon on the Indus. In southern India, three Tamil states were also of political consequence. The first is the Chera state, which ruled the seacoast from Calicut to Cape Comorin, where the marts of Muziris and Nelcynda were the main attraction for the Roman traders, especially the pepper trade. The second, Muziris, was the main trading port for the Roman ships. Gold was exchanged for the pepper grown in the nearby hills and the interior. In the south and southeast, the north coast of the Gulf of Manaar to the Palk Strait was under the control of the kingdom of Pandya, where the export concentrated on pearls and pepper. Its main port was Nelcynda, located inland along the Pambiyar River. The large Roman ships would moor in its estuary near Becare, whereby the cargoes from Nelcynda would be transported and loaded on them for the return trip to the Red Sea and beyond. Along the eastern coast of India, from the Veliyar to Nellore, is the Chola kingdom, specializing in muslin as its primary export. For the latter, trading goods from Sri Lanka were also parts of the array of items for exchange. The Chola kingdom had three commercial ports on the eastern coast: Puhar, Poduke, and Sopatma. They serviced trading ships from Roman Egypt, Indian merchant ships plying the eastern coast of southern India, and ships that also sailed to Southeast Asia bearing goods from Roman Egypt and India.

Within these trading complexes of south India was the island of Sri Lanka. Sri Lanka, known to the Romans and Greeks as Taprobanê, was also a source for spices and other products, though the island might not be the only place of cultivation. Taprobanê exported spices and other products to the South Asian ports for onward transfer to the Gulf and Red Sea ports, and finally to Roman Egypt. Some of these products most likely came also from Southeast Asia, especially from the various islands of Indonesia and the Malayan archipelago. The evidence of deposits of Roman coins excavated provided the confirmation of this trade, and most of the coin deposits were those of the fourth century AD (Young 2001). It has also been known that by the time Ptolemy was compiling his geography, Roman ships were already making ocean trips from the Gulf of Aden to Taprobanê (McLaughlin 2010). Bopearachchi (2011), however, suggests that the Greek/Roman merchant ships never sailed as far as Sri Lanka because they had to take advantage of the monsoon winds for the voyage to India in July from the Red Sea, thus reaching the Indian ports by September/October, with the return journey to be taken in November to take advantage of the northeast monsoon. Such timing meant that the Roman merchants had only a month to exchange their wares in South Asia, and is not considered to be enough time by Bopearachchi (2011). Thus, it was the Indians in an intermediary role and Sri Lankan merchants who transported their goods to southern Indian ports and marts for the exchange of goods with the Greeks/ Romans. Such reasoning of Bopearachchi's might be an explanation based on the limited finds of Roman coins, but the idea of Greek/Roman ships reaching Sri Lanka and eastward should not be jettisoned without careful consideration. There have been numerous literary sources indicating foreign merchant colonies being established in South Asia, East Africa, island Southeast Asia, and southern China where foreign merchants spent a period of sojourn among the littoral communities of the Eurasian world system waiting for the monsoon winds to change so that they could continue their onward or return voyages.

Further east from Sri Lanka is Southeast Asia. Roman trade contacts were initiated after voyages by Roman ships passed Sri Lanka and sailed into the Bay of Bengal and the region where the River Ganges flowed. During the time of Ptolemy, Roman ships from the Ganges had reached the Burmese coast from Paloura, India, that was the launching point for ships to Burma (McLaughlin 2010). The route to Burma had been reached by Indian sailors seeking commodities such as gold, diamonds, sandalwood, and cinnamon from Southeast

Asia. McLaughlin (2010: 58–59) has determined that Roman ships explored beyond the Malay Peninsula a few decades after AD 139, reaching Vietnam looking for supplies of rhinoceros horns, pearls, ivory, and fragrant woods. According to the Chinese court document *Hou-Han-shu*, Rome was known as Ta-Ch'in to the Chinese (Leslie and Gardiner 1996) and was interested in pursuing economic and political relations with Han China. On this subject, in the document Wei-Lü provided a detailed account of the Roman products that were imported into China (Leslie and Gardiner 1996). According to Chinese sources, an official delegation from Rome to China arrived in the Middle Kingdom around AD 166. McLaughlin (2010) also states that by AD 166 during the Han dynasty, Roman subjects reached China sailing from Southeast Asia. Whether these Romans belonged to the same delegation or were of different delegations dispatched to the Chinese court is not clear. What is clear is that from the Antonine period onward, during the third Dark Age of collapse, Roman trade with the East tapered down as reflected by the coin hordes discovered in India and a sharp decline in trade of the Red Sea ports.

From the Indian Ocean to the South China Sea

As much as the Roman and Indian ships sailed east toward Southeast Asia and China, ships from Southeast Asia were also sailing west toward India, Sri Lanka, and the East African coast. Notwithstanding maritime trade, the land trade routes radiating from the eastern Mediterranean toward central Asia, India, Southeast Asia, and China were also used to conduct trade in the Eurasian world economy.

Various timings have been pinpointed of trade connections between the East and the West of the Eurasian world system. According to Kennedy (1898) and Tibetts (1956), trading connections between Mesopotamia and China existed as early as the seventh century BC, and Glover (1996) notes exchanges between mainland Southeast Asia and India between 360 and 390 BC. Wang (1998: 13) states that Chinese trade with India started toward the end of the first millennium BC. Within Asia, localized exchange networks in Indonesia and the Malay Peninsula existed from the second millennium BC (Chew 2001, 2007; Glover 1979, 1996). Southeast Asian merchants and trading communities were already participating in the trading world by 1000 BC and had substantial commercial contacts with India and Madagascar by the second part of the first millennium BC (Christie 1990; Hall 1985; Leong 1990: 20–21; Taylor 1976). Archaeological excavations have indicated that perhaps as early as 500 BC the polities in the Malay Peninsula were already participating in regional trading networks.[4] It is clear that with the material evidence unearthed from archaeological finds, regional Southeast Asian trade was quite robust before the arrival of Indian influence in the later parts of the early historic period, further underlining the formation of developed kingdoms in mainland and island Southeast Asia (Jacq-Hergoualc'h 2002).

In East Asia, intraregional trade routes were established by the fifth century BC (Higham 2002; Hung and Bellwood 2010; Sarabia 2004). Within East Asia, Chinese goods were exchanged by land to the Korean Peninsula and via shipping to the Japanese islands. Imamura (1996) and Sarabia (2004) have traced the exchange between China and Japan in the archaeological bronze finds unearthed in Japan that had northern Chinese origins. There were raw materials exchanged between Taiwan and Southeast Asia (c. 500 BC), and nephrites of Taiwanese origin have been excavated in southern Thailand, the Philippines, and other parts of insular Southeast Asia (Hung and Bellwood 2010).

Given the above different periodizations, within the Asian region, we can assume that trade occurred between China and the ports on the Indian Ocean by at least the second half of the first century BC when, following unification of China in 221 BC, the Chinese pursued expansions to the south (Wang 1958: 21). Wheatley (1959: 19) writes of Chinese envoys being sent by the Han emperor Wu (141–87 BC) to explore the South Seas as far as the Bay of Bengal. The establishment of commanderies in the south helped to facilitate and establish trade exchanges (Wang 1998). Evidence of Chinese trade in Southeast Asia has been revealed in recent excavations in southern Thailand of the Malay Peninsula (Murillo-Barroso et al. 2010). With these different timings of trading connections between the eastern and western zones of the Eurasian world system, it would be safe to assume that the connection of Southeast Asia and East Asia with the eastern Mediterranean can be seen from the era of the Chin dynasty (around 221 BC) onward.

The various seas and straits in Southeast Asia and East Asia circumscribed the trading connections conducted in the eastern zone of the Eurasian world economy. Like the land (silk) routes that linked the West with the East, the Bay of Bengal, Andaman Sea, Straits of Malacca, Java Sea, Makassar Strait, Molucca Sea, Celebes Sea, South China Sea, East China Sea, Yellow Sea, and Sea of Japan became marine routes linking the East with the West. The two major seas of importance in these maritime routes between East and West were, of course, the Indian Ocean and the South China Sea. Regionally, the Straits of Malacca and the South China Sea were of particular significance, for they bordered the major land masses of Southeast Asia and East Asia whereby the global trade was conducted. Networks of local and regional trading ports and centers existed from 200 BC onward or perhaps even earlier, and from these local and regional networks the trading was linked to the trans-Eurasian maritime routes of the global system from the East China Sea to the Mediterranean (see figure 2.3).

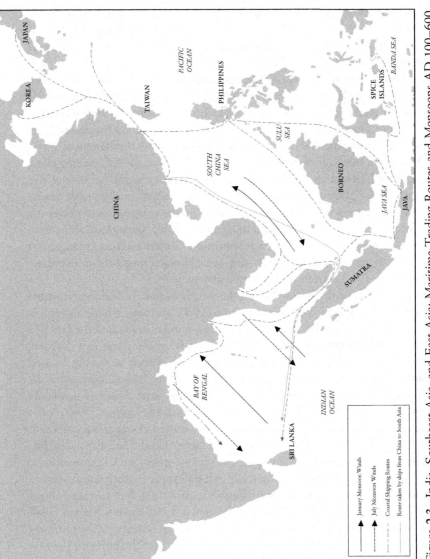

Figure 2.3. India, Southeast Asia, and East Asia: Maritime Trading Routes and Monsoons AD 100–600. Courtesy of Annie Thomsen, Cartographer.

From the Roman Mediterranean through to India, merchants used the above shipping routes from the Indian Ocean, the Bay of Bengal, and the Andaman Sea to mainland and island Southeast Asia, seeking products that Southeast Asia had in abundant supply. The reverse occurred as well. Those sailing east had pepper, aromatics, cloves, various food items, marine products, exotic feathers, and pearls on their trading orders (see, e.g., Hall 2011; Hoogervorst 2013; Manguin 2004; Wang 1958; and see figure 2.4). Usually for shipping from India and Sri Lanka, the port call would be the Isthmus of Kra near Peninsula Malaya, whereby goods were then transferred by land portage across the Isthmus to eastern Malay Peninsula ports and kingdoms located on the western edge of the Mekong Delta, such as Funan with its port of Oc Éo. From Funan, ships would call on Pan Pan, located on the eastern part of the Isthmus of Kra; Linyi and Chiao-chih, located in Vietnam; and Hepu and Xuwen on the Gulf of Tonking (Borell 2013; Glover 1990). Sailing along the Straits of Malacca and avoiding the land portage across the Isthmus of Kra would only take place in the fourth century AD onward. Traders took advantage of the monsoon winds, which, depending on the season, would power the ships toward the east or west toward India and onward. Sailing east, ships from Southeast Asia would reach ports in southern China, such as Guangzchou (Borell 2013), and, in turn, Chinese ships would reach the ports on mainland Southeast Asia and eastern Malay Peninsula.

Further south of the Malay Peninsula are the islands of Indonesia, where a regional networks of export centers provided the aromatic woods and spices that symbolize the Southeast Asian trade. The Sunda Straits and the Java Sea were the main shipping routes, where products from Sumatra, Java, Borneo, and the Celebes would be collected at regional centers such as Koying, located in southern Sumatra, and from Koying to Funan on mainland Southeast Asia.

Various polities and ports dotted mainland Southeast Asia and peninsula and island Southeast Asia. Funan, located on mainland Southeast Asia, was a center not only for the trans-Eurasian maritime routes; it was also a collection point for the intraregional trade that flowed from island Southeast Asia. Funan's port of Oc Éo handled the shipping traffic. According to Chinese sources, Funan was quite developed economically and politically by the second century AD. Its stage of development even allowed it to send a fleet to take control of some of the smaller polities located in Thailand and eastern Malaya (Hall 2011; Manguin 2009). This was to change by the fifth century, as the products from island Southeast Asia started to bypass Funan and the ports on the east coast of the Malay Peninsula, with direct sailing from Koying and other collection centers in Borneo and Indonesia to the ports of southern China. Prior to its decline (from the mid-fifth century onward) as a main trading center for Southeast Asia, Funan had developed as an urban center with shipbuilding facilities (Hall 2011; Manguin 2009). Founded, according to Chinese sources,

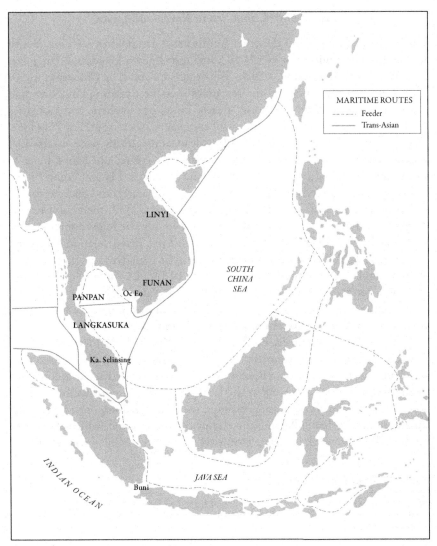

Figure 2.4. Southeast Asia and East Asia: Maritime Trading Routes 200 BC–AD 500. Courtesy of Annie Thomsen, Cartographer.

around the first century AD, Funan had walled cities, palaces, storehouses, port facilities, and even hostelries for visiting foreign merchants (Hall 2011). Its capital had a moat surrounding it and a six-kilometer-long wall. It had an established agricultural economy as well. The latter was developed further when the regional trade of Southeast Asia and those coming from India and Sri Lanka started to bypass Funan on their way to the trading ports of southern China.

From South China Sea to Korea and Japan

Further east of Funan and the other Southeast Asian polities is China. South China, prior to unification in 221 BC, had four known kingdoms: Tung Ou, Min Yueh, Nan Yueh, and Lo Yueh. The expansion south by Chinese emperor Shih Huang-ti was to obtain the resources that these trading kingdoms had access to, such as rhinoceros horns, pearls, kingfisher feathers, and aromatics of Southeast Asia. Following successful campaigns, these southern kingdoms were defeated. Chinese military and civil administrations were established on the coastal regions, and four commanderies were set up: Min-Chung at Fuchou, Nanhai at Canton, and Kwei-lin and Hsiang at Hanoi (Wang 1958). Political disruption followed the end of the Chin dynasty, and declarations of independence were made by the four commanderies. With the establishment of the Han dynasty, political struggle ensued among the four commanderies, with Nanhai emerging victorious and establishing vassal relations with the Han Emperor. With the ascension of Wu-ti to the Han dynasty's throne, Nanhai was finally incorporated into China by 114 BC. By the first century BC, trade was conducted between China and India (Wang 1958). The number of commanderies by now had increased to seven, and they were of different sizes in numbers of households and individuals (see table 2.1).

Trade relations continued, but according to Wang (1958), there was a slowdown in trade with India toward the end of the Han dynasty. This slowed pace continued until the later Han dynasty and was only revived at the second half of the second century AD, when the land silk routes in northwestern China were disrupted. Such disruption fostered the Wu kingdom, one of the three kingdoms established following the end of the Han period, which controlled lands to the south of the Yangtze to initiate trade of the Nanhai with India and

Table 2.1. Number of Commanderies

Name of Commandery	Households	Individuals
Nanhai	19,613	94,253
Yu-lin	12,415	71,162
Ts'ang-wu	24,379	146,610
Chaio-chih	92,440	746,237
Ho-p'u	15,398	78,890
Chiu-chen	35,743	166,013
Jih-nan	15,460	69,485
Total	215,448	1,372,290

Source: Wang, 1958: 17.

the Roman Orient. Chiao Chou was the terminus of the sea trade with the West. From here, the merchants connected to Funan and Lin-Yi on mainland Southeast Asia. Trading exchanges slowed again between AD 300 and 400, which further underscores the contraction of the whole system being experienced then.

Whereas the Nanhai imported products from the southern Chinese commanderies, and ports supplied the urban environments along the Yangtze and the Hwang Ho rivers, there were also relations between China, Korea, and Japan as early as seven thousand years ago (Meiyuan 1971; Tongko 1971). The normal route was via the East China Sea, from the Yangtze to Korea and Japan. There was also a sea route between Nanhai in the south and Jiankang in northeast China. From here, the route goes from Jiankang, Liuzi, and Yan via land routes on the coast that were connected to Korea's Lolang, Hangsong, and Kyongju, and by sea between Yan in China and Lolang in Korea. The land trading route then turns again to a maritime route between Kyongju in southern Korea and Nagasaki in the Japanese islands, ending at Tokyo. The sea routes between Southeast Asia and Taiwan were also used, especially for the exchange of raw materials from Taiwan to Southeast Asia.

Transportation

The transportation of goods is a key feature in structuring the trading exchanges between the regions of this evolving Eurasian world system. Various modes were utilized, depending on the costs, the locations, and surrounding landscapes where the goods were to be delivered (Sidebotham 1986, 2011; Warmington 1928). The two main forms were animals and ships. For the land trading routes of the Eurasian world system, pack animals such as donkeys, horses, and camels (Arabic and Bactrian animals) were the main beasts of burden used to transport the goods across vast stretches of land linking the trading marts of Europe, the eastern Mediterranean, central Asia, Arabia, East Africa, India, Persia, and China. Depending on the monsoon winds, it was more economical and efficient with the scale of goods that were moved in terms of volume and weight to be transported in ships via the vast maritime routes of the various oceans and seas that surrounded the Eurasian world economy (Chew 2007). In addition to the consideration of size and weight of goods to be transported, costs for overland routes were high, especially for distances over 120–160 kilometers (Sidebotham 2011). Because of this, when the items to be shipped were not luxuries that would secure a high profit, but were goods for mass consumption, the maritime route was the modality of transportation of choice. In certain cases, it was a combination of both maritime and land routes during periods when there was a hiatus for sailing between March and

October while waiting for the wind directions to change. Under these conditions, whenever possible, the land route was chosen if the required goods were consumed year round. Estimates of animal power that were contracted exhibit the scale. For 220 tons of cargo transported between Berenike and Alexandria, traders would use over a thousand camels and 160 camel drivers, along with armed guards (McLaughlin 2014: 90).

Being dependent on the winds to propel the ships during this period of world history, shipping times and costs were contingent on the wind directions that prevailed during certain times of the year. Prior to the discovery of the monsoons, the sailing times were much extended as the ships had to hug the coasts of the various continents that circumscribe the Eurasian world economy in order to reach the distant shores, such as from Alexandria in Egypt to Berenike on the Red Sea, and onward to Barbaricon and Barygaza on the northwestern part of India. Likewise, Indian shipping from Barbaricon and Barygaza would need to sail following the coast to the Persian Gulf, and along the coast of Arabia to reach Okelis, located on the entrance to the Red Sea. It is clear that with the discovery of the monsoon winds, the sailing times would be reduced as the ships then could sail directly from one land mass across the ocean to another, provided that their construction was of suitable strength and durability (Hourani 1995; Parkin and Barnes 2002; Tomber 2008). Ships from east African ports could sail directly across the Indian Ocean to Barbaricon, and ships from the Red Sea ports could sail directly to northwestern India or southern India and Ceylon. As well, ships from Southeast Asia could take advantage of the monsoon winds to sail from Southeast Asia to India and beyond, undertaking their return journeys during a different period of the monsoon season. Likewise, shipping from India could sail from southern and eastern Indian ports via the Straits of Malacca to eastern mainland Southeast Asia and southern China. Given such natural environmental parameters as the changing directions of the monsoon winds, the extended period between the direction of the wind change, and the state of technology existing then for shipping propulsion, an explication of the shipping utilized would be useful to understand the social exchanges and institutional structures along these trading routes across the Eurasian world economy.

Ships of the Maritime Eurasian World System

Without prioritizing by importance or types of the ships that plied the oceans of the Eurasian world economy, our explication begins in the West and moves eastward. The seminal works of Hourani (1995), Manguin (1980, 1993), Ray (2003), and Hoogervorst (2013) provide us with an overview of the cultures and technologies that were involved in the maritime transportation from the ancient times. The maritime sphere of the Eurasian world system has a long tradition of seafaring. The Eastern Mediterranean has a long history of maritime activities with the Minoans, Greeks, Phoenicians, and Romans, depending on the historical period, dominating the sea lanes of the trade routes (Casson 1991, 1994, 1995). The Red Sea, East Africa, and the Arabian Sea regions had their Arabic seafaring culture and included Greek/Roman sailors and merchants (Hourani 1995; Sidebotham 2011; Young 2001). The South Asian region also had a long history of South Asian sailors and shipping owners (Mookerji 1987; Ray 2003). Southeast Asia, especially the island Southeast Asian region, has been noted by various archaeological studies for its seafaring sailors and ships reaching as far as the East African coast by the first millennium BC (Manguin 1980, 1993a, 1993b; McLaughlin 2011; Ray 2003). The East Asian region, especially China, has also a long historical practice of voyaging sailors and ships plying the South China and East China Seas and the Indian Ocean as far as East Africa, depending on the time period (Deng 1997).

Hourani's (1995) focus on Arab seafaring offers a view of the early origins of this maritime activity undertaken by Arab sailors. Because of the lack of good timber suitable in this region for the construction of ships that could undertake voyages over large expanse of oceans, Arab shipping initially was restricted to coastal routes along the Red Sea, the Arabian coast, the Persian Gulf, and East Africa. According to Hourani (1995), only when Indian shipping reached the Red Sea and Persian Gulf region and opened up the possibility of importing timber from India for ship construction was it possible for shipping from this region to sail directly across the oceans and seas to distant lands such as South Asia. Prior to this, during the time of Alexander, the Phoenicians and Greeks were the seafarers in the Red Sea and the Persian Gulf. Greek/Roman sailors, plus those of Arabic origins, dominated the seafaring trade of the region. On the whole, Arab, and Greek/Roman merchant ships plied the Red Sea and the Arabian coast (Young 2001). With the conquest of Egypt by the Romans, Greek/Roman ships, as well as Arab ships, dominated the Red Sea, the Arabian Coast, and East Africa. In his *Geography*, Ptolemy noted that Greeks were sailing to Ceylon, and it has been suggested that they even sailed as far as the Malay Peninsula (Hourani 1995: 35). Such voyages reduced in frequency by the third century AD with the collapse of the western part of the Roman Empire during the third Dark Ages (Chew 2007). Persian shipping in the Arabian Sea and the Persian Gulf received a boost with the rise of the Persian Sassanid Empire in AD 225. Persian shipping went as far as Ceylon for exchange of trade goods from Southeast Asia and China.

Arabic and Greek/Roman ships were constructed of wood of different varieties. Arabic ships were made of teak or coconut wood. Teak was not a tree that grows in the region but was imported from India, probably from the Himalayan region, and its importation has been continuous since 3000 BC

(Chew 2001). This practice of importation of teakwood was also reported in the *Periplus* (Casson 1968). Teak was chosen because once seasoned it does not split or crack, or shrink and lose its shape. Besides teak, wood from the coconut tree was also used in the construction of Arabic ships. The wood was from Southern India, Ceylon, the Maldives, Laccadives, and perhaps even from Indonesia. According to Hourani (1995), either the wood was imported or the ships were built in the Maldives and the Laccadives.

The typical Arab ship for the seafaring trade was the dhow. "Dhow" is a general term applied to all sailing vessels of the western Indian Ocean (Hourani 1995). Traditional Arab vessels were constructed by laying the keel on the ground and fastening horizontal planks to the keel on each side with fiber stitches. Using fiber to tie the planks together instead of nails were typical of the shipbuilding technique for ships built along the Red Sea, the East African coast, the Persian Gulf, the Malabar and Coromandel coasts of India, and the islands of the Maldive and Luccadive (Hourani, 1995: 93; Sheriff 2010). Iron nails were only used after AD 1500, following the arrival of Portuguese and Chinese ships that had visited the western region of the Indian Ocean. After that, boats that were fiber-attached were seen only along coastal routes and used primarily for fishing. This technique of building ships produced vessels that were not strong enough to meet strong winds and high seas, for the stitches would often snap, and the vessels would have to undergo constant repair to keep them seaworthy. The probable reason that stitching was continued was its relative cheapness compared to vessels that were built with iron nails, even though the manufacture of iron had been discovered in India, Iran, and Egypt. During the early periods, iron making was a small-scale, expensive process and the use of iron in shipbuilding was not pursued on a grand scale until it was necessary to build vessels that could compete with the growth of commerce in the Indian Ocean following the arrival of the Europeans. The rationale for the need to switch to iron nails and the resultant robustness of the constructed ships explained by Hourani (1995) as outlined above is a possible explanation. How accurately it explains the changing construction practice needs to be reconsidered in light of what has been discovered in maritime archaeology and shipwrecks in Southeast Asia (Flecker 2005; Manguin 1993a, 1993b). Stitching continued to be used on Arab and Indian ships, albeit with evolved construction technology for ocean-going ships, as late as AD 800, as the Belitung shipwreck has shown (Flecker 2005). The practice was also continued in Southeast Asian shipbuilding.

The masts of ships were made of similar types of wood as the hulls. Teak or coconut wood was used, with some masts supposedly measuring seventy-six feet in length. Cotton cloth or even palm or coconut leaves were employed as the materials for the sails.

The Greek/Roman ships plying the waters of the Red Sea and the Indian Ocean were usually less than seventy-five tons, though some were as large as 200–350 tons and up to 120 feet long (McLaughlin 2014; Sidebotham 2011; Young 2001). The piers at Berenike had docking space up to this length. In terms of construction, the shell-first method was employed, with timbers joined edge to edge with dowels and nails. The hulls of these ships were sheathed with pitch, and even lead was used to retard the marine organisms from invading the hulls. Later on in the Roman period, ship construction was changed: first the internal ribs were assembled, and the hull was then built around these ribs. Supposedly, this change in construction technique enabled the vessel to be built much more quickly and cheaply. Large-sized timbers of either cedar or teak were used for the ribs to strengthen the ships, and cheaper planking formed the hull. Cedar from Lebanon, as well as teakwood, was used during construction in Roman Egypt. The teakwood was either imported from India or employed in repairs during port visits to western India. Indian cotton was used for the sailcloth. Usually a large, centrally placed sail on the ship was the design to catch the monsoon winds and, at the same time, to withstand the waves caused by the rough seas during the monsoon season.

Insular Southeast Asia also has a long tradition of maritime activities. Manguin (1993a, 1993b: 190) highlights this indigenous shipbuilding tradition: "The evidence shows an original, structurally unique technical assemblage which was developed as early as the Chinese or Indian Ocean neighbouring traditions." In an earlier publication, Manguin (1980: 276) suggested that the Southeast Asian tradition of building of ocean-going ships was adopted and adapted by Chinese shipwrights in the eighth to ninth centuries AD, when China started to build ocean-going ships. Before this the Chinese had only coastal or river ships and crafts, and these vessels did not have the necessary features of ocean-going ships. From this, Manguin (1993a, 1993b) reasons that it was the Southeast Asian ships that visited southern Chinese ports that became exemplars (rigging of multiple masts and sails, v-shaped hulls with keel and stem post, and fastening of several sheaths of planks to the hull) that the Chinese shipwrights adopted. Deng (1997) and Guangqi (2000), however, note that the Chinese had established long-range sea routes to the Arabian/Persian Gulf region by the time of the Western Han dynasty, and by the beginning of the early first millennium AD, Chinese ships had reached Ceylon and beyond. Since these timings of their works were based on literary accounts, the question still remains whether it was Chinese merchants and travelers sailing on Arabic or Southeast Asian vessels or on Chinese ships that reached the Arabian/Persian Gulf region and even the eastern provinces of the Roman Empire. Supporting Manguin's (1993a, 1993b) view of Southeast Asian nautical technology, Hall (2011: 44–45) notes the contributions of Southeast Asian seafaring in connecting the maritime silk trade routes between India and China, particularly that Southeast Asian ships provided the transportation vessels. Hoogervorst's (2012) seminal study summarizes concretely via archaeological and linguistic analyses the contributions of Southeast Asian seafaring technologies to the shipbuilding traditions of the Indian Ocean, such as methods of plank-fastening, rigging, outrigger device, and a specific type of paddle. The Southeast Asian influence was much stronger in the eastern part of the Indian Ocean, in the Bay of Bengal area, than in the Arabian Sea. In turn, the Southeast Asians were adopting the seafaring technologies of the South Asians. To this end, exchanges and communications in the form of trade on the maritime silk route have fostered the hybridization of shipbuilding and nautical technologies among different cultures and littoral groups of the Eurasian world system.

The Southeast Asian ocean-going vessel, the jong, or known to the Chinese as Kun-lu bo, was constructed using the stitched plank and lashed-lug technique (Manguin 1980, 1993a, 1993b). The earliest Southeast Asian vessel excavated in Pontian (Malaysia) has been dated to be between the third and fifth century AD (Booth 1984). Similar to Arabic and Indian shipping construction, stitching continued to be used to hold the planks of the ships together. The stitches and lashings were made from the fiber of the sugar palm (Arenga pinnata). The technique has protruding lugs carved out of the inner side of the planks to allow lashing to hold the planks together. This construction technique changed as time progressed, with wooden dowels replacing the sewing of the planks together. The dowels gave more rigidity to the hull for ocean travel.

According to Chinese literary accounts of Southeast Asian vessels and excavation discoveries, the main features of these ships are the following: (a) they were large, about fifty meters in length, with a carrying capacity of five hundred to a thousand persons and perhaps 250 to 1000 tons; (b) iron was not used in their construction; (c) the vessels have several layers of planks; and (d) they were rigged with multiple sails and masts for efficient ocean travel. Given the size and tonnage of these ships, Manguin (1993a: 264) has suggested that these vessels were constructed by the "incipient coastal states such as those that appeared on the Malay Peninsula around the beginning of the Christian era."

By the Chinese Han period (206 BC–AD 220), a maritime silk route from southern China to South Asia was established (Guangqi 2000). China, with its long history of maritime tradition by the period of the Western Han dynasty (206 BC–AD 24), had multideck ships sailing the coastal waters (Deng 1997). Their length was approximately fifty meters, and they carried six hundred to seven hundred passengers. Instead of stitching to secure the planks of the vessel, iron nails and clamps were employed by the eighth century AD. There was also multiple sheathing of the hulls. The axial suspended rudder was commonly employed. Lug sails were also mounted. The ocean-going vessels, known as junks, became associated with Chinese shipping, and the shape and style of this vessel, according to Manguin (1993a), is usually associated with Chinese ships. That should be reconsidered in view of the cross-pollination of Southeast Asian and South Asian shipbuilding technologies (Hall 2011; Manguin 1980, 1993a, 1993b). Most of China's shipping expansion and ocean-going activities developed during the Tang-Song dynasty period (AD 617–1279) and reached its peak during the Ming Dynastic period (AD 1368–1644).

The extensiveness of the maritime networks linking the trading exchanges of the Eurasian world system over the expanse of Mediterranean Sea, the Red Sea, the Persian Gulf, the Indian Ocean, and the South China and East China Seas, as well as their associated polities/communities, indicates trading exchanges and communications continued over long periods of world history, starting from the late prehistoric times. These polities in the different regions of this system participated in this system-wide exchange using their available resources, whether occurring naturally or derived from technologies that they developed or adopted in this trade. In terms of shipping construction, which is key to the maritime trading system, Southeast Asia exhibited technological prowess (to be discussed in chapter 3) that has to be noted in comparison to the other regions of the Eurasian world system. By no means does this reflect the characteristics of a peripheral region of the world economy. Even the tonnage and size of the Southeast Asian ships, as noted in the previous pages, suggest the developmental progress of the Southeast Asian region.

Besides the above discussion of the construction, tonnage, and size of Southeast Asian shipping, the study of the type and volume of trading exchanges of the Eurasian world economy has focused overwhelmingly on the core polities and littoral communities located in the geographic areas of Europe, India, and China. What have been neglected are the polities and littoral communities of Southeast Asia that have participated in this global trading system. In terms of scale and extent, Southeast Asia's contribution, in terms of volume and type of trade exchanges, has been much overlooked. The following chapters try to address this imbalance.

Notes

1. To say that Crete was in an expansionary mode during this time of the first phase of the Dark Age, starting about 2200 BC, requires clarification. This expansion during a Dark Age suggests that only the southern portion (southern Mesopotamia, the Gulf, and northwestern India) of the trading system was deeply impacted by downward trends and that Crete was not in the core of the system at this time.
2. Thompson (2001) has periodized the pulsations of the expansion and contraction of this trading world of the Near East.
3. For a periodization of long-term economic downturns of the system, see Chew (2007).

The Economy

CHAPTER 3

Southeast Asia in the Maritime Eurasian World Economy

Introduction

Linked by maritime and land trade routes, the Eurasian world system evolved and expanded with the rise of multiple core polities (empires and kingdoms) that developed over world history. The ascent of multiple cores was the result of accumulation of surpluses derived through economic exchanges, wars, or tributes obtained from political/military dominance. System expansion was contingent much on the exchange of goods generating surpluses within and between regions of the Eurasian world system. Natural landscape assets, environmental and climatic conditions, and the stage of economic development conditioned the goods that were produced for exchange, creating product specializations by particular polities. The production of these goods was also dependent on cultural lifestyles and military and mass consumption needs. In other words, a range of goods and food items was produced for exchange in this Eurasian world system for both elite and mass consumption. A system-wide division of labor existed related to the type of products exchanged within and between regions of the world economy, and the maritime and land trading routes were the conduits by which these trading goods flowed from the Mediterranean Sea to the South China Sea and from Byzantium (Antioch, Petra, and Palmyra) to Loyang. Likewise, the reverse flow also occurred, albeit with different types of goods.

Southeast Asia's input in this global trade network has often been underemphasized. Instead, scholars and specialists have awarded world economic expansion to the initiatives taken by Chinese, South Asian, Greek/Roman, and Arabic merchants and the respective core polities in the different regions of this Eurasian world system. There have been some exceptions to the above common understanding of Southeast Asia place in this world history (Hoogervorst 2013; Manguin 1980, 1993a, 1993b). Unfortunately, these studies are among the very few that offer us a reevaluation of Southeast Asia's contribution and role in the evolving Eurasian World system in world history. The overwhelming intellectual stance in Western and Asian scholarship continues to portray Southeast Asia as a region that is the recipient of socioeconomic and cultural influences from South Asia, Arabia, and China, and as an intermediary, or distribution point/entrepôt, instead of envisioning it as a region that has played a contributory and productive part in the Eurasian world economy throughout history (see, e.g., Bellina 2004, 2006; Coedes 1966, 1968). We will address this neglect by examining Southeast Asia's materialistic practice of producing trade goods for exchange to meet system-wide needs, including those of the core centers of the Eurasian world system, thus emphasizing the contribution and influence of Southeast Asia to the economic expansion of the Eurasian world system instead of treating it as just an intermediary or distribution point/entrepôt. In this chapter, and the subsequent one, we will provide evidence contrary to this latter economic depiction of Southeast Asia.

The Circuit of Maritime Trade Exchanges

The globalizing Eurasian world economy from the late second millennium BC onward was circumscribed by circuits of trade routes linked to different regions, cities and towns, and rivers and oceans, forming a trading matrix with developed nodes of urban areas with ports. Throughout history, these nodes were urban centers located within core developed polities, whether they were empires or kingdoms. Some of these trading routes in the Eastern Mediterranean, the Red Sea, and Persian Gulf areas, along with the northwestern portion of the Indian Ocean, existed as early as the third millennium BC, as I have identified in chapter 2.

The core centers of the system determined its dynamics of accumulation of surpluses, geographic expansions through trade and conquests, and cultural and social consumption trends and tastes that influenced goods produced or harvested from terrestrial and maritime sources. From the late second millennium BC onward, the cores of the Eurasian system centered regionally in the Eastern Mediterranean, South Asia/Iran, and China. These centers with their urban nodes were connected via the matrix of trade routes (land and maritime), determining a division of global production and consumption. In the previous chapter, I have traced these urban nodes, especially the littoral communities from the Eastern Mediterranean to the South China Sea. Southeast Asia's location in this Eurasian maritime trading matrix is one situated between two core regions (South Asia and China) with developed urban centers and ports. It produced trade items that were highly sought after, and its geographic position between two core regions, whereby trading ships would sail past, provided the area with an added advantage, unlike other more remote areas (such as Australia) that are off the ancient trade route circuits. Southeast Asia is not just a region of entrepôts, as most Asian and Southeast Asian specialists and scholars have categorized it (see, e.g., Leong 1990; Lughod 1989).

Trade Exchanges between Regional Cores: Rome and India

Toward the end of the second millennium BC, the western zone of the Eurasian world system had two core nodes of the trading network: Rome and India. The Romans knew about South Asia but were not that cognizant about the Far East until the first century BC, when silk started to reach the Mediterranean in larger volumes by way of the Parthian Empire. With the annexation of Egypt in 31 BC following the civil war of the Roman Republic, the Romans finally gained access to the Red Sea and the shipping lanes of the Indian Ocean and beyond. The peak of the Roman-Indian trade was from the first century BC to the third century AD (Tomber 2008). Vast quantities of goods, including gold and silver, were exchanged starting from the eastern part of the Roman Empire, via the Arabian Peninsula, the Persian Gulf, and eastern Africa (what is now Ethiopia and Somalia), with the Indian subcontinent and Taprobanê. The trade was conducted mostly via the sea routes as we have identified in the previous pages. Land routes from the eastern part of the Roman Empire connecting with those in Central Eurasia and China, with tracks veering south to the Indian subcontinent were also used; though in these latter routes the exchanges were more restricted to products of China and Central Eurasia.

Roman trade with the East, including South Asia and Eastern Africa, was financially rewarding for Rome. The quarter-rate import tax (tetarte) imposed yielded enormous revenues for the Roman state. McLaughlin (2015: xix) has estimated that by the first century AD, the tax on foreign trade provided about a third of the income to finance the administration of the entire Roman Empire.

The trade between India and Rome covered different types of goods, from preciosities to necessities, as we have briefly covered in the previous chapter. It was mostly focused not only on natural resources, but manufactured products as well. Coined money of gold, silver, and copper of Roman origin was part of the trading transactions (Charlesworth 1970; Deo 1991; Tomber 2008; Warmington 1928; Young 2001). Large quantities of merchandise were exchanged starting from the reign of Roman Emperor Augustus (27 BC–AD 14) onward, occurring during a period of economic expansion of the world economy (Frank and Gills 1993). The types of products imported by Roman and Greek merchants, with some of them based in Alexandria, Egypt, were wide ranging. Live animals and animal products, such as lions, tigers, rhinos, elephants, parrots, draft animals, and Indian ivory, were sought after by the traders. In certain cases, such as the wild animals, the goods were not from India, but were transshipments, with their points of origin being locales such as Aksum in eastern Africa (Ethiopia). It is clear that this wildlife was consumed in households, and used as well for transportation purposes and as instruments of war, as in the case of the elephant.

Other goods traded were not only luxuries for elite consumption, but also necessities for use in manufacturing and cooking or for medicinal and religious purposes, such as plant products and aromatic spices (McPherson 1995; Sidebotham 1986; Tomber 2008; Warmington 1928). These included pepper, cinnamon, ginger, cardamom, myrrh, sugar, and raisin-barberry, indigo for coloring, cotton for clothing, ebony, and rice as cereal. Mineral products and precious stones were also exchanged, such as diamonds, onyx, carnelian, amethyst, garnet, pearls, and conch shells. Indian manufactures such as cotton textiles and Chinese silk were also part of the imports exchanged by the Roman, Greek, and Arab traders.

Exports to Rome from India

Plant Products

Spices and aromatics have, since the dawn of the first millennium of the current era, been the driving forces of commerce between the West and the East. The voyages of discovery (or commerce) in the fifteenth century AD by the Portuguese and the Spanish seeking a reliable route to the East for its spices were just a continuation of a commercial quest that started fifteen hundred years before. Pepper and cinnamon were not only from the Indian subcontinent. For example, cinnamon also came from Ceylon, Southeast Asia, and southern China. It seems that true cinnamon came from India and Ceylon, and the poorer grade cassia was from Southeast Asia and China (Cappers 2006; Dalby 2000; Tomber 2008). These different source origins of spices underscore the global trade connections that extended beyond India and Ceylon to Southeast Asia and southern China. Hence we see another indicator of a global system of trade that spans from the Mediterranean, the Red Sea, the Persian Gulf, the Indian Ocean, through to the South China Sea rather than just ending at the Indian Ocean.[1] Pepper can be considered one of the most sought after spices for its wide range of uses in the Roman lifestyle. Two species of pepper (Piper nigrum and Piper longum) were imported. Long pepper, black pepper, and white pepper had different monetary values. The most expensive was long pepper, which was almost three times the price of black pepper and half as much as white pepper. Pricing cost was due to long pepper having the quality of being the hottest, and also its use for medicinal purposes. For the latter, it is found as an ingredient in all kinds of Roman medicines and drugs. During Pliny's times, black pepper was four denarii a pound, and white pepper was seven denarii a pound, with long pepper costing the most, at fifteen denarii a pound (Warmington 1928: 183). Black and white pepper came from India, whereas long pepper came not only from India but also from Ceylon and the Malay Peninsula (Tomber 2008; Warmington 1928). It has been recorded, according to the *Periplus Maris Erythraei*, that bags of pepper were traded for with gold bullion by Greek and Roman traders (Casson 1989). The spice, according to Warmington (1928: 182), probably formed half the cargo of a Roman ship. Such vast profits were received from the spice trade that a ship's captain would load up with pepper and set sail even in bad weather. From inland trading houses, these sacks of pepper would find their way back to the Roman Empire via the Red Sea, and even by camel from Coptos down the Nile to Alexandria, with forward shipment across the Mediterranean to Puteoli and Rome.

Ginger (Zingiber officinale), another plant product of high demand, was also part of the spice trade. Its source of origin was Southeast Asia and Ceylon, and perhaps India. India and Arabia were mostly the transshipment points for ginger from the Southeast Asian trade, in which India was part of the trading conduits. Its pricing was about that of white pepper, at six denarii a pound. Ginger, according to Pliny, was used in food with dried fish and was (and still is) considered a digestive. Cardamom (Elletaria cardamomum) was another spice that was traded, though it was almost ten times the price of ginger, about sixty denarii a pound. Grown in Malabar and Travancore, it was used by the Romans in medicines and perfumes. Pliny noted the shipment of it to the Roman Empire was via both the sea and land routes (Warmington 1928).

Cinnamon (Cinnamomum zeylanicum), a plant product from India, China, Tibet, Burma, and Ceylon, was one of the most prized imports of the Romans. Used as a perfume, incense, condiment, and medicine, its wide range of application meant that it was a very important spice. The very best brought almost three hundred to fifteen hundred denarii per pound. As part of the aromatics of the Roman trade, the root of costus (Saussurea Lappa), used for scenting shawls and perfumes, seasoning food, and for sacrificial ceremonies, was also a popular trading item. It was exported from Kashmir in India. Another popular item was cloves (Eugenia caryophyllata). Shipped from Moluccas in Southeast Asia to Ceylon and India, this aromatic was used not only for consumption but was also treated as rent from Egyptian estates to the churches in Rome around the fourth century AD.

Frankincense (Boswellin sacra) and myrrh (Commiphora myrra) were valued gum resins. From India, Arabia, and East Africa, these items were among the goods imported into the Roman Empire. In the first century AD, Pliny the Elder valued frankincense at ten silver denarii per pound, while resin-oil myrrh was valued at fifty denarii (two hundred sesterces), to put it into context. Besides the resinous products, other Indian plants used for coloring and in foods and medicines formed the long list of imported plant products. Indigo (Indigofera tinctoria), a plant that provides a coloring of black and blue, was sought after by the Romans. The price for a pound varied. For black indigo, the cost was seven denarii per pound, and the blue was twenty denarii per pound. There was also raisin barberry (Beberis sinensis from China, B. allichiana and B. siatica from Nepal, B. floribunda from India), which produces a yellowish color dye (lyceum). This plant product had its origin in the Himalayas, China, and Nepal.

Cotton and muslin were exported either in the form of textiles or in raw condition. Most of these types of textile materials were shipped to Egypt for the manufacture of cotton cloth, stuffed mattresses, and pillows for sale in the Roman Empire. In this context, the global division of labor continues with the manufacturing process undertaken in Egypt from raw materials from India and Ceylon.

Continuing a practice that had been going on for quite some time since the second millennium BC, the import of wood products from India to Mesopotamia and the eastern Mediterranean was extended into the first millennium AD. Two classes of wood products were traded: (a) ornamental and timber wood, and (b) fragrant wood for medicinal and religious practices and ceremonies. From the Indian port of Barygaza, according to the *Periplus*, sandalwood, teakwood, black wood, and ebony were exported mainly via Arabia to the Roman Empire (Casson 1989). Wood imports to the empire also came from eastern Africa (where modern day Ethiopia is located). The hardwood imports were used mainly for building construction and for shipbuilding. Sandalwood (Santalum album), a fragrant wood from south India, Ceylon, and Indonesia, was also part of the trade (Fuller 2006; Warmington 1928). Whatever the origin, sandalwood was sought after for various decorative purposes. Other wood products, such as camphor from Sumatra and Borneo, were also part of the array of wood being exchanged.

Mineral Products

Beyond the necessities of plant products that formed part of the Roman trade, precious stones and other mineral products were also part of the exchange process. As luxuries, these mineral products were sought after by Roman elites. Diamonds and sapphires were exported from India for elite consumption throughout the trading system, from the Indian Ocean to the Red Sea and the Mediterranean. Quartzes, opals, agate, carnelian, and onyx were also in great demand. The port of Barygaza on the eastern Indian coast was the export point. Parthian and Arabian mineral products were transported via the land routes to Barygaza for shipment by sea to the Red Sea and beyond. Other sources of the precious stones, such as ruby, were from Ceylon and Burma in

Southeast Asia, thus underlining the trading linkages southwards and east-wards from India.

Amethyst and opal found in India and Ceylon were favorites among the elites. Along with quartz, which was obtainable from Ceylon as well as the Urals, they complemented the various precious mineral products that formed the list of gems and stones that were traded. Other precious stones included in the list are sapphire, emerald, beryl, and aquamarine, which are found in India. Lapis lazuli, with its source in Persia, Tibet, China, and Scythia, was also part of this mineral product trade. Though not of Indian origin, lapis lazuli (from Afghanistan and the Iranian Plateau) was transshipped through the port of Barbaricon on the western Indian coast on the way to the eastern Mediterranean via the Red Sea. Rock crystal, used for ring stones and also made into drinking cups and large bowls, was manufactured in India and exported for elite consumption in the Roman Empire.

Humans, Animals, and Animal Products

The trade between Rome and India in the exchange of slaves, animals, and animal products did not take up a large share of the overall trading volume. The import of slaves and their appearances in Roman elite households as cooks, trainers, and attendants were noted in the writings of Ptolemy and in the *Periplus* (Warmington 1928). However, there were far more slaves exported from Rome than from India to Rome. Live animals imported into the Roman Empire were usually transported via land routes, and, because of geographic proximity, they most often came from Africa. Exotic birds, such as Indian parrots, and other mammals, such as lions, tigers, monkeys, and rhinoceroses, were also part of the menagerie of live animals sought for by Romans in exhibitions, *venationes* (animal hunts, usually staged in amphitheaters), and as household pets. Snakes such as pythons were brought from India, Ceylon, Burma, and Southeast Asia.

According to Herodotus, Indian and Tibetan hounds were also imported for hunting (Warmington 1928). Indian humped cattle and camels were exchanged for use as draft animals. The elephant, however, which played a part in the history of wars even during Roman times, was never adopted by the Roman military as part of its ensemble of war strategy or equipment for the conduct of warfare. Instead, its presence was mainly for transportation of heavy loads or for ceremonial functions. According to literary accounts, elephants were exported from Africa and Ceylon. Because of their size and transportation considerations, they were mostly from Africa. Besides the live animals, the ivory tusk of the elephant was an important product in the Roman-Indian trade. Ethiopian and Indian ivory were most often mentioned in trading accounts. The exuberant living of the Romans led to wide usage of ivory in statues, furniture, scabbards, chariots, jewelry, combs, doors, musical instruments, etc., making this a high-demand trade item among the elites of the Roman Empire. The ivory, though imported from Africa and India, was transformed and crafted into the various manufactured items in the urban centers of the Roman Empire.

Animal products transported on the sea routes were imported to the eastern part of the Roman Empire. Hides and furs were popular items. Early accounts identify the main sources as India and China. Wool was also an item that was sought after, and it was mainly imported from places in northern India, such as Kashmir. The wool was processed in Egypt in imperial manufactories, where the wool was first dyed and then spun into textiles. The production of wool highlighted the global division of labor at that time, whereby the wool from animals in northern India was dyed and spun into textiles in Roman Egypt, and transferred for exchange and consumption in the eastern and western parts of the Roman Empire and beyond.

Exports to India from the Roman Empire

Exports to India from the West included slaves, red coral, flax clothing, papyrus, wine, medicinal items, pottery, glass, and precious metals. Slaves exported to India for the Indian princes came primarily from the eastern Mediterranean and from locations such as Syria. They were also transshipped as far as China.

Fine red coral from the Mediterranean was sent to South Asia. The coral was exported to the Indian ports of Barbaricon and Barygaza via the Arabian port of Cane, and it was in high demand, according to the *Periplus* (Casson 1989). Red coral was highly prized by the Indians and was used extensively in amulets.

Flax clothing exported to India and China was made mostly in Egypt and Syria (Warmington 1928). The Chinese preferred Egyptian-made flax clothing instead of that manufactured in Mesopotamia. Papyrus made in Egypt was also exported to India. According to ancient sources such as Pliny, it was a profitable trade in the early part of the third century AD (Warmington 1928).

Wine was one of the major Roman exports to India, Arabia, and East Africa. The wine had the added function of being the ballast of the ship on its outward journey to India. It was shipped all over the trading network, including the regions of Africa and Arabia, and then forwarded to India. The wine exported was mostly stored in Roman amphorae, and various archaeological excavations in India have unearthed these amphorae pottery sherds (Begley and De Palma 1991; Tomber 2007, 2008; Will 1991; Young 2001). It seems that the amphorae were not only from Rome, but from Mesopotamia as well (Tomber 2007). Besides wine, the amphorae also contained oil and garum for

Indian consumption. Storax, a sap from Liquidambar orientalis (sweetgum tree) used in medicines, was exported from Egypt to India via the Indian ports of Barbaricon and Barygaza.

Other pottery items exported to India were both coarse and fine table wares. The coarse table wares were of Egyptian origin. Roman glass was also an export product to India. Tyre, Sidon, and Alexandria were manufacturing centers of these glass items and were the main sources of these wares. Glass vases imitating metal vases were exported from the Roman Orient to as far as China.

Precious metals such as gold and silver were imported by the Indians as bullion or as coins that were part of the transaction process in exchange for Indian imports. Lead and copper were sent to India as base metals for local currency even though gold and silver coins were also used in local exchanges. Lead from Spain and Britain were shipped to the western port marts of India. Required for local currency, lead, tin, and copper were much sought after by the Indians. The copper was derived from the mines of Roman Cyprus and North Wales, and the tin was from Spain. These sources outlined the extent of the trading networks that extended as far as the northern parts of the Roman Empire in the West. According to the *Periplus* and Pliny, these metallic ores were imported in large quantities (Casson 1989; Warmington 1928).

Balance of Payment

The volume of Roman trade has not been fully documented. Scholars such as Miller (1969), Hopkins (1988), and Warmington (1923) have noted that there was an adverse balance of payment between the Roman Empire and India (and even China) in its trading exchanges. Warmington (1923: 273) puts it this way: "The Empire taken as a unit was often unable to offer foreign regions in general and to oriental nations in particular sufficient products of its own to balance the article imported from them in large quantities, and the result of this was the draining away from the Empire of precious metals in the form of coined money without any adequate return."

According to Pliny, the amount of funds transferred to India to pay for the imports were about fifty million sestertii (Warmington 1923; Young 2001). This amount might not reflect the total adverse balance, as Warmington (1923) has argued that the accumulation of wealth by notable Romans such as Seneca was about three hundred million sestertii. The total amount to pay for the imports from India, China, and Arabia, according to Pliny, was a hundred million sestertii. If the point made by Warmington (1923) holds, then this amount for three countries would have to be more than this. In spite of the differences in balance of payments, such volumes would also suggest that huge profits were made (Tchernia 1997). In view of these estimates, the issue of an adverse balance of trade between Rome and India must have been greater. We can also surmise the size of the imbalance by looking at the volume of trade between Rome and India. Sidebotham (2011) provides an estimate for the cost of each cargo that a seventy-five-ton-capacity Roman merchant vessel carried in the first century AD between India and Rome. A vessel of this capacity can potentially carry up to 147 million drachmas worth of cargo. The Muziris Papyrus, a Greek document dated back to the second century AD, revealed another set of figures for a Roman ship involved in the Indian Ocean trade, showing the Roman vessel carried over 220 tons of Indian merchandise (McLaughlin 2014: 89). When the cargo was removed from the ship so that taxes could be levied, the cargo was worth the equivalent of nearly seven million sesterces. McLaughlin (2014: 94) suggests that in addition to the main cargo carried on the ship Hermapollon, there were also lightweight preciosities, such as pearls, gemstones, and silk. With these, the total cargo would probably have amounted to ten million sesterces. Scaling up from a single ship, as noted in the Muziris Papyrus, to the estimated 120 ships that plied the Indian trade with Roman Egypt, the scale and type of goods exchanged per annum were sixteen thousand tons of pepper and cotton (556 million sesterces), ten thousand tons of malabathrum and other spices (158 million sesterces), seven thousand boxes or fifty tons of nard (32 million sesterces), 360 tons of turtle shell (18 million sesterces), and 576 tons of ivory (over fourteen thousand tusks costing 60 million sesterces) (McLaughlin 2014: 93). Given Strabo's figure of about 120 ships involved in the Roman-Indian trade each year, a total of 17.64 billion drachmas were estimated to be involved in this trading exchange (McLaughlin 2014; Sidebotham 2011). This is equivalent to 17.64 billion sestertii. If this is the estimated volume of trade transacted, then the fifty million sestertii amount for the adverse balance of trade Rome suffered must be underestimated. In terms of scale of the adverse balance of payment, one can obtain a feel for this by noting that four sestertii would be one and a half days of pay for a Roman legionary, and a skilled workman in Roman Egypt had a monthly salary of twenty-five sestertii.

This adverse balance is reflected in the size of shipping required for the Roman-Indian trade. Larger vessels were required to carry the voluminous goods from India compared to the smaller ones for the transport of goods to India and the East from the Roman Empire (Casson 1989; Warmington 1928). In this regard, in order to balance (pay) the exchange of voluminous products from India to the Roman Empire, and the smaller volume from Rome to India, precious metals such as gold and silver made up the difference in the balance of trade. The gold and silver were shipped to Barygaza, Muziris, and Nelcynda.

Such import transactions resulted in large archaeological finds of hoards of gold and silver coins in southern India, especially in the southwest (Deo 1991; Meyer 2007; Raman 1991). These coins were mostly dated at the start of the first century to the third century of the early Roman period (MacDowall 1998; Turner 1989). The coins were mostly silver denarii, aurei, and gold solidi (Turner 1989). Local silver punch-marked coins were also found with the Roman coin hoards and looked like fine imitations of Roman ones (Tomber 2008; Turner 1989). The dating (63 BC–AD 217) of most of these coins (from Augustus to Carracalla) as belonging to the first two centuries of the early Roman period does suggest that the world economy must have been in a period of economic expansion (Bopearachchi 2011; Tchernia 1997; Turner 1989). In contrast, very few Roman coins of later periods (third century AD onwards) have been unearthed in archaeological excavations in India (MacDowall 2011; Tchernia 1997; Turner 1989) other than Ceylon (Bopearachchi 2011), suggesting that the world economy must have receded from its expansionary phase (Parker 2002). This dovetails with the periodization of the long-term expansion and contraction of the world system that has been noted in the literature on the world system's pulsations (see, e.g., Beaujard 2012a, 2012b; Chew 2007; Frank and Gills 1992).

Southeast Asia's Trade in the Maritime Silk Route of the First Eurasian World Economy

The geographic location and ecology of Southeast Asia established its economic attributes for its participation in the Eurasian world system. With a mainland that has terrestrial connections with India and southern China, coupled with a peninsula and an archipelago of islands that offer potential harbors and ports, Southeast Asia's location commanded the various maritime trading routes connecting the eastern part of the Eurasian world system to the western segment. As such, the ships transporting goods and peoples from the eastern part of the Eurasian world system to the western portion necessarily had to sail through the waters of Southeast Asia. Before the advent of steam power and with wind being the only source of ship propulsion, Southeast Asia's geographic locale ideally positioned it for visits from trading ships, which stopped for economic exchange at the various ports located on its coasts and peninsula, and for sojourns of the merchants and traders waiting until the monsoon winds changed their direction.

Endowed with marine resources and a terrestrial ecology that provides optimum conditions for growing and wild harvesting of crops and plant materials sought after in both the western and eastern portions of the Eurasian world system, the various polities of Southeast Asia produced and harvested these materials for exchange. Furthermore, according to archaeological analyses, the peninsula and island parts of Southeast Asia, surrounded by seas, developed various shipping crafts and seafaring technologies that were transferred historically to other maritime communities outside the region (Blench 2010; Fuller et al. 2011; Hoogervorst 2013; Manguin 1993a, 1993b). Location and ecology therefore determined the socioeconomic pattern and trajectory of Southeast Asia's participation in the evolving world system.

When did these trade links between the western and eastern parts of the system—and Southeast Asia's participation in it—begin? According to Kennedy (1898) and Tibetts (1956), based on literary sources, trading connections between Mesopotamia and China were known to exist as early as the seventh century BC. Trade between the Far East and the West were noted as early as 138 BC, though these early indications of trade contacts were between China and the West, and in an indirect fashion via Central Asia and India (Evans 1992). China secured its presence on the trade routes in Central Asia by its conquest of Ferghana and its vicinity in 101 BC (Lattimore 1940). With these different timings, it would be safe to assume that the connection of East Asia and Southeast Asia with the evolving Afro-Indo-Eurasian world system began during the Chin dynasty (around 221 BC) or earlier. Southeast Asia was the sea linkage between the West, the Mediterranean basin, and Han China (Glover 1996; Hall 1985, 2011; Hung and Bellwood 2010; Hung et al. 2007).

For Southeast Asia, there is archaeological evidence of trade exchanges between mainland Southeast Asia (such as Thailand, Vietnam, Cambodia, and Malaya) and South Asia as early as the fourth to second centuries BC (Glover 1990; Glover and Bellina 2011; Hung and Bellwood 2010; Miksic 2013). Within Asia, localized exchange networks in Indonesia and the Malay Peninsula existed from the second millennium BC (Chew 2001, 2007; Glover 1979, 1996). But some have even suggested that Southeast Asian merchants and trading communities were already participating in the trading world by 1000 BC and had substantial commercial contacts with India by the second part of the first millennium BC (Christie 1990; Hall 1985; Leong 1990: 20–21; Miksic 2013). Archaeological excavations have indicated that perhaps as early as 500 BC, the polities in the Malay Peninsula were already participating in regional trading networks.[2]

Given the above different periodizations, within the Asian region, trade occurred between China and the ports on the Indian Ocean by at least the second half of the first century BC when, following unification of China in 221 BC, the Chinese pursued expansions to the south (Wang 1958: 21). Wheatley (1959: 19) writes of Chinese envoys being sent by the Han emperor Wu (141–87 BC) to explore the South Seas as far as the Bay of Bengal. The establishment of commanderies in the south helped to facilitate and establish trade exchanges (Wang 1998). Evidence of Chinese trade has been revealed in recent excavations in southern Thailand of the Malay Peninsula (Miksic 2013; Murillo-Barroso et al. 2010). Wang (1998: 13), however, states that Chinese trade with India started much later, toward the end of the first millennium BC—the second half of the first century BC.

Despite the various timings suggested, what is clear is that by the beginning of the first century AD, trade flourished between the West and the East of the world system as we have stated above (Christie 1990; Colless 1969; Glover 1996; Hall 1985; Tibetts 1956). By the first century AD, Malay and Indonesian sailors were known to have settled along the East African coast (Blench 2010; Hall 1985, 2011; Taylor 1992). Marshall (1980) even suggests that Indonesian merchants and seafarers were involved in the Indian Ocean trade as far as Madagascar by the late first millennium BC; and Blench (2010) and Dorian et al. (2010) have noted the long-distance transfer of agricultural species such as plantains (Musa paradisiaca), water yam (Dioscorea alata), and Taro (Colocasia esculenta) to the East African coast from Southeast Asia prior to the first century AD.

Clearly, the various datings of trade linkages identified above rely on archaeological finds and the various Indian and Chinese literary sources; and it should not be surprising that future archaeological investigations might reveal even earlier trade connections. More important to consider are the types of commodities produced and exchanged. What was shipped westward and eastward and did the composition of commodities change over the historical period? What were the technologies developed, transferred, or imported that shaped the socioeconomic and political patterns and trajectories of the polities of prehistoric and early historic Southeast Asia?

Southeast Asia's Trade with the Western Part of the First Eurasian World Economy

Southeast Asia's participation in the global Eurasian system was connected to its location to the then core consumption areas of India, the Roman Empire, and China. Its ecology afforded both terrestrial and maritime products for export. From the seas, pearls and tortoise shells were some of the commodities exported, and from the land, spices, food crops, timber, metals, precious stones, textiles, swords, sewn boats, and animal products made up the rest of the export equation. In the previous chapter, we have indicated that some of the spices and food crops that were shipped from India and Ceylon to the western part of the Eurasian world system, and especially to the Roman Empire, were not solely of Indian origin. Rather, some had their beginnings in Southeast Asia. Recent studies by Blench (2010), Dorian Fuller, Nicole Boivin et al. (2010, 2013), and Tom Hoogervorst (2013) have provided further material, textual, and linguistic evidence of such origins and transfers.

Spices and Food Crops

The perishability of Southeast Asian spices, aromatic woods, and food crops or raw materials that were immediately consumed or converted to other products, such as jewelry, has resulted in a significant imbalance in Southeast Asia's already sparse archaeological record compared to another region's export records consisting of pottery, metal figurines, etc., that have been archaeologically unearthed. Because of this perishability, as well as the lower level of archaeological research on Southeast Asia's prehistoric and early historic periods, the volume of spices and food crops that formed a large bulk of the Southeast Asian maritime trade with the western and eastern segments of the Eurasian world economy have not been fully revealed, other than excerpts from merchant trading reports or from the Roman or Chinese imperial import notations. Nevertheless, we can get a feel of the volume and the level of profits by proxy from the balance of payment issues faced by the Roman Empire in its trading activities with India, as we have discussed in the previous pages.

In addition to spices, aromatic woods, and other maritime products, Southeast Asian food plants were translocated to east Africa over the prehistoric period (see, e.g., Blench 2010; Boivin et al. 2013). Recent archaeobotanical studies have suggested that plantains (Musa paradisiaca), water yam (Dioscorea esculenta), taro (Colocasia esculenta), sugarcane (Saccharum spp.), and coconut (Cocos nucifera) were transferred to the East African coast prior to the beginning of the historic period as part of the trade flows (Hoogervorst 2013).

Spices, as we have mentioned in the previous pages, have many uses, depending on the sociocultural context. Their uses extend beyond that of elite consumption as luxuries to the level of the layperson who consumed them for medicinal or religious-cultural purposes (Sidebotham 2011). The Southeast Asian ecology provides optimum conditions for the perpetuation and growth of the spice trade that defined the maritime silk routes from the Indian Ocean to the South China Sea. The "Spice Islands" of Maluku, the rainforests of Sumatra, Java and the Southeast Asian Malay Peninsula and mainland were the optimum geographic locale for cloves, nutmeg, pepper, cinnamon, and cardamom.

The famous pepper trade of Southeast Asia, which supplied the western portion of the Eurasian world economy from India, Ceylon, East Africa, and Arabia to the Eastern Mediterranean was mostly of the Java long pepper (Piper retrofractum), which was different from the Indian long pepper (Piper longum) that was also shipped to the Roman Empire from India. As a spice, it was used as seasoning and for medicinal purposes by the Romans. For seasoning, it was sought after in India and the western and eastern parts of the Eurasian world system. The second most prevalent Southeast Asian pepper that formed a large part of the pepper trade was the cubeb (Piper cubeba), which, like the Java long pepper, was also used for medicinal purposes, and as well as an adulterant for the black pepper intended for the Roman market (Dalby 2000; Hoogervorst 2013).

Cloves are the dried unopened flowers of the clove tree (Syzygium aromaticum), and for a very long period could be obtained exclusively from the islands of Ternate, Tidore, Motir, Makyan, and Bachan in the Moluccas (Glover 1990). They were exported to India, Ceylon, East Africa, Arabia, Rome, and China. They were grown much later in East Africa and South Asia only after the Dutch arrival in Southeast Asia. Used as incense, seasoning, condiment, and for medicinal purposes, cloves played an important part in the sociocultural lifestyles of the maritime Eurasian world system. According to the list of commodities subjected to tariffs in the port of Alexandria, cloves were imported into the Roman Empire around AD 176–180 (Miller 1969). As a condiment and seasoning, it was in high demand in China, and it was an important commodity traded for by Chinese merchants in Southeast Asia. Gingerroot, of the ginger plant (Zingiber officinale), was another item that was consumed in India, and from India, it was transmitted to the Middle East, Africa, and Europe (Hoogervorst 2013). Besides being a popular consumable in these places, it was also sought after in China. The ginger exported from India to the West was mostly derived from Southeast Asia, and, according to Parker (2008), they were from Java and Thailand. Cinnamon, a popular item shipped to India and the Roman Empire, was mostly grown in Madagascar and Indonesia (Parker 2008).

Aromatic woods and gum resins from the tropical forests of Southeast Asia were also major exports. The consumption of these products was completed in the urban core areas of the Eurasian world economy from the western Mediterranean to China. Of these aromatic woods, Sandalwood from the sandalwood tree (Santalum album) was used for its fragrance, and also as a cosmetic. Its use over time permeated the cultural and religious practices of India and China. Benzoin, a resin from the trees of the genus Styrax, was also shipped to India and China, and as an ingredient for incense and perfume was used for religious practices and elite consumption. Other aromatics that were quite popular in the western and eastern ends of the Eurasian world system were myrrh (Commiphora spp.) and storax (Liquidambar spp.).

Bronzes, Metals, Timbers, and Stones

By no means were spices and food crops the only products that were exchanged between Southeast Asia and the western Eurasian world economy. Mainland Southeast Asia's bountiful supply of timber, metal ores such as tin and gold, and bronzes were also part of the commodity flows from Southeast Asia to India and other regions of the Indian Ocean (An 1996; Francis 1996; Glover 1990; Wheatley 1964).

The abundant sources of tin in Thailand and Malaya were mined and exported to India, which had a scarcity of tin (Rajan 2011; Wheatley 1964). As the Indian economy expanded, there emerged a need for bullion as a form of accumulation. Bronze vessels that had a high tin concentration were also part of the list of trading items of the Southeast Asia-India exchange (Rajan 2011).

Given the scale of trading activities, by the first century AD or even earlier, the Malayan peninsula was undergoing radical socioeconomic changes (Manguin 2004; Saidin 2011, 2012; Wheatley 1964a). They occurred primarily because Southeast Asian and Indian merchants and traders were exchanging their merchandises and wares along the coastal areas of Southeast Asia and India, with the Indians seeking gold, which in the past they had obtained from the Mediterranean or Central Asia (Wheatley 1964). Gold, which was widely available in mainland Southeast Asia, became a part of the Southeast Asian trade with the western part of the Eurasian world system, especially with India. The prohibition on the export of gold imposed by Roman Emperor Vespasian (AD 69–79) spurred the Indian merchants to search for gold bullion in Southeast Asia (Hall 1985). Indian ships that weighed about seventy-five tons and could carry up to two hundred persons were sailing between South Asia/Ceylon and China by the beginning of the first century AD (Wheatley 1964b). Metallic ores such as tin and gold were absorbed in the production and accumulation processes, and thus their origins can never be completely ascertained from archaeological finds other than determining from geological surveys the historical presence of the mineral in the landscape of the geographic space. In view of this, the volume of these ores and their contribution to the production, accumulation, and consumption processes of the Eurasian world system on the part of Southeast Asia can never be fully realized.

In the area of the fabrication and production of metals, besides the manufacture of bronze items, the knowledge of iron smelting reached insular and mainland Southeast Asia between 500 and 400 BC from China and India, though local innovations of iron smelting, according to Higham (2014), cannot be ruled out entirely. Regular trade contacts between India and China further expanded the ferrous metallurgical process both on mainland and peninsular Southeast Asia (Hoogervorst 2012).

Notwithstanding the export of metals such as tin and gold and the production of bronze and iron objects, beads and glass were also produced locally for the regional trade with India (Bellina 2007; Manguin 2004; Miksic 2013). Besides the existence of glass, agate, and carnelian beads that have Indian and Southeast Asian origins, recent studies of excavated garnet beads in Cambodia represent a local beadmaking tradition (Carter 2012). The growing dynamics of regional trade between India and Southeast Asia suggest different historical origins for bead production. Studies have revealed beads of Indian origins, and some that were produced locally in Southeast Asia. Francis (2002) has traced the manufacturing and trading of beads between core centers and civilizations on a global scale starting from 300 BC onward, with India and Southeast Asia as major production centers. The production of beads underscored the development of manufacturing capacity, thereby emphasizing the emergence of core type activities and status for Southeast Asia. Francis (2002: 149) describes such a developmental trajectory: "The bead evidence throws into sharp contrast the regions which we may consider core and periphery. At the beginning of our analysis all of Southeast Asia was peripheral, while the core areas were India and China. In time, core areas arose within Southeast Asia Funan, the Malaysian Peninsula, Srivijaya, and Java, and these areas became beadmakers. Beads, after all were important trade items, and as manufactured items they may be considered to have been markers (not makers) of emerging core areas or states."

Numerous studies (Bellina 2003, 2007, 2014; Bellina and Silapanth 2006a, 2006b; Bellina et al. 2014) of bead production in Southeast Asia have outlined the bead manufacturing process, and how it has been carried out within a social political landscape comprised of Indian migrant craftsmen and perhaps locals trained by the Indians. The presence of Indian craftsmen based in Southeast Asia manufacturing beads as suggested by Bellina (2003, 2007, 2014a, 2014b, 2014c) was based on an examination of the quality of Indian beads that were found with the beads manufactured in India via an inspection of the local Southeast Asian manufacturing techniques. Other than this, no other material evidence of the presence of Indian craftsmen has been provided by Bellina (2003, 2007).

Excavation of Khao Sam Kaeo, a site in southern Thailand, revealed beads of carnelian and agate that were manufactured on site (Bellina 2003, 2007). The various sites of bead production located in Burma, Thailand, Thai-Malay Peninsula, Java, Bali, Vietnam, and the Philippines suggest an intratrade network linking these places to the exchange markets within Southeast Asia and beyond (Bellina 2007, 2014; Bellina et al. 2014; Miksic 2013). Some of these centers—coordinated perhaps, according to Bellina (2007), by the Indians—were either importing Indian-manufactured beads and/or manufacturing local beads. Eventually, these centers started to produce local beads of somewhat good quality, and were also manufacturing mass-produced beads for export. It suggests, as well, that beads viewed as luxuries consumed by the elites gave way to more of a mass-consumption item. Such a transformation occurred in the early historic period.

The bead production centers were dependent and connected to urban centers that enabled the distribution and exchange of this product with the rest of the Eurasian world economy. The coastal polities in Southeast Asia, such as Funan, had ports through which the bead trade could be conducted intraregionally and interregionally among Southeast Asia, India, and China.

Southeast Asia's Trade with the Eastern Part of the First Eurasian World Economy

As part of the Eurasian world system, Southeast Asia traded not only with the core urbanized centers in the western portion of the Eurasian world economy; its proximity to China, Korea, Taiwan, and Japan through its land and sea connections meant that its maritime trade networks with the eastern portion of the system were firmly connected by the end of the prehistoric era. In East Asia, intraregional trade routes were established by the fifth century BC (Higham 2002; Hung and Bellwood 2010; Sarabia 2004). They were primarily centered on products such as silk and ceramic wares. Within East Asia, Chinese goods were exchanged by land with the Korean peninsula and via shipping to the Japanese islands. Imamura (1996) and Sarabia (2004) have traced the exchange between China and Japan in the archaeological bronze finds unearthed in Japan that had northern Chinese origins. One can also assume that the products of Southeast Asia that were shipped to China for consumption would have found their way to Korea, Taiwan, and Japan. For example, Taiwanese nephrite has been found in southern Thailand, indicating the exchange of raw materials between Southeast Asia and East Asia (Hung and Bellwood 2010).

Trade Connections with China

Different type of products characterized the trading exchange. From China, silk, pottery, and other manufactured wares were exported in exchange for natural resources such as wood products, spices, preciosities from the sea, and mineral resources of Southeast Asia. The sea trade routes were as follows: frankincense, myrrh, camphor, spices, gharuwood, sandalwood, ivory, rhinoceros horns, kingfisher feathers, tortoise shells, birds such as parrots, and pearls were transshipped from Southeast Asian sources for exchange in the ports of southern China in exchange for Chinese manufactures, particularly silk, and pottery; the latter was then shipped westward to India, Arabia, and the Mediterranean.

The maritime trade route from the Southeast Asian region to southern Chinese ports conveying spices, aromatics, wood, pearls, rhinoceros horns, tortoise shells, etc. was known as the Nanhai trade; the goods were shipped from various polities located on mainland and island Southeast Asia (Wang 1958). One such polity in Southeast Asia was Fu-nan, which was a center of accumulation from the first to the sixth century AD (Hall 1985, 1992; Stark 1996).[3] By the third century AD, Fu-nan consolidated all the trading centers on the Malay archipelago, making it the unrivalled polity in the region (Hall 1985, 1992; Wheatley 1964b). The Southeast Asian polities, such as Tun-sun, Chu-Po, P'an-p'an, Tung Tien, Ch'u-tu-k'un, Chiu-Chih, T'ai-p'ing, Yu-lan, Sui-Shu, Pien/Pan-tou, Pi-Sung, Chin Lin, and Chu-li, played significant roles in this long-distance maritime trade with China on the one hand, and with India on the other (Wang 1958; Wheatley 1964a).

From the first to the third century AD, the trade in wood products grew in Southeast Asia. Gharuwood was imported to southern China, involving merchants from the Malay archipelago, Sumatra, and even as far as Ceylon (Hall 1985). Polities such as Lo-yueh were the collection centers for forest products, while P'eng-feng shipped lakawood (Hall 1985; Wheatley 1961). Tun-sun on the Malay Peninsula, a dependency of Fu-nan, was the emporium whereby the goods from the western part of the Eurasian world system were shipped to southern China and the manufactures from southern China were conveyed to India and the Mediterranean.

By the second century AD, the power of China was recognized by the polities in Southeast Asia, which led to diplomatic or tribute missions from these countries to the Chinese court. Such diplomatic missions were to obtain political and economic concessions from China (Wang 1958, 1989). They came from as far as Sumatra and Java (Dunn 1975; Hall 1985; Wang 1989). The size of exchange varied from the offering of wood products and luxuries such as pearls, to gold, silver, and copper. For example, a mission from Lin-yi— founded around AD 192 and situated on the Vietnamese coast (what is modern day Danang)—brought ten thousand kati of gold, one hundred thousand kati of silver, and three hundred thousand kati of copper (Wang 1958: 52; Yamagata 1998).[4] The number of diplomatic or tribute missions from Southeast Asian countries varied according to the state of political affairs in China with the rise and fall of dynasties. Missions were lowered during years when China had political unrest, reducing its pursuit of trade exchanges and relations, and they were increased during times of peace and prosperity, such as during the era of the Tang dynasty, when sixty-four missions were recorded (Wang 1958: 122–123). Miksic (2013: 4), however, counted a larger number of such diplomatic missions between the fifth and sixth centuries AD, a total of 78 (see table 3.1). With such political relations, the Nanhai trade flourished.

According to Wang (1998: 111), the Nanhai trade was distinguished by three phases of development. The first phase, which began in the first century AD and lasted five centuries, was dominated by a concentration in preciosities consumed by the court and the lords. The second phase had a more religious emphasis whereby "holy things" were imported into China in addition to preciosities and natural resources. This occurred for two centuries, with the third phase extending for three centuries from the Tang through the Sung dynasties. In this third phase, there was a shift to spices and drugs that were introduced earlier but by this period had generated a consumer demand. The increase in market demand of the Nanhai trade products from the fifth century AD onward reveals the establishment of a wider consumer market that was emerging in the urban centers of China. Some of this urbanization was facilitated further

Table 3.1. Diplomatic Missions to China

Kingdom	Location	Number of Missions	Dates (AD)
Holodan	Java	6	430–440
Pohuang	Southeast Sumatra	7	445–464
Gantoli	South Sumatra	5	455–564
Poli	Bali	3	470–524
Panpan	Malay Peninsula	12	455–589
Langkasuka	Malay Peninsula	3	515–556
Champa	South Vietnam	25	420–589
Funan	South Mekong Valley	17	43–589

Source: Miksic (2013: 4).

by China's global trading relations within the region, and with the West via both the sea and land routes. The Nanhai trade had grown to such a scale that by AD 987 (during the Sung dynasty), the southern maritime trading relations provided a fifth of the total cash revenue of the state (Hall 1985; Wheatley 1959: 24).

The Seafaring Technologies

For Southeast Asia, the various seas that surrounded its land mass also conduced the technologies that were developed to sustain its political-economic activities. Widely known in the eastern portion of the Eurasian world economy for its seafaring capacities and connection to the seas—as were the Minoans and Mycenaean Greeks in the second millennium Bronze Age Mediterranean—Southeast Asia's maritime nautical technological innovations were adopted and transferred to the Indian Ocean littoral communities and to China (Fuller et al. 2011; Hoogervorst 2013; Manguin 1993). To summarize Hoogervorst's (2013) and Manguin's (1985a, 1985b, 1993) findings, South Asia, East Africa, and China adopted and modified some elements of Southeast Asia's nautical technological innovations, such as vessel types, plank fastening, rigging, and devices such as the outrigger. The adoption process was not unidirectional. The Southeast Asians were also open to adopting nautical technologies from South Asia and Arabia.

Chinese ships, up to the Han Dynasty, according to Manguin (1985a, 1993), were mostly designed for coastal and river shipping. Péronnet (2013) notes the development of maritime navigation in southern China around Canton. Later on, when China started to be involved in the Nanhai trade, Chinese ships were patterned after foreign ships that seem to have been of Southeast Asian origin. Descriptions of large foreign ships with four sails set to the wind and that took advantage of the monsoons were discussed in Chinese literary accounts (Manguin 1993).

Construction of ships and boats involved fastening the planks together for the hull via the method of sewing. This manner of ship construction was much different from the ship construction undertaken in the Mediterranean whereby iron nails were used to hold the planks together. Sewing the planks together requires that the cords be passed through lugs. Such a design is often called the lashed-out method, which I mentioned in chapter 2. In addition to the stitching of the planks, dowelled edges were also introduced to hold the planks together. This lashed-out dowelled design is a technique that was much in use in Southeast Asia from the Philippines to Indonesia and the Malayan archipelago, and, according to Hoogervorst (2013), was introduced to other regions of the Eurasian world economy.

Sails designed to maximize wind propulsion replaced oars and paddles. The sail design that was in use for Southeast Asian vessels had the shape of a rectangle. Hoogervorst (2013), citing Richard LeBaron Bowen (1952), suggested that this design was probably invented in Indonesia, and the use of unfixed sprit spars to hold the sail was certainly a Southeast Asian invention.

For making ships seaworthy for the speed generated by the use of the winds for propulsion, a design for balancing the craft was important. Different construction designs were used; the outrigger device, which stabilized the craft from capsizing during maneuvers, was of Southeast Asian origin. The use of the outrigger device was evident in crafts in the Indian Ocean from places such as Ceylon and the East African and South Asian coasts.

It is clear from the distribution and quality of archaeological finds and the evidence of shipbuilding advances discussed above that the Southeast Asian region developed a level of social, economic, and political complexity that does not allow it to be easily categorized as just a place composed of distribution centers or entrepôts. The volume of trade flows it had with the western and eastern segments of the Eurasian world economy must lead us to realize that a substantial level of socioeconomic and political transformations had taken place, and that there were polities involved not only in extracting and cultivating of natural resources, minerals, plants, and food crops, but also in manufacturing beads, pottery, bronze wares, iron items, figurines, jewelry, etc., and in undertaking political relations with other core centers in the Eurasian world system. Given these socioeconomic and political trends, the next chapter outlines the developmental patterns and linkages of Southeast Asian polities in the Eurasian world system in the late prehistoric and early historic era of the social evolution of the world.

Notes

1. Studies and discussion of historical globalizations over world history have focused overwhelmingly on the trading world of the Mediterranean Sea and the Indian Ocean as a world-economy (see, e.g., Beaujard 2005, 2010, 2012a, 2012b; Boivin 2009; Braudel 1981, 1982, 1984; Chaudhuri 1985, 1990). These studies tend to attribute the Mediterranean Sea or the Indian Ocean as a "unified" economic system with a set of particular dynamics and socioeconomic practices instead of visualizing these seas as part of the world economy (economy of the world) comprised of global trade routes and exchanges that spanned from the Mediterranean to the South China Seas since the advent of the first millennium AD or earlier.
2. For example, the discovery in the eastern part of the Malay Peninsula of the Dong Son drums similar to those of the earlier Dong Son culture located in the Red River Delta of Vietnam is indicative of how much distance these drums have traveled (Jacq-Hergoualc'h 2002; O'Reilly 2007).
3. Roman coins and products have been discovered among the ruins of Fu-nan (Stark 1996; Wheatley 1964a).
4. One kati is equivalent to 1.1 lbs.

The Polities

CHAPTER 4

Political Transformations
in Southeast Asia

Introduction

From the optics of most past scholarly treatises on Southeast Asia, albeit with some exceptions, the region's place in the world economy was viewed mainly as a way station populated by diverse groups of people of no consequences. Accordingly, the sociocultural and economic transformations that occurred in Southeast Asia in the late prehistoric and early historic periods were outcomes of trade, religious, and political contacts with the core centers of India and China (see, e.g., Coedes 1966, 1968). That Southeast Asia was known as Farther or Greater India, for example, reinforced further the view of Southeast Asia as nothing more than an extension of India spatially (Majumdar 1952). To Southeast Asian specialists in the mid-twentieth century, and even to some now, it was Indian colonization through economic and religious contacts that engendered socioeconomic and political transformations of the Southeast Asian region. As Glover (2007: 3) remarks on the expositions on Southeast Asia's long-term change, "The received opinion was that the process started only in the early centuries of the Christian Era and through the extension of complex mercantile and political systems projecting their sphere of influence eastwards from the South Asian sub-continent into a region of technologically backward small-scale egalitarian societies."

Given this overarching conceptual view, such explanations of the socioeconomic and political development of (prehistoric and early historic) Southeast Asia have painted the Southeast Asian region as an area of "peripherality." Upon examination, this socioeconomic developmental stance parallels the scholarly position of Western modernization theorists in their depiction of the socioeconomic and political potential and developmental capacities of so-called Third World countries in the post–Second World War period (Hoselitz 1960; Lerner 1965; McClelland 1967; Parsons 1964; Pye 1962; Rostow

1960).[1] Whereas Latin American and African scholarship had an efflorescence of vociferous counter-responses to the articulation of their peripheral conditions and their potential as depicted by modernization theorists, in the case of Southeast Asia, especially for our period in question, it was rather silent; the concept did not received the level of scholarly countering, attention, and interest compared to post–Second World War Latin America. There have been some voices in the quiet. Though not rejecting the external South Asian influence, scholars such as Jacques Van Leur (1967) awarded a level of resourcefulness and initiative to local Southeast Asian elites in this interactive process. The negation of the passivity of Southeast Asians, for example, was also questioned by the works of Benda (1962) and Smail (1961), followed by Kulke (1990) and Wolters (1999) discussing the dynamic and interactive character of Southeast Asian relations to South Asian trade and cultural influxes. In spite of these interventions, the standard orthodox understanding of Southeast Asia prevailed and continues today to determine the intellectual consensus on the writing of Southeast Asian socioeconomic and political development. Such a persistent viewpoint does not, in my view, give Southeast Asia its due, especially during the period circa 200 BC– AD 400/500. The region is treated as little more than an area of "peripheral" entrepôts or distribution centers/trading posts between China and India (see, e.g., Hall 1982, 2011; Abu-Lughod 1989; Leong 1990).

In addition to the viewpoint of the region as a peripheral way-station in the Eurasian world economy, the prehistory and early history of Southeast Asia also has enjoyed a lower level of archaeological initiatives compared to other regions of the world, such as the Fertile Crescent, Egypt, Europe, and the Mediterranean. Southeast Asia's acidic soil and tropical climate have also caused poor retention of the material evidence of the Southeast Asian human communities' socioeconomic practices (Kim 2013). For this time period, therefore, the information on Southeast Asian communities has mostly been derived from foreign Chinese and Indian literary sources, religious texts, linguistic mapping, art, inscriptions, and travel records. There is no question that these sources do provide useful ethnographic information about the materialism of life in Southeast Asia. There are some issues associated with relying only on these types of sources, however, such as the periodization of significant milestones of socioeconomic transformation that tend to start only when the foreign contacts were made and usually not before, and the gaps in information, especially that these accounts often noted only what was important to the foreigners and seldom addressed indigenous development. Because of these concerns, archaeological stratigraphic studies and dendrochronological and pollen analyses can aid us with a clearer material account of the socioeconomic and political landscapes of Southeast Asia over a continuous longer-term horizon provided that careful archaeological studies are undertaken.

Unfortunately, dendrochronological and palynological analyses on this period are relatively few.

Notwithstanding a lower level of archaeological initiatives for Southeast Asia compared to other regions of the world as stated above, the recent works of Higham (2014), Bellwood (2004), Glover (2011), Kim (2013), and Stark (2004) have unearthed rich evidence of Bronze Age and Early Iron Age Southeast Asia. Their archaeological studies, especially those of Higham (2014) and Stark (2004), show how highly developed Southeast Asian societies and polities rose and declined in mainland, archipelago, and island Southeast Asia over the course of world history. Their work underscored what Christie (1990: 42) wrote close to two decades ago about Southeast Asian polities: "Thus it seems that not only were Southeast Asians themselves active and often sophisticated participants in, rather than primitive and passive recipients of long-distance trade well before the period of Indianization, but also that the most culturally significant trade remained regional rather than foreign in origin into the early centuries AD."

With a lack of extensive written records and archeological studies, the burden of understanding the nature of Southeast Asian sociopolitical and economic formations has been quite dependent on models from more recent historical and ethnographic investigations (Bellina and Glover 2004; Christie 1990; Leong 1990). Nevertheless, as stated in the prior chapters, archaeological excavations have indicated wet rice cultivation in Southeast Asia as early as the mid-third millennium BC (Higham 2006, 2014; Higham and Lu 1998; O'Reilly 2007). Evidence of subsistence communities has been unearthed at Ban Na Di, Non Nok Tha, Ban Chiang Hian, and Khok Phanom Di, where a widespread exchange network existed as early as the Bronze Age with bronze being forged around the eleventh century BC (Bayard 1984; Hall 1985; Higham 1989, 1996, 2014, 2015; O'Reilly 2007; Taylor 1992). Centers producing bronze, beads, and jewelry, such as Khao Sam Kaeo, were established on the mainland and archipelago Southeast Asia since the sixth century BC (see, e.g., Bellina 2007; Bellina and Glover 2011; Higham 2002; Higham and Thosarat 2012).

Given such archaeological evidence (see Glover and Bellwood 2004; Higham 2014; O'Reilly 2000, 2003, 2008, 2014), we find from the Bronze Age to the Iron Age the progressive development of chiefdoms into kingdoms, and later the formation of empires on mainland Southeast Asia. Comparatively speaking, at the world-historic level, the socioeconomic and political development of Southeast Asia (mainland and peninsula) parallels that of other regions of the Eurasian world economy. For Bronze Age central Europe, it was between 2000 and 1900 BC. that tin bronze emerged, and the Middle Bronze Age for central Europe was around 1600 BC (Kristiansen and Larsson 2005). For Southeast Asia, bronze working started in the Mekong and Red River deltas and some parts of coastal Vietnam around 2000–1500 BC (Pigott and Ciarla 2007). In northeast Thailand, according to Higham (2014, 2015) the transition to the Bronze Age was in the eleventh century BC. Analyses of lead isotopes in the copper slag and excavated cast artifacts found at Ban Non Wat showed that there was local sourcing of copper, indicating that copper ore was exploited in the Khao Wong Prachan valley by about 1000 BC (Higham 2014, 2015; Pryce et al. 2011).

Historically, we know that trade connections between Southeast Asia and the rest of the Eurasian world economy from at least 200 BC onward traversed eastward and westward and within Southeast Asia itself (see, e.g., Chew 2015; Higham 2014). Intraregionally, a myriad of trading networks connected the mainland, the peninsula, and the archipelago with coastal trading ports linked to hinterland communities that were also tied to agrarian urban settlements. These networks waxed and waned in relation to the dynamics of the Eurasian world economy, and the shift in the trading routes along with the rise and fall of the Southeast Asian polities.

Besides the trajectory of developmental sequences from agriculture to metals fabrication and long-distance trade, another indicator of socioeconomic transformation is urbanization. As V. Gordon Childe (1942, 1950, 1952) once remarked, human societal development occurred in phases, and with the Neolithic Revolution and its generation of surplus, the other major structural transformation for human civilizations that followed was the Urban Revolution. The Neolithic Revolution was to Childe (1950) a significant human innovation, for it provided the material basis for the generation of surplus resulting in the formation of stratified groups possessing a differential specialization in labor skill-sets. With the Urban Revolution, changes in socioeconomic complexities of human organizations and structures (such as cities) emerged. Childe (1950) distinguished various dimensions to depict the urbanization process that, according to him, the ancient cores had achieved:

1. Growing population sizes and population concentration in cities
2. Production of surplus in terms of food, etc.
3. Large building structures
4. Complex division of labor leading to development of full-time craft specialists (itinerant experts) perhaps going from city to city or resident specialists
5. Social stratification
6. Writing and record keeping and the sciences, with specialists providing artistic expression beyond naturalism
7. Development of foreign trade and importation of raw materials
8. Appearance of a state organization that craftsmen can belong to economically and politically.

On the human social evolutionary scale, urbanization provides the benchmark for distinguishing civilizational complexity. To paraphrase Childe (1950), the city has always been associated with human civilizations. Across scholarly disciplines, "urbanization" depicts a certain status and stage of socioeconomic transformation of a given social community in world history. Southern Mesopotamia, Egypt, and northwestern India (Harappan civilization) five thousand years ago are the key exemplars noted for such an achievement.

In earlier works (Chew 2001, 2007, 2008), I found that this urbanization process did not proceed in a linear fashion. It proceeded through phases of expansion and decline contingent on the changing relationships between Culture and Nature. Global economic systemic crises, environmental stresses, and climate changes have significant impacts on the dynamics of the global urbanization process, even for Southeast Asia. Thus the rise and decline of Southeast Asian polities because of their links to the Eurasian world economy should not be explained by just focusing on regional/local socioeconomic and political linkages. The other factors—climate changes and environmental stresses as a consequence of the historical-global human community's relations with the natural environment—have to be given equal weight; only then can we have a more thorough explanation of this expansion and decline process. The expansion and decline of polities need to be accounted for beyond the typical explanations offered by Southeast Asian specialists. The rise and fall are not only due to the changing economic conditions in China or India or to other factors such as a shift in the trading ideology of a new dynasty, new emperor, or new mandarins. Other vectors at the world systemic level, such as climate, global historic economic downturns, and the decline and upheavals of centers of the Eurasian world economy, such as Rome and China, etc., need to be considered. It is this interpolation of factors, I believe, that conditions the rise and decline of Southeast Asian polities.

In summary, in accordance with a social evolutionary trajectory whereby the tendency is toward increasing systems complexity, Southeast Asia's developmental arc paralleled those of the other regions of the Eurasian world system, albeit perhaps in some parts of Southeast Asia the socioeconomic and political transformations occurred later. Furthermore, in this case, increasing complexity entails not only intensifying urbanization and reproduction/production of goods for consumption and trading exchanges, but also increasingly structured and institutionalized distribution of power between and within social formations (Kristiansen 2014).

The aforementioned dimensions of complexity that have been used as guiding measures of evaluating socioeconomic and political complexities in other regions of the Eurasian world system can assist, but should not determine solely, our evaluation of Southeast Asian polities in our attempt to revise the understanding of Southeast Asia's place in the prehistory and early history of the Eurasian world system.

Polities and Trading Communities

Our knowledge of trading communities/polities located on mainland, peninsula, and island Southeast Asia and of the structure of Southeast Asian trade has been based on hypothesized generalized analytical frameworks, developed from a more recent historical period than that of the prehistory of Southeast Asia, as very few archaeological evidences are available to guide us. The coastal state model by Bennet Bronson (1978) has been widely accepted and utilized by others, such as Leong (1990), Christie (1990), and more recently Hall (2011). There are also many other conceptions of Southeast Asian polities and trade structures suggested, such as those of Van Leur (1967), Wheatley (1983) and Wolters (1999) for example. The pitfalls of using a generalized model to understand Southeast Asian historical structures, coupled with a lack of written records, can pose some challenges for a materialist understanding of world-historical transformation. Bellina and Grover (2004: 69) have also voiced such worries: "With a lack of written records, we cannot analyse in the same detail as India the structure of exchange within Southeast Asia for the thousand years from the fifth century BC onward. Good archaeological documentation is still scarce and we depend over much on models based on analogies from more recent historical and ethnographic situations. For instance, Bronson, Wheatley, Wolters, Miksic and Wisseman Christie have all proposed evolutionary or structural models for Southeast Asian exchange systems. Although useful, these are generalized and abstract and, for the most part, lack firm support from empirical data from the past."

Methodologically, materialist interpretation of world history should be responsive to what Eric Wolf (1982) has suggested, that "theoretically informed history and historically informed theory" must be joined together within the framework of a world system so that even the people/region "without history" can be accounted for in the making of the modern world. With this in mind, we need to be open to all accounts from different sources to identify and map the extent of the evolution of polities and structures in place from late prehistory that were established in mainland, peninsula, and island Southeast Asia within the context of a world economy.

Between 500 BC and AD 500, Southeast Asia had established urban centers across the region; we find canals, ramparts, and moats encircling these built-up areas. The moats not only provided irrigation in areas that experienced dryness, such as in certain regions of mainland Southeast Asia, but also defense from external parties (O'Reilly 2014). These urbanized areas have been excavated from Burma to Vietnam, suggesting comparable scale to those of the ancient civilizations of southern Mesopotamia and northwestern India (Stark 2006, 2015).

It is clear from numerous Indian and Chinese historical accounts that there were a number of kingdoms established by the period of the Han dynasty on mainland Southeast Asia, the Malay Peninsula, and perhaps even island Southeast Asia (see, e.g., Christie 1990; Coedes 1966, 1968; Leong 1990; Wheatley 1964a; Yamagata 1998). From such descriptions we can discern that a defined hierarchical structure of control was in existence, such as kingship and a standing military, as well as the establishment of urbanized communities with ports and production centers involved in maritime trading activities.

Various models of political and economic structures have been proposed to distinguish the political economic models for the different regions of Southeast Asia. The proposed models have been on the whole determined by what has been deemed the nature of economic activities undertaken by Southeast Asia in the global division of labor of the Eurasian world system, and by the penetration of Southeast Asia by other centers, such as India and China. The early works of Coedes (1964, 1966), Van Leur (1967), Wolters (1999), and Wheatley (1964) distinguish the socioeconomic and political structures based on the individual scholar's interpretation of Southeast Asian prehistory and early history. Coedes's work (1964, 1966) is guided by the assumption that developed core powers such as China and (especially) India shaped the developmental formation and trajectory of Southeast Asia's socioeconomic and political transformations, which naturally followed the "universal" trajectory of kingships evolving to states. Van Leur's examination (1967) focused on the rise of Indonesia and its early trade relations, revealing economic and political structures that are conditioned by the trading activities as well as the geographic landscape of Indonesia, dominated by islands and their various riverine systems. Wolters's (1999) analysis of Southeast Asia provides us with an articulation of political, economic, and cultural arrangements. As a geographer, Wheatley (1964a) was guided by geographic dimensions such as urbanization and cultural interpretations of the transformations of Southeast Asia via trade and religion by Arab, Indian, and Chinese sources.

On the whole, the above early developmental frameworks of Southeast Asia are less articulate of the specific nature and networks of the socioeconomic and political structures of prehistoric and early historic Southeast Asia. If we review the historical narratives and the limited archaeological assemblages of prehistoric and early historic Southeast Asia, the overarching model is a social evolutionary trajectory of increasingly complex political structures, from big man/chiefdoms to kingdoms to states. Associated with these political structures is the assumption of socioeconomic activities that are conditioned by the nature of the landscapes and climate. Mainland Southeast Asia had a more diversified economy that included agriculture, natural resource extraction from both terrestrial and marine sites, and production of luxury and mass-consumption items. In this context, Java, even though it is classified as part of the island Southeast Asia region, is also included in this matrix. Peninsula and island Southeast Asia's political and economic structures, conditioned by the landscape and climate, were deemed to have more specific political structures and distribution of power and control.

In the case of mainland Southeast Asia, the general model is a popular one—developed by Wittfogel (1957) and Weber (1987) and widely embraced by both Marxists and non-Marxists—of early agrarian (Asian?) civilizations that used hydraulic systems within the political matrix of king/emperor and a retinue of religious and aristocratic elites who determined the political economy. With the discovery of moats and embankments in urbanized settlements in Northeast Thailand, this model of the nature of early polities in Mainland Southeast Asia gains further support (Higham 2014; Moore 1988; Mudar 1999; O'Reilly 2014; Stark 2004).

Refining Van Leur's work further, Bronson (1978) proposed a model of economic and political development (state formation) for peninsula and island Southeast Asia that is different from mainland Southeast Asia's development, including Java. The nature of the landscape and the lack of settlement persistence beyond a limited period of time (no more than two hundred years) led Bronson to suggest a political and economic structure that was organized differently from that of mainland Southeast Asia. The reasons (land infertility and lower population) for the lack of settlement persistence given by Bronson (1978) need to be further scrutinized. Leaving this aside, the political economic matrix put forth by Bronson consists of core centers located at the mouths of the various riverine systems of peninsula and island Southeast Asia. The center is determined to be a port polity, with kingship as the political authority. The assumption is that this port polity assumed the role of an entrepôt (Hall 1982, 2011; Leong 1990). Political relations, authority, and control were reduced as the distance increased further upstream of the watershed (Bronson 1978: 41–52). Furthermore, the port polity was connected to other core centers, such as those in China and India, that were deemed economically superior to the port polity, whereby their products were exchanged with those produced in the vicinity of the port polity. Accordingly, with the vast number of river systems in island and peninsula Southeast Asia, we can surmise that there were numerous port polities controlling their respective hinterlands and, via trading systems, were linked to the economically superior core centers in China and India, and perhaps some to regional cores in mainland Southeast Asia and beyond. Perhaps, within this ambit of political and economic development, the perceptions and understanding of archaeologists, historians, geographers, political scientists, and sociologists have been shaped to regard the role of Southeast Asia in world history as that of a trading entrepôt.

From such a model, we can understand how theory-infused historical accounts of the political economy of Southeast Asia caused it to be categorized as one of "peripherality" in the Eurasian world economy of trading exchanges. In certain ways, this model parallels the "dependistas" model used to explain the developmental trajectory of Latin American countries core-periphery relations with centers in Europe and the United States in the 1960s and 1970s (see, e.g., Dos Santos 1970; Frank 1966; Prebisch 1959; Sunkel 1973). The assumption is that Europe and the United States were developed cores and the countries in Latin America were underdeveloped peripheries, and every explanation of power and socioeconomic and political relations were understood with this uneven association in mind.

In the case of Southeast Asia (mainland, peninsula, and island), we have sociocultural exchange relationships occurring between Southeast Asia and India and China defined as processes of Indianization and Sinicization, since it is already assumed that India and China are politically and economically superior in their development (Vickery 2003). Conceptually, such models determine perceptions of the exchanges by presenting Southeast Asia as a passive periphery.[2] From a political economy approach within a world economy stance, however, such exchanges can also be viewed as one of active selection of socioeconomic, political, and cultural inputs that are conditioned by the balance of power, technology, degree of social complexity, long distance trade, and population by the specific Southeast Asian polity at a particular historical conjuncture in world history.[3] Along this vein, Southeast Asian polities, within the context of the Eurasian world system, participated in the global maritime economy specializing in economic activities and trade based on the character of its geographic landscape and the technology generated and adopted over the course of world history.

Mainland Southeast Asia

Southeast Asia as a region from the late prehistoric period onward was contributing to the ongoing socioeconomic and political dynamics of the Eurasian world economy. Its natural resources and products fed the growing consumption of the different cores located in Europe, South Asia, and East Asia. The urbanization processes in these regions facilitated the increase in mass consumption of the products of the Southeast Asian region as well as the luxuries that were consumed by the elites. This world demand for Southeast Asian goods naturally also transformed the polities located in mainland, peninsula, and island Southeast Asia.

The wide availability of copper, tin, and iron ore in the river valleys made possible the widespread development of chiefdoms on the mainland, the peninsula, and the archipelago of Southeast Asia from the Bronze Age onward. By the first century BC, political economic development on mainland Southeast Asia was spurred further by the Han dynasty's expansionist policies in the south leading to the incorporation of Yunnan and Vietnam into Han China's imperial schemes. A surge in militarism was followed by the rise of powerful local chiefdoms investing their energies in warlike actions. One can clearly see this in the chiefdom of Dian in Yunnan. The graves of the elites and royals of this period contained extraordinary wealth. The lacquered coffins were filled with bronzes and drums of thousands of exotic cowrie shells (Higham 2004, 2014). Female elite graves that were uncovered contained superb bronze weaving instruments. In the Red River plains of northern Vietnam, the graves excavated included weaponry of bronze spears and axes, imported Chinese coins, and woven clothing.

The excavations of Southeast Asian mainland, peninsula, and archipelago settlements of the early Iron Age have revealed great urban centers. They are of comparable scale to those of the earliest cities found in Egypt and Southern Mesopotamia (Chew 2007; Stark 2006). For example, that at Angkor Borei, in the lower Mekong region of Cambodia, has indications of a large urbanized complex, of which the later kingdom/state of Funan was part (Stark 1998; Wheatley 1964b). The estimated time of occupation of these sites is as early as 500 BC, with an end point of around AD 500 (Stark 2001a; Stark et al. 1999). Angkor Borei was settled in the late centuries BC, and its formation paralleled urban structures with moated sites excavated in the Mun River valley of Thailand, such as Ban Chiang Hian. Archaeological investigations focused on the period between the first to the eighth centuries AD in Cambodia have outlined the formation of complex socioeconomic and cultural systems with an indigenous writing system and monumental architecture that also participated in international trade, underscoring Childe's (1950) dimensions of urbanization outlined in the previous pages (Stark 1998, 2004). Of particular importance is the kingdom of Funan. The urban complexes at Funan had a developed division of labor, and many remains have been collected from the excavations of Malleret (1962). Potters, glass workers, goldsmiths, jewelers, and bronzesmiths formed the artisans that were involved in production processes. Their tools, refuse, and work materials have been excavated on a particular quarter of the urban complex. Other centers, such as the port of Oc Éo, had walls, moats, and reservoirs. The discovery of Roman artifacts indicates Oc Éo's role as a port city. Gold and bronze coins and medallions have been unearthed from the ruling periods of Antonius Pius and Marcus Aurelius (Malleret 1962).

According to Chinese records, Funan was in existence starting from the third century AD to the early seventh century AD (Wheatley 1964b). Coedes

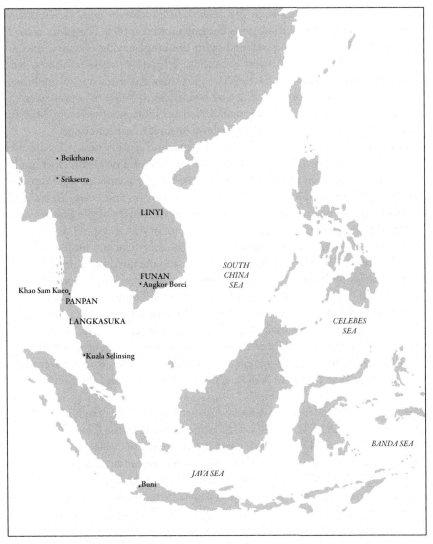

Figure 4.1. Urban Sites: Late Prehistoric and Early Historic Southeast Asia. Courtesy of Annie Thomsen, Cartographer.

(1966) dated its founding in the first century AD. Power and authority were developed from the second century AD onward. The power structure was an overall big man/chieftain who had vassal relationships over a set of chiefs.[4] It has been suggested that Funan was organized along the manner of an Indian kingdom, with vassal kingdoms politically associated with it (Coedes 1966). Vickery (2003) offers an alternate narrative for the foundation of Funan, one with no Indian roots. As time progressed and socioeconomic development continued, the hierarchical relations became more complex. Kingship, according to Wheatley (1964a), developed, with the kings having executive and judicial powers that they, on most occasions, delegate to their ministers, who were most often Brahmans. Stark (2015) sketches out the scope of the Funan sovereigns' actions—from building elite residences to house his retinues, to directing the construction of public works such as canals, reservoirs, etc. Military expeditions were sent to Malaya for tribute or diplomatic functions.

Historically, in the case of Funan from the second century onward, a number of small chiefdoms was brought under the tutelage of a powerful chieftain by the name of Hun P'an Huang (Wheatley 1964a). A paramount chief replaced Hun P'an Huang and attacked neighboring territories and even dispatched a naval expedition against other principalities on the shores of the South China Sea. Supposedly, the seat of government for Funan was about 500 li (250 km) from the sea. According to Coedes (1966), the extent of the limits of Funan stretched from Nha-trang, Vietnam, in the east to the northern part of the Malay Peninsula, to as far west as Lower Burma. It has been suggested by others, such as Hall (1982), that Funan's influence extended over these areas, intimating that it had hegemonic control over these territorial areas. Such an expanse of territorial control ensured that Funan had command of the land and sea trading routes that were part of the maritime trading routes of this portion of the Eurasian world trading system. The maritime silk sea routes covered the Bay of Bengal, the Straits of Malacca, the Gulf of Siam, and the South China Sea.

By the middle of the third century AD, settlements were established at several points on the Mekong delta. Descriptions made in the *Chin-shu* (written much later, about AD 646) discussed the existence of enclosed settlements, palaces, and dwelling houses, with wooden palisades for city walls. Funan covered about 300 to 500 hectares and had canals. A degree of cultural sophistication was achieved, with its ports and towns being the locus of the local and regional trade, and its agricultural base located in the interior mainland.

By the middle of the third century, Funan's commercial prosperity reached its peak. This is also reflected by the dispatch of embassies to India after AD 225 and to China in AD 268 and between AD 285 and 287. Missions were also undertaken to ensure good relations with the Chin emperors, reflecting the formation of state-like governance and structures. Further embassies were recorded for AD 434 and 484. Return Chinese delegations to Funan recorded lifestyles of the population paying their taxes in gold, silver, pearls, and perfumes, and using eating utensils made of silver. Emissaries also noted that the kingdom housed book depositories and archives. Additionally, they mentioned ships built that were eighty to ninety feet long and six to seven feet wide.

Changes in the Eurasian world economy by the fourth century had severe consequences for Funan. When the Chin dynasty lost its access to the overland northern silk routes to the west, great efforts were made by China to use the maritime routes to satisfy their trading needs. As a result, not only was Funan involved in this trade, but other Southeast Asian polities, such as those in northern Java, were also drawn into this maritime trading system. By then, the land portage route across the Kra Isthmus, which usually took about five days, was replaced by a route via the Straits of Malacca, which meant that ships using this Straits of Malacca route—which often needed six weeks to sail through—could, after crossing the straits, sail directly across the South China Sea to the southern Chinese ports, bypassing the trading ports of Funan located in the coastal areas of Cambodia and Vietnam. Polities that in the past were bypassed, such as Ko-ying and Yeh-p'o-t'i, located in the Sunda Straits area, benefited from this shift. Evidence of this choice of routing can be seen in the voyage of Fa-Hsien (1965) during the fifth century from Borneo to China.

Funan's decline continued in the fifth century. The reason that has thus far been provided is the arrival of ships capable of sailing both legs of the route between India and China along the Straits of Malacca and the South China Sea, bypassing coastal ports on mainland Southeast Asia under Funan's control. According to Hall (1985), Funan's decline was exacerbated further by the spread of wet rice agriculture throughout island Southeast Asia, thus unraveling the monopoly that Funan had as a supplier of rice with its location on the Mekong delta. No one, however, has given as a reason for Funan's demise the collapse of the Eurasian world system starting in the second century AD onward, nor has a reason that is climatologically based been proposed. In the later section of this chapter, I will put forth an argument correlating world-systemic socioeconomic downturns and climate changes with the demise of the Southeast Asian polities.

Other urban complexes have been unearthed in Vietnam. Five sites (Thanh Ho, Chau Sa, Thanh Loi, Tra Kieu, Oc Éo) have occupation periods from AD 1 to 1000 and sizes ranging from 160 to 850 square hectares (Stark 2006). These kingdoms were walled cities with moats surrounding them. Along the coastal and riverine landscape of the Indochinese coasts, 350 groups of sites dating back to the first half of the first millennium AD have been discovered (Manguin 2004). Vietnamese archaeologists have categorized these sites as belonging to the "Oc Éo culture." In the Red River valley, Co Loa, encompassing over six hundred hectares, appears to be an early state-level society in existence since 200 BC (Hilgers 2016; Kim 2013: 217). Emblematic of the urban transformation in mainland Southeast Asia, Co Loa had monumental constructions of rampart fortifications, moats, and hydraulic systems. Such constructions exhibit the various functions that such large-scale projects were meant to achieve, from irrigation for dry seasons to defense. They also underscore the scale of labor expenditure. Kim (2013: 231) provides estimates of such labor commitments from a plausible workforce of a thousand to ten thousand persons depending on the length of time it would take to complete construction, from three to fifty years at a very conservative rate of five persons per cubic meter. Therefore, the size and scale of these systems reveal the tremendous expenditure of labor and the social organization and complexity of the urbanism established in northern Vietnam during the late prehistoric period.

Lin-yi, situated on the Vietnamese coast (Yamagata 1998), was supposedly the center of the Cham country, emerging around AD 192. Archaeological excavations have yielded numerous items, such as jars and other items reflecting stamped patterns of Han-style pottery, roof tiles, and bricks. The roof tiles were similar to Han-type roof tiles discovered in southern China, whereas the bricks were of similar design to those excavated at Oc Éo in southern Vietnam. Excavations of two tombs unearthed bronze mirrors, Chinese-style pans, and coins. A shard of pottery and rouletted ware similar to that produced in India were also uncovered. Such a range of products from different locations reveal to us the extent of the trading connections Lin-yi had with countries within and outside the region. The presence of different types of pottery pieces suggest that there were indigenously developed skills in Lin-yi.

These polities participated in the Nanhai trade that was discussed previously. Tung-Tien in the third century AD had over twenty thousand families, which would give it a population of eighty to a hundred thousand persons. We can get an impression of their strength and vitality by the amount of tribute some of these states dispatched to China. For example, as we have previously noted, in AD 445, Lin-yi offered to China ten thousand katis of gold, a hundred thousand katis of silver, and three hundred thousand katis of copper (Wang 1998: 48).

Similar urbanization processes can also be detected in Thailand. In central Thailand, at the excavation site of Ban Don Te Phet, the graves contained much wealth. Iron spears, harpoons, axes, bronze ornaments, and billhooks were found. Similar level of sociocultural transformation were uncovered at another location in Thailand, Noen U-Loke, which was first occupied during the late Bronze Age and later abandoned between AD 400 and 500. Graves unearthed contained extremely rich wealth. The excavated grave of a male showed the interred person wearing 150 bronze bangles, bronze toe and finger rings, and three bronze belts. His ear coils were made of silver covered by gold. Pottery and glass beads were also buried with him.

In northeastern Thailand and the Chao Phraya valley, archaeological investigations using aerial photography have revealed moated settlements from about 400 BC to AD 200. The moats were constructed primarily for two main purposes: irrigation (water harvesting), aquatic resource extraction, and territorial occupation and defense (Moore 1988; Mudar 1999). Mudar (1999) also suggests that the presence of these moats underscores the ability of these centers to mobilize human and material resources. Settlements with moats for irrigation covered about 32.5 hectares at Mu'ang Fang, whereas the moated settlements at Mu'ang Sema, which are territorial in nature, were much more extensive, encompassing about 112.5 to 150 hectares. Archaeological assemblages reveal the usage of metals such as iron for manufacturing, derived from the geological deposits of the lateritic soil. Wet rice cultivation using the water from the irrigation moats made possible the generation of surplus, leading to population expansion and social stratification. Moore (1988) hypothesizes that these physical evidences, along with the distribution of these moated settlements in northeastern Thailand, point to the formation of chiefdoms in late prehistory or the early historic period. Recent studies have also attested to this development of political complexity (O'Reilly 2014; Scott and O'Reilly 2015). No central places, such as citadels, have been discovered. The low level of archaeological activity so far does not preclude the possibility of finding such formations and structures in the future. The extensive size of these settlements does underline that this region was situated on the land trading routes to southern China.

In Burma, six sites (Maingmaw, Beikthano, Halin, Sriksetra, and Dhanyawadi), ranging in size from 208 to 1477 square hectares and with occupation periods from AD 1 to 800, have been excavated (Moore 2007; Stark 2006). Beikthano occupied 859 hectares, Maingmaw 625 hectares, Halin 629 hectares, and Sriksetra 1,452 hectares. By the early historic period, the excavated sites in Upper and Lower Burma were walled and moated. These walled sites, commonly called "Pyu" and "Mon," with the former located in Upper Burma and the latter in Lower Burma, represent urban development with irrigation and water control (Moore 2007). The distribution of Pyu sites in Upper Burma is more extensive than the Mon sites in the lower region of the country. Excavations reveal the transformation of the Bronze Age culture to Buddhist social formations (Moore 2007). The Pyus practiced Sarvāstivādin Buddhism, whereas the Mons were Theravāda Buddhists, with the arrival of Buddhism in 300 BC (Moore 2007; Tarling 1999).

For Burma (Myanmar), the kingdom/state of Tircul had a number of urbanized centers established in the early centuries of the first millennium from the second to the ninth century AD (Hudson 2004; Luce 1985; O'Reilly 2007). The emergence of this kingdom/state can be traced to the first and second century AD (Stargardt 1990). These centers were fortified and furnished with hydraulic works and temples. The sphere of influence of this kingdom stretched about 1080 kilometers from west to east and 1800 kilometers from north to south in central Burma. Excavations show substantial urban remains and a rich material culture. By the ninth century AD, the extent of control stretched from the Chenla kingdom (successor of the Funan state) in the east to eastern India in the west, and from Nanchao (Yunnan, a kingdom founded in the seventh century) in the north to the ocean in the south. Within this sphere of influence were eight fortified cities (Hla 1979). The dominance of Tircul meant that it had a number of dependencies under its control. Eighteen dependencies and thirty-two tribes recognized it as their overlord. In terms of overall control, the excavated sites exhibited a hierarchy of urbanized settings. Dominance was exercised by nine garrison towns overseeing at least three hundred settlements (Wheatley 1983).

The scale of these urban centers can be seen in the city of Beikthano, an area of nine square kilometers surrounded by a wall about 2.5 meters thick and punctuated by twelve gates that are six meters across. These gates form the entrances to the city. Guardrooms were constructed behind the gates. Within the city are religious structures and bead workshops. A palace or citadel of 480 by 360 meters has also been excavated (Moore 2007), along with nearly a hundred buildings associated with the palace structure. Presumably, these building structures were for purposes ranging from religious, ceremonial, and funerary to administrative. Radiocarbon dating indicated that these structures were from the first/second century to the third/fourth century AD; however, habitation could have started as early as circa 200 BC (Moore 2007). The city was apparently destroyed by fire in the fourth to fifth century AD.

Other urban centers, such as Sriksetra and Halin, exhibited similar scale of development and material culture, with gold and silver coins, jade, ruby, carnelian, and agate beads found among the ruins. Sriksetra had the largest citadel-palace complex, measuring 575 by 375 meters, of all the urban sites excavated to date (Moore 2007). Overall urban development covered thirty square kilometers at Sriksetra. At Halin, Chinese emissaries had noted that the brick-walled sites required 319,147 cubic feet of bricks to build one kilometer section of the wall. Habitation lasted from AD 60 to 870 (Moore 2007). South Indian influence started around the eighth century AD, evidenced by the discovery of Indian script on the walls starting from this period. Wheatley (1964) has noted that these Pyu urban settlements numbered about sixty to one hundred thousand persons, according to the *Old Book of Tang*. Halin had an outer wall measuring 3.2 kilometers long and a width of 1.6 kilometers with a circumference of about 9.5 kilometers. The thickness of the wall was about 4.9 meters.

The establishment of urban areas on Mainland Southeast Asia can be seen in a tabulated summary listed in table 4.1. Given the estimated site areas of these urban complexes, and assuming a density of fifty people per hectare (Higham and Thosarat 2012), the population levels would range from seventy-four thousand persons for Sriksetra in Burma to seventy-one hundred persons for U-Thong in Thailand. Table 4.2 provides the estimated population levels for excavated sites in mainland Southeast Asia.

Table 4.1. Southeast Asian Polities and Site Sizes

Region	Date Range	Site Name	Site Area
1) Burma	AD 1–500?	Maingmaw	222 ha
2) Burma	AD 1–500	Beikthano	291.7 ha
3) Burma	AD 100–780	Halin	208 ha
4) Burma	AD 400–800	Sriksetra	1477 ha
5) Burma	AD 450–800	Dhanyawadi	572 ha
6) Vietnam*	300–100 BC	Co-Loa	600 ha
7) Vietnam	AD 400–700	Thanh Ho	490 ha
8) Vietnam	AD 600–800	Chau Sa	160 ha
9) Vietnam	AD 500–600	Thanh Loi	250 ha
10) Vietnam	AD 100–800	Tra Kieu	850 ha
11) Vietnam	AD 1–1000	Oc Eo	450 ha
12) Cambodia	AD 1–1000	Angkor Borei	300 ha
13) Cambodia	AD 500–800	Sambor Prei Kuk	400 ha
14) Thailand	(early Dvaravati)	Nakhon Pathom	300 ha
15) Thailand	(early Dvaravati)	Sri Thep	176 ha
16) Thailand	(early Dvaravati)	U-Thong	142 ha

Source: Stark (2006: 21.12); *Derived from Kim (2013: 218).

Table 4.2. Southeast Asian Polities and Population Levels

Region	Date Range	Site Name	Est. Population (Persons)
1) Burma	AD1–500?	Maingmaw	11,100
2) Burma	AD 1–500	Beikthano	14,600
3) Burma	AD 100–780	Halin	10,400
4) Burma	AD 400–800	Sriksetra	73,850
5) Burma	AD 450–800	Dhanyawadi	28,600
6) Vietnam	AD 400–700	Thanh Ho	24,500
7) Vietnam	AD 600–800	Chau Sa	8,000
8) Vietnam	AD 500–600	Thanh Loi	12,500
9) Vietnam	AD 100–800	Tra Kieu	42,500
10) Vietnam	AD 1–1000	Oc Eo	22,500
11) Cambodia	AD 1–1000	Angkor Borei	15,000
12) Cambodia	AD 500–800	Sambor Prei Kuk	20,000
13) Thailand	(early Dvaravati)	Nakhon Pathom	15,000
14) Thailand	(early Dvaravati)	Sri Thep	8,800
15) Thailand	(early Dvaravati)	U-Thong	7,100

Source: Stark (2006: 21.12); figures in fourth column of table 4.2 are not from Stark (2006).

Peninsula and Island Southeast Asia

Peninsula Southeast Asia also had a number of polities on both its eastern and western sides. Trading ships from India came through the Straits of Malacca bordering the western side of the peninsula and docked in the ports along the western coast, and ships from China docked in ports on the eastern portion of the peninsula. Chinese historical sources indicate that sophisticated social systems existed in the Malay Peninsula from the early centuries of the first millennium of the current era. Other literary historical text accounts, such as Ptolemy's ([150 AD] 199) *Geography*, note other maritime polities along the coastline of the peninsula. According to these texts and recent archaeological excavations, as early as the first century (perhaps even earlier) to the fifth century AD, urban centers enclosed in palisades or walls, with rulers living in palaces, existed along the coastlines of the peninsula.

In the *Golden Khersonese*, Paul Wheatley wrote of the Han dynasty envoys visiting what was then the kingdom of Funan and claiming to have visited or heard of more than a hundred kingdoms in the Southern Seas. This claim was noted later by the *Liang-shu* (Annals of the Liang dynasty AD 502–557), which also listed four kingdoms located on the Malay Peninsula. According to the Liang-shu, one of the kingdoms located in the Malay Peninsula used its military to subdue the neighboring kingdoms: "Once more [a ruler named Fan-man] used troops to attack and subdue the neighboring kingdoms, which all acknowledged themselves his vassals. He himself adopted the style of Great King of Fu-nan. Then he ordered the construction of great ships, and crossing over the Chang-hai attacked more than ten kingdoms, including Chu-tü-k'un, Chiu-chih and Tien-sun. He extended his territory for five to six thousand li.[5] Then he attacked the kingdom of Chin-li (a country seemingly situated on the northern shores of the Gulf of Siam)" (Wheatley 1964: 15).

The four other kingdoms that were supposedly located on the Malay Peninsula and established by the early historic period of the Han Dynasty were also noted in other historical sources, such as the *Ch'ien Han Shu*, *Nan-shih*, and *T'ai-p'ing Yü Lan*. Described as substantial kingdoms, these polities, such as Tien-Sun or Tun-Sun (situated on the peninsula), had political and trade relations with Funan. The account of Tien-Sun is as follows:

> More than 3,000 li from the southern frontier of Fu-nan is the kingdom of Tun-sun, which is situated on an ocean stepping stone. The land is 1000 li in extent; the city is 10 li from the sea. There are five kings who all acknowledge themselves vassals of Fu-nan. The eastern frontier of Tun-sun is in communication with Chaio-chou (T'ong-king), the western with Tien-chu (India) and An-hsi (Parthia). All the countries beyond the frontier come and go in pursuit of trade, because Tun-sun curves round and projects into the sea for more than 1000 li. The Chang-hai (Gulf of Siam) is of great extent and ocean-going junks have yet

crossed it direct. At this mart East and West meet together so that daily there are innumerable people there. Precious goods and rare merchandise—there is nothing which is not there. Moreover, there is a wine-tree which resembles the pomegranate. The juice of its flowers is collected and allowed to stand in a jar: after a few days it becomes wine. (Wheatley 1964: 16)

Tun-sun was supposedly to be the locale on the Malay Peninsula where the East met West, and at its mart there were more than ten thousand people meeting daily (Wheatley 1956).

Of the other three kingdoms, Ch'u-Tu-K'un (or Tu-K'un) was situated on the Malay Peninsula on the opposite shores of Funan, about three thousand li (fifteen hundred kilometers) beyond the great bay of Chin-lin; Chiu-Chih (or Chu-Li) was positioned southward from Tun-Sun, a voyage of about eight days; and Pi-sung was situated across the Gulf of Siam from Funan, about three thousand li (fifteen hundred kilometers) southward. In addition to the four kingdoms, there was another: P'an-P'an (Tan-Tan).

According to Malay folklore, there was another kingdom, Langkasuka (Lang-ya-hsiu), established on the west coast, which extended across the peninsula from sea to sea. This kingdom was founded, according to the *Liang shu*, in the second century AD. It experienced a period of decline in the first half of the third century AD (Jacq-Hergoualc'h 2002). Subsequently, there supervened a period of eclipse (Dark Age!). By the second half of the fifth century, the fortunes of Langkasuka were restored. The urbanization of Langkasuka was similar to the urban areas on mainland Southeast Asia. Earthen ramparts as fortifications have been excavated, along with canals dug possibly for agriculture, and buildings of bricks formed the urban areas. A great variety of bricks with moldings have been unearthed. Objects found indicate one building might have been a Buddhist sanctuary. The urban area was connected to coastal ports (Jacq-Hergoualc'h 2002). Coins made of bronze of Chinese and Arab origins have also been uncovered, indicating external trade relations. Langkasuka was an independent kingdom, sending four embassies to Chinese court in AD 515, 523, 531, and 568. Its ascendance followed the decline of Funan in the sixth century. By the seventh century, it was a regular port of call on the sea route to India, and after this period it became a unit in the Sri Vijayan thalassocracy (Wheatley 1964: 262–264). A description of the kingdom, along with details of its history, is given by Wheatley (1964: 253–254):

The kingdom of Lang-ya-hsiu is situated in the Southern Seas. Its frontiers are thirty days' journey from east to west and twenty from south to north. It is twenty-four thousand li distant from Kuang-chou (Canton). Its climate and product are somewhat similar to those of Fu-nan. Aloeswoods, Barus camphor and suchlike are especially abundant. It is customary for men and women to go with the upper part of the body naked, with their hair disheveled down their backs, and wearing a cotton kan-man. The king and his high officials add cloths of yün-hsia to cover their shoulders, wear golden cords as girdles, and insert gold rings in their ears. Their kingdom is surrounded by walls to form a city with double gates, towers and pavilions. When the king goes forth he rides upon an elephant. He is accompanied by banners, fly-whisks, flags and drums and is shaded with a white parasol. The soldiers of his guard are well appointed. The inhabitants of the country say that their state was founded more than four hundred years ago. Subsequently the descendants became weaker, but in the king's household there was a man of virtue to whom the populace turned. When the king heard of this he imprisoned this man, but his chains snapped unaccountably. The king took him for a supernatural being and, not daring to injure him, exiled him from the country, whereupon he fled to India. The king of India gave him his eldest daughter in marriage. Not long afterwards, when the king of Lang-ya died, the chief ministers welcomed back the exile and made him king. More than twenty years later he died, and was succeeded by his son, P'o-ch'-ieh-ta-to (possibly Bhagadatta). In the fourteenth year of the T'ien-chien period (AD 515) he sent an envoy, A-ch'e-to, to present a memorial to the Emperor.

At Langkasuka, trade was focused on native products such as ivory, rhinoceros horn, camphor, lakawood, and gharuwood (Wheatley 1956). Foreign merchants traded for them with wine, porcelain vessels, and cotton.

The mention of these kingdoms—with their wide array of socioeconomic and political relations—as early as the period of the Han dynasty suggests that there were established polities at least on the Malay Peninsula, if not also on island Southeast Asia, in addition to the kingdoms in existence on mainland Southeast Asia. Unfortunately, we do not have much description of the scale of urbanization of these polities and their socioeconomic transformation because there have been few archeological activities pursued to date, other than those undertaken by Bellina (2007, 2014) of Khao Sam Kaeo (c. fourth century to second century BC) on the isthmus, and by Saidin et al. (2011) at Sungai Batu, Malaysia. These excavations do call into question the type of port polity structure proposed by Bronson (1978), which depicts the typical political and urban settlement established in island Southeast Asia.

Archaeological excavations undertaken from 2009 onward have revealed urbanized communities on the northwest Malaysian coast of the peninsula at Sungai Batu as early as 50 BC that covered a thousand square kilometers, with continuous settlement until the sixth century AD (Chia and Naziatul 2011; Saidin et al. 2011). An astonishing find of a 1,900-year-old monument built with detailed geometrical precision (possibly for sun worship) was excavated at Sungai Batu (Chia and Andaya 2011; Saidin 2012).[6] Such a monument suggests a highly developed "civilization" existing at the dawn of the current era, very much earlier than the well-known powerful kingdom of Sri Vijaya (700 AD), which dominated this region. Warehouses with tile roofs and port jetties have also been found. Iron slags, iron furnaces, and clay tuyeres (air-blast nozzle for iron production) have also been excavated, indicating the urban community was also undertaking the production of iron and the distribution of iron ingots. Earlier finds in northwest Malaysia have also uncovered building structures of a large kingdom (Jiecha) dating to the third century AD.

In addition to the urban settlements at Sungai Batu, there are other communities on the peninsula that practiced agriculture, had skilled craftsmen, and also hosted Brahmin and merchant communities. According to the Chinese accounts, they have names such as Takola, P'an P'an, Tun-Sun, Chieh-ch'a, Ch'ih-tu, etc. Described as city-states, these complexes each had a large urban settlement. By the fifth century AD, these polities had developed to become full-fledged city-states that were sending and receiving embassies from India and China.

Specifically, the urban center Tun-Sun covered an area of about 370 kilometers (Wheatley 1961). It is said that Tun-Sun hosted foreign nationals, such as a colony of South Asians. Another kingdom, Panpan, situated on the east coast of the peninsula near what are now the Malaysian states of Kelantan and Trengganu, was a city-state that later sent embassies to China. During the early centuries of the current era, one of the other urban centers that participated in the trading networks in a significant way was Langkasuka, with its walled city and dense concentrations of canals and moats. These canals connected the city to the sea, about ten kilometers away. Bronze coins from China and the Arab world have been found at Langkasuka, which is located in the northern part (near Songkhla) of the peninsula—what is now southern Thailand (Jacq-Hergoualc'h 2002). Later on in the millennium, Langkasuka sent a total of five trading missions to China. Kedah, Ko Kho Khao, Kampung Sungai Mas, and Kuala Selinsing were urban centers that have also been excavated on the west coast of the Malay Peninsula, and Chitu and Pulau Tioman have also been discovered on the east coast.

Besides the building structures at Bujang Valley (northwest Malaya) and the other city-states located on the Malayan peninsula, there were also other maritime polities located along southwest peninsular Thailand and the Malayan/Sumatran coastlines by the first half of the first millennium CE. These polities, like those in southern Thailand, were producing beads and glass for regional trade with India (Manguin 2004). The establishment of glass and bead production in Southeast Asian coastal polities indicates the growing dynamics of regional trade, especially between India and Southeast Asia, by this time.

The bead production and urban centers at Khao Sam Kaeo, located on the eastern part of the Kra Isthmus in southern Thailand, along with its counterpart Phu Khao Thong/Bang Kluai Nok on the western end, were considered port polities equivalent to Malacca, Banten, and Pasai of the later historical period (Bellina et al. 2014). Khao Sam Kaeo has been classified as a complex coastal polity dating from the early fourth century to the second or first century

BC. It is about thirty-five hectares in area, surrounded by walls and palisades. The surrounding areas were used for dryland cultivation of rice and the cultivation of millet and mung beans. Archaeobotanical finds suggest these crops had origins in China and India. Besides agrarian activities, manufacturing of glass, beads, bracelets, and high-tin bronze bowls were also evident. Copper was imported, whereas tin was sourced locally. The scale of agrarian and production activities underline the development of a complex and stratified social structure. Coordinating and managing such a range of socioeconomic undertakings meant that a developed coastal port polity existed that was linked to the various trading centers in Southeast Asia and beyond.

On the western side of the Kra Isthmus, Phu Khao Thong and Bang Kluai Nok were similar centers to Khao Sam Kaeo. The archaeological assemblages of Phu Khao Thong around the third to the first centuries BC and those of Khao Sam Kaeo are reportedly quite comparable. Indian ceramics of fine wares and steatite containers have been unearthed. The Roman-like intaglios, pendants, and glassware discovered suggest trading connections that are further west than South Asia (Borell 2014).

Beyond Sumatra, a site complex has also been discovered at Buni in West Java. Still active in the third century AD, it was one of the gateways for the Indian trade. Known as Ko-Ying from Chinese sources, it is said to have been densely populated.

The tropical weather and the acidic soil in the Southeast Asian region has been quite debilitative to the preservation of material evidence and records of these ancient socioeconomic and cultural systems that existed more than two thousand years ago. Nonetheless, what has been archaeologically excavated/discovered so far underlines the complexity and developed nature of these ancient polities. From Chinese and Indian records, we can determine the functions and socioeconomic and political activities undertaken by these kingdoms and city-states in the Eurasian world economy at the beginning of our current era until the wide-scale collapse of the world system and the arrival of another Dark Age (see Chew 2007, 2008) starting from the fourth century AD onward. For example, the urban settlement at Sungai Batu (northwest Malaysia) showed site abandonment by the sixth century AD and was not used again for iron smelting until the seventeenth century AD (Chia and Naizatul 2011).

Indian Colonization and Indianization: Hybridization?

The scholarly understanding of the character of political and social development of Southeast Asian polities since the early 1960s has been shaped by an overall perception of Southeast Asia's "peripherality status" within the Eurasian world economy. Furthermore, that Southeast Asia was called "Greater India" or "Farther India" by nationalist South Asian scholars, such as Majumdar (1952), and deemed Indian colonies by others, such as Coedes (1966, 1968), has framed our interpretations of Southeast Asian sociopolitical development. As a result, the Southeast Asian political institutions and structures have been viewed as being either transplants of Indian institutions or the result of Indian influences.

How do we make sense of the above characterizations of sociopolitical development of Southeast Asia in the late prehistoric and early historic periods between 200 BC–AD 500? To assess the characterizations that have been put forth over the years, we need to consider first on what basis these attributions of sociopolitical development were made, besides the ideological orientation of the respective scholars. It is clear that the writing and understanding of sociopolitical development of Southeast Asia, especially the mainland, were based on and informed by Indian and Chinese texts and inscriptions, and on archaeological evidence. The textual documentation was derived mostly from merchants and traders, travelers, pilgrims, and state officials on missions to Southeast Asia. The accounts would have been embellished—especially the travelogues, but even the Chinese official reports—according to the personal and official interests of the sources from which they were obtained. Notwithstanding this, the earliest documents did not survive the times, and therefore the accounts were written in a later period, after their occurrences.[7] In the case of Indian documents and sources, scholars have not even considered them as historic documents but rather a mixture of stories and epics (see, e.g., Higham 2014). In a materialistic sense, archaeological evidence would be the most reliable in providing material support of the historical transformations. Even these types of indications can pose an issue, as the interpretation of the archaeological assemblages is always guided by a theoretical framework or model; and we know that different models can prompt a different understanding and interpretation of the archaeological evidence. And as we have mentioned previously, in Southeast Asia's case, there have been too few archaeological studies covering the early prehistoric and historic period; thus we the need to consider different sources of information and data in order to reach a more in-depth, faithful understanding of the historical changes that transpired. The few archeological assemblages that cover the later prehistoric and early historic periods have led most of the Southeast Asian scholars from Coedes onward to provide historical accounts of the sociopolitical structures and processes based on evidence that are dated for a later period of Southeast Asian history. Vickery (2003) has shown the conflicting names of kings and place names that make it difficult for us to have an understanding of the historical formation of Funan, for example. Does this undermine the historical interpretations and explanations that have been made and widely accepted as historically "factual"? This issue must be grappled with and deliberated on, and a conclusion must be reached within a reasoned context.

Given the above, we can therefore appreciate what earlier studies of sociopolitical development were faced with in order to offer an interpretation and understanding of the character of the development of Southeast Asian sociopolitical institutions. A close examination of the studies of Coedes (1966, 1967), for example, reveals that they are based primarily on Indian and Chinese source texts. Steeped in the view that external influences—mostly from India, and to some extent from China—determined the sociopolitical institutions of Southeast Asia, Coedes (1966: 53–54), shaped by the European orientalist mentalité of the times, openly declared that "very little is known about how these (Southeast Asian) kingdoms came into being," but then proceeded to argue that one should "assume either that Indians imposed their form of political organization on an indigenous society, or that an indigenous society which had been affected by Indian cultural influence created a political organization on the Indian pattern." This sociopolitical trajectory was rationalized by Coedes based on evidence he had obtained in Chinese accounts and epigraphic materials that do not necessarily represent the historical period he was discussing. Such an interpretation and understanding on Coedes's part naturally frames and labels mainland Southeast Asia during the late prehistoric and early historic period as a peripheral region in the Eurasian world economy, or a region with a less developed set of social and political institutions. As Vickery (2003: 120) suggests, "This is part of the old orientalist prejudice that all cultural progress in Southeast Asia had to start with an import from India."

To promote this interpretation, Coedes articulated two hypothetical routes that could satisfy the colonization or Indianization process. The first is that of an Indian becoming the ruler of the Southeast Asian kingdom by marriage to an indigenous female person of royalty. The other is one whereby the native chief uses an Indian Brahman as an advisor to help him legitimate his rule, resulting in the establishment of a kingdom based on the Indian monarchy. According to Coedes (1966, 1967), both paths were taken, depending on the local contexts. Several historical interpretations from Coedes (1966, 1967), Hall (1982), and others suggest that the foundation of the famous kingdom of Funan was based on the first path, whereas there are many examples of kingships established, especially in island Southeast Asia, such as Indonesia, that followed the second route. Either path requires further distinction of whether there was a transplantation of the Indian superstructure onto the local culture, or an interaction between the local culture with the Indian elements brought by Indian visitors.

According to the early scholarly analyses of the trajectory of sociopolitical development in Southeast Asia, Indian colonization was most intense in the second and third centuries AD and came to fruition in the fourth and fifth centuries. Another narrative of intense Indian influence suggests a period much later—fourth to fifth centuries AD—and that both Southeast Asian and South Asian traders were involved actively in the maritime trade (Hall 1982; Smith 1999; Vickery 2003). Leaving aside the route of marriage between an Indian and a local princess or the import of Brahmans that led to formation of kingdoms, another trajectory of sociopolitical development leading to state formation was mainly as a consequence of commercial expansion by South Asians (Coedes 1967; Hall 1982; Mabbett 1997a; Smith 1999). As traders in the Indian Ocean economy and with links to the Arabian and Mediterranean trade, the Indians were spurred to seek Southeast Asian products that were much sought after in the West. Such impetus was facilitated by the availability of shipbuilding technologies and the construction of ships capable of trans-porting six to seven hundred passengers (Coedes 1967: 20). Trade led either to colonization or Indianization, and the two paths of sociopolitical develop-ment of institutions and structures discussed in the previous pages can fit with this explanation of the dynamics of trade that led to the arrival of Indians in Southeast Asia. Whether the Indians came via the maritime route and/or by the overland trading route has not been shown distinctly. The general consen-sus is the maritime route across the Bay of Bengal and the Andaman Sea via the Straits of Malacca (land portage across the Isthmus of Kra) and onward to the Gulf of Siam, the South China Sea, and the Java Sea. A trip of this na-ture would extend about two years, with sailing through the Straits of Malacca usually taking about six weeks (Francis 2002). Some traders preferred the land portage route that usually cost about four days, with a day for unloading the cargo and reloading it back on board ships at both ends of the Isthmus of Kra, notwithstanding the length of the sea journey from India to China. This land portage route across the Isthmus of Kra was first undertaken by Chinese offi-cials during the Western Han period of Emperor Wudi (140–87 BC) though these officials traveled from China to India (Jacq-Hergoualc'h 2002; Wheatley 1961).

Others, such as Van Leur (1967) and Wolters (1999), to name a few, have offered a more refined determination of the nature of the sociopolitical devel-opment of Southeast Asia by sketching a view of a more robust indigenous political development in place prior to the arrival of the Indians, and, following the Indian arrival, an active interaction between Indian and South Asian influ-ences. Over the years, others such as Benda (1962), Mabbett (1977a, 1977b), Hall (1982), Kulke (1990), Smith (1999), Wheatley (1982), etc., have also contributed to the characterization of the sociopolitical institutions of South-east Asia.[8]

The work of Van Leur (1967), focused mainly on the island of Java, paints a picture of the indigenous sociopolitical development that veers away from how it was characterized by Majumdar and Coedes. Whereas the latter two scholars view Southeast Asian polities as less complex and passive prior to the arrival of the South Asians, Van Leur (1967: 93–95) articulates a characterization of the sociopolitical institutions and structures as well developed and formed:

> Judging from the evidence of these few stray forms, the "pre-Hindu" communities would seem to have been already in essence on the same level as what is still encountered in social structure and socio-economic life in many regions of Indonesia at the present time. From the existence of irrigation farming and the administrative system connected with it can be deduced the existence of patrimonial, bureaucratic states conceived on a larger or smaller scale. . . . From the existence of navigation can be deduced trade and the forms of social structure, inter-communication, and authority connected with it. . . . There can only be one conclusion, however—the Indonesian peoples, scattered over the islands of the archipelago, each group in its own historical and geographic milieu, have exhibited processes of long-lasting, independent historical "development" in a multiplicity of forms of government, legal, and social organization and socio-economic life, forms the inner power of which vary according to circumstances, but which in the course of history have been subjected to the greatest tests of strength and have proved to have power of resistance.

What the above implies is an active social interaction and the exchange of ideas, customs, and social practices among the South Asian merchants, Brahmins, and the local elites. The use of the word "colonization" to depict the process of external influences on Southeast Asian sociopolitical institutions and structures by South Asians does not characterize the social interactions that took place according to Van Leur. Instead of considering the Indonesian sociopolitical institutions as less complex prior to external contact, Van Leur (1967: 98) suggests that they were fully developed, and even went as far to suggest that the Indonesian rulers and aristocrats, in order to facilitate their trading practices and their legitimacy "*summoned* [my emphasis] the Brahman priesthood to their courts."

Following Van Leur's line of attributing sociopolitical development to the active interaction between the local and the foreign, Wolters (1999) introduced the term "localization" to describe the absorption of Indian influences into the cultural matrix of Southeast Asian social systems. The Indian materials were restated and localized before they were fitted into local religious, social, or political complexes. These foreign fragments in their new environment would only then make sense and be deemed unique by the Southeast Asian elites and their subjects. This characterization, instead of reflecting passivity, underscores the active nature by which Southeast Asian social systems interrelated with external/foreign (i.e., Indian) influences. Following this trend of explaining social and political formations in Southeast Asia, Hall (1982) offers a more nuanced explanation to state formation in the case of Funan. Instead of placing South Asians as the overall force and impetus toward state formation as

Coedes (1966, 1967) proposes, Hall attributes the process of state formation to Funan's location in the maritime trading routes facilitating local and regional trade exchanges, and its inland agrarian system ensuring a stable revenue flow for its rulers, thus enabling the basis for financing statecraft. These economic activities and assets facilitated the diffusion of Funan's political and cultural achievements to other secondary areas of Southeast Asia. For Hall (1982: 91), "Funan is indeed the first Southeast Asian 'state.'" Rather than, as Coedes argues, South Asian traders, merchants, and Brahmans leading to political development, Hall suggests the active dynamic of a Southeast Asian sociopolitical and cultural matrix that provided the momentum for state formation. It is only later in the fourth to fifth century AD that South Asian influences emerged in concert intertwined with the Southeast Asian sociopolitical and cultural matrix to further the development of the state. Historically, therefore, one can characterize this cultural intertwining as a process of hybridization,[9] instead of Indianization, for the latter connotes a process of adaptation whereby South Asia provided the overall distinctive cultural matrix.

Located between two stratified and complex civilizations of India and China, it is quite understandable that the interpretations of Southeast Asian sociopolitical development were framed within the context of a trajectory either derived from Indian impulses or developed in interactions with it. Whether there was plentiful solid evidence to substantiate such interpretations was seldom questioned; it was always assumed by most of the Southeast Asian scholars that socioeconomic and political development had to start with an import from South Asia. Such an interpretation would fall under what one would classify as the process of Indianization of the region. Another model to depict the interactions of two cultures that does not give more weight to one culture but views the process as a cultural interchange would be the hybridization model that that has been put forth above. This model would fit better with the various interpretations of the trajectory of sociopolitical development Southeast Asia following the work of Van Leur and Wolters. Recently, however, in view of recent archaeological assemblages unearthed in mainland Southeast Asia, Higham (2014: 336) has suggested that "the Indian colonialist and Indianisation models are no longer tenable" for our characterization of the development of sociopolitical institutions leading to the formation of states. Higham's (2014) assessment was that Southeast Asia's political development in the late prehistoric and early historic period was one whereby the Indian presence was only one of several variables in mutual interplay, and therefore should not be considered as the only factor that determined sociopolitical development of Southeast Asia, as others in the past, such as Coedes (1966, 1967), have posited.

Can the recent archaeological excavated assemblages in Malaysia (Saidin 2012) and southern Thailand (Bellina 2003, 2007, 2014) during the late prehistoric age of Southeast Asia help us to understand, decipher, and explain these "cultural exchanges" further? In spite of the varied and substantive evidence of indigenous Southeast Asian socioeconomic development occurring in the late prehistoric period, most contemporary Southeast Asian specialists, such as Ray (1996) and even Bellina (2003, 2007, 2014) to a lesser extent, continue to rationalize and explain the socioeconomic transformation of prehistoric Southeast Asia within the mentalité of Indianization even before the impact of Indian influence became visible from the fourth to fifth century AD onward. Bellina's (2003, 2007, 2014) excavations of sites in southern Thailand, such as Khao Sam Kaeo (KSK), offer an example of how this mentalité of Indianization has influenced the examination, analysis, and conclusion of the late prehistoric sites of southern Thailand: that it was Indian influence even at the start, perhaps via Indian specialist craftsmen who were responsible for the manufacture of beads that were widely exchanged and sought after in Southeast Asia as early as late prehistory and early history of Southeast Asia. Not much archaeological evidence of Indian origin has been provided for the presence of Indian craftsmen in these prehistoric sites (KSK) in southern Thailand (see, e.g., Bellina 2007: 52, 54) other than an assertion of similarity in the bead manufacturing process to that of Indian craftsmen in Gujerat in northwestern India. Bellina (2014) tends to favor the Indian connection and believes that bead manufacturing in late prehistoric and early historic southern Thailand could not have been indigenous in origin but rather were Indian products or products produced by Indian craftsmen in Southeast Asia. Thus we can understand how the mentalité of Indianization emerges to rationalize the sophistication of the produced beads in spite of the fact that little archaeological evidence of the presence of Indian craftsmen was ever discovered at KSK. Bellina (2007: 54) mentions the absence of Indian craftsmen at KSK in her doctoral dissertation: "the fact that no concentration of production by-products has been found, as well as the absence of any other type of archaeological material of Indian origin indicative of the presence of a group of Indians." To smooth over this absence and to continue to maintain the Indocentric mentalité, some attribution is given to local indigenous craftsmen who might be the producers of the agate and carnelian beads, but the emphasis and rationale remain that it had to be Indian craftsmen that produced the high quality beads, and, perhaps in a later period, excavated beads of a coarser kind had been manufactured locally in Southeast Asia.

In a recent comparative study of excavated beads, Bellina (2014) continued such an Indocentric mentalité in her attempt to reveal the cultural exchanges and networking that occurred as a consequence of the regional trade networks in place during this period of late prehistoric and early historic Southeast Asia. Four groups of beads were ranked and categorized by their manufactured quality and distinct production process. No new evidence of the existence of Indian skilled craftsmen at KSK was provided, and conclusions made about the quality of beads and the production process continued to be based on Bellina's earlier study (2007), though in these current ones (Bellina 2014; Bellina et al. 2014) she and her colleagues suggest other skilled Asian and Southeast Asian craftsmen were residing in KSK, reflecting KSK's cosmopolitan character. In spite of this presence of Asian and Southeast Asian craftsmen, Bellina (2014: 346) continues to assert "the introduction of skilled exogenous technologies in Southeast Asia."[10]

What does this all mean for our understanding of Southeast Asia's place in the first Eurasian world system? With a lack of written records and archaeological documentation still being scarce, even the current analysis of prehistoric Southeast Asia is based mostly on models utilizing analogies from more recent historical and ethnographic situations to account for the prehistoric period of Southeast Asian history. Although these models are useful to us as an academic comparative exercise, they pose significant issues of interpretation, and are open and susceptible to ideological framing that specialists have in terms of their modes of orientation or mentalities. If such is the case, it's likely the history of the people without history has yet to be written.[11]

What if we do not adopt the mentalité of Indianization, but frame our analysis along the lines that indigenous Southeast Asian craftsmen in the prehistoric and early historic periods were manufacturing items for exchanges tied to a regional network of exchanges within Southeast Asia, and beyond this geographic locale to the Eurasian world system? In commenting on socioeconomic transformations in Central Vietnam between 500 BC to AD 500, Lam Thi My Dzung (2011: 11) proposes this line of interpretation: "I argue that the spread of goods and culture from India and China reflected the grafting of Indian commerce onto a pre-existing infrastructure of Southeast Asian networks. Such an explanation implies that earlier phases of development in various areas of Southeast Asia were characterized by indigenous processes of trade expansion and increasing social stratification." The work of Lankton and Dussubieux (2006) also points to the possibility of an early tradition of glass manufacturing in Southeast Asia.

The existence of a wide distribution of Dong Son drums throughout Southeast Asia reflects the indigenous capacity to manufacture bronze wares of significant sophistication. Supposedly made in the Bac Bo region of northern Vietnam by the middle of the first millennium BC, the Dong Son drums and the other types of bronze drums found throughout Southeast Asia clearly substantiate the fact that indigenous socioeconomic transformation and manufacturing capacity and metallurgical skills in Southeast Asia did not require an "import" from South Asia to stimulate indigenous Southeast Asian development, for we know that visible Indian presence in Southeast Asia occurred at a much later period. The manufacture of the Dong Son drums shows us that a high degree of indigenous metallurgical skills were in place by the middle of the first millennium BC. Furthermore, the wide distribution of Dong Son drums all over Southeast Asia (with the exception of the Philippines and Borneo) reflect that perhaps there were migratory movements of mainland Southeast Asians to island and peninsula Southeast Asia and that their presence all over Southeast Asia was the result of the intraregional trade (Chew 2015; Miksic 2013).

If such a line of reasoning is considered, Theunissen, Grave, and Bailey's (2000: 85) geochemical analysis of agate and carnelian beads archaeologically excavated in Thailand, and their search to discover their geographic origins, needs to be added to this endeavor to understand and explain the Indianization process that has dominated and determined the conclusions of so many studies of late prehistoric and early historic Southeast Asia's socioeconomic and political transformations. Theunissen, Grave, and Bailey (2000: 85) conclude that, with regards to bead production, the emphasis placed on Indian influence even as a catalyst "should be moderated with a greater consideration of indigenous contributions." The results from this study suggest that the vast majority of the Thai beads used in the geochemical analysis came from another non-Indian source. For Theunissen, Grave, and Bailey (2000: 98), the analysis "represents perhaps the best evidence thus far that carnelian beads were being manufactured in Southeast Asia from early in the Iron Age, and given the use of local material, that this manufacture was most likely under the control of Southeast Asian people." This non-Indian source of some of the glass beads excavated in Thailand, especially those found at Ban Don Ta Phet, is echoed in a recent reinterpretation in which Bellina and Glover (Glover and Bellina 2011) support the findings of Theunissen and his colleagues.

It is clear that theoretical frameworks, worldviews, mentalities, and hegemonic ideologies shape our interpretations, explanations, and acceptances of what we consider as truthful descriptions of what happened in the past. They mold and influence our view of the place of early Southeast Asia in world history. Whether these received accounts reflect truthfully what occurred historically can never fully be determined because historical, anthropological, and archaeological findings have always been guided by the local or regional social, political, and economic order of the times, as we have noted in the previous pages of this chapter. Beyond the local and regional dimensions of the social, economic, and political, we also need to delve into the deep structures and the rhythms of *global* social, political, and economic trends and tendencies, such as the Dark Ages, that we have referenced in many instances in the previous chapters to explain and account for what happened in Southeast Asia. There are also other elements, such as the climate and natural landscape transformations, that can provide us with a more robust explanation of polity formation in Southeast Asia than if we include in our deliberations only the usual socioeconomic and political factors. From this, a clearer understanding of Southeast Asia's place in world history can be derived.

Climate and Landscape

There have been some attempts of exploring climate as a factor of socioeconomic changes in Southeast Asian polities, though they are fewer in number than studies that use socioeconomic and political factors to explain transformations. Recently, however, there have been some archaeological and geographical studies (see, e.g., Boyd and Chang 2010; Boyd and McGrath 2001; O'Reilly 2014) that have focused on the historical interactions between culture, landscape, and climate to account for the transformed physical and socioeconomic landscapes of prehistoric and historic periods of mainland Southeast Asia. Such studies go beyond the standard socioeconomic explanations to offer us a more nuanced explanation for polity changes in Southeast Asia.

The climate of mainland Southeast Asia is of the humid tropical type (see, e.g., Stark 2001b). Rainfall from the monsoons is the main determinant of the seasonal pattern of dry and wet periods. Nearly all of mainland Southeast Asia experiences a dry season followed by a wet one. Inland areas of mainland Southeast Asia, such as northern Burma and eastern Thailand, tend to experience an even more arid environment. There are occasions that this arid condition can extend to an even longer dry season in comparison with island Southeast Asia. Besides convectional rain, the monsoons bring moisture to the region, especially during the monsoon seasons. Usually the wet season starts from July to December, followed by a dry season between January and March. The monsoon winds bring increased moisture to the region between July and December on the mainland. Sometimes, if the monsoon winds are drawn further south than what they normally prevail, the arid conditions on the mainland could extend even longer. Over world history, this has occurred in Asia and South Asia (Chew 2001, 2007). Such are the vagaries of the weather that mainland Southeast Asia experiences. Historically, therefore the polities located on mainland Southeast Asia had to adapt their socioeconomic activities to this climatic environment.

Mainland Southeast Asia, as we have discussed in the previous pages of this chapter, had an array of developed urban settings exhibiting intensive landscape transformations to meet the socioeconomic needs of the various centralized political organizations that dotted the landscape from Burma to Vietnam from the early Iron Age onward (Boyd and McGrath 2001; Kim 2013; O'Reilly 2014; Scott and O'Reilly 2015). In northeastern Thailand, these early Iron Age urban centers were the forerunners of the vast kingdoms (such as Angkor, etc.) that emerged on the mainland in the later Iron Age Southeast Asia. World history has clearly shown that with increasing urban development, what most often results is large-scale landscape transformation (Chew 2007). In Southeast Asia's case, we note this from the archaeological assemblages discovered in Northeastern Thailand and northern Vietnam. Canals, ramparts, moats, and hydraulic works were constructed to meet the socioeconomic needs of these urbanized centers throughout the Iron Age. These constructive activities naturally led to deforestation, sedimentation, and siltation. Grasses replaced trees. In addition to construction works that generated deforestation, intensive agriculture, such as rice cultivation, also led to landscape changes, requiring more irrigation works and canals (Boyd and McGrath 2001). We find evidences of these outcomes throughout mainland Southeast Asia, especially in northeastern Thailand and northern Vietnam.

In northern Vietnam during the Iron Age—for example, in the Red River delta—forests were removed for agriculture, building construction, and fuel (Li 2016). The deforestation led to increased soil erosion, resulting in sedimentation occurring downstream. The eastern part of the Red River delta accelerated in area to twice the size of the western portion over the course of ten centuries, from the first century AD onward. This transformation of the landscape has implications for the region in the area of agriculture and human habitation. Reduced fresh water flow often leads to salt water intrusion. In the end, it impacts human-induced activities such as agriculture.

Northeastern Thailand underwent similar landscape transformations. From the early Iron Age onward, forest disturbance was followed by rice cultivation and, over time, forest regeneration. Continuous transformation of the landscape through building construction from the early Iron Age onward, coupled with rice cultivation until the mid-Iron Age (c. AD 300), resulted in a very transformed landscape. Uninterrupted deforestation has consequences. Palynological analysis has revealed that there was no longer any forest regeneration by the late Iron Age (AD 500–600) in northeastern Thailand; instead grassland and scrubby vegetation became the replacement (Boyd and Chang 2010).

The urban settlements on mainland Southeast Asia from the early Iron Age onward, especially in northern Vietnam and northeastern Thailand, have been surveyed for their construction complexity and their high-density settlement, suggesting a hierarchical and town-based society. These urban settlements, as we have discussed in the previous pages, have been distinguished by the moats that ring these sites. There have been different speculations as to the functions of these moats. Military defense, monumentality, aquatic resource extraction, water storage, and irrigation have all been proposed (Kim 2013; Moore 1988; Mudar 1999; Scott and O'Reilly 2015). Depending on which factor is used to explain the basis for the construction of these moats and ramparts, different plausible rationale for their constructions can be surmised. What follows reflects this.

Among the various moated sites in mainland Southeast Asia, Co Loa is one of the largest (six hundred hectares), located in northern Vietnam's Red River valley region. Built with rampart fortifications and moats, it is, according to Kim (2013), emblematic of mainland Southeast Asian urbanism. These fortifications were clearly intended for military defense, according to Kim (2013). This rationale for the existence of ramparts and moats fits with the orthodox understanding for the construction of such types of structures, for it is always assumed that ancient social systems experience conflicts and warfare along with the need for social enforcement and control (Moore 1988). In the case of Co Loa, the immediate threat from neighboring kingdoms and, of course, from southern China is easily recognizable and assumed (Kim 2013).

If we veer away from such an orthodox understanding for the existence of these structures, we find another explanation has been offered, one based on the dimension of climate. Focusing on northeastern Thailand with its vast number of moated urban settlements, recent studies (O'Reilly 2016; Scott and O'Reilly 2015) suggest that the construction of moats was a response to climatic changes. In the case of northeastern Thailand, there was a drop in the rainfall pattern between 200 BC–AD 500. It was a drier environment, with high levels of water lost through evaporation. Overlaying the distribution of the moated sites on a rainfall distribution map, the studies have shown that the majority of the moated sites were located in regions with the lowest precipitation. Besides rainfall distribution, the analysis has further indicated that water loss is also an important factor in determining the location of moated sites. Moats were built as storage areas for water. Therefore, soil permeability (in terms of seepage over time) has to be considered as a factor in moat construction. Examining the distribution of the moated sites, those areas in northeastern Thailand that have low or low-medium soil permeability have the highest concentration of moated sites compared to areas that have high soil permeability. Such close significant correlations, according to Scott and O'Reilly (2015), suggest that moats were constructed for water storage in order to respond to climatic changes such as irregular rainfall and long periods of drought conditions.

Given such conditions, these moats could provide the means by which political power could be exercised and maintained. If the polity's economy was agriculturally focused, the control of water availability could provide the elites with the ability to exercise command of a hierarchical social complexity because of the environmental circumstances. O'Reilly (2014) posits such a possibility in the political economy of northeastern Thailand, where arid conditions predominate. Therefore, we should realize that socioeconomic and political transformations are necessarily tied and circumscribed by changes in climatic and environmental parameters, and that the latter changes are just as important in our understanding of the social evolutionary trajectories of mainland Southeast Asian polities. Unfortunately, the limited number of long-term analyses of the climate and environmental conditions of early Southeast Asia will continue to hinder us in following such a tack in our attempt to understand and explain the early socioeconomic and political transformations of Southeast Asia. Hopefully, these lacunae can be filled in the future.

Notes

1. For a rebuttal of the modernization theory's position, see, e.g., Amin (1974); Dos Santos (1970); Frank (1966); Furtado (1971); Presbich (1959); and Sunkel (1973).
2. For an approach to understanding socioeconomic and cultural transformation different from the world-systems model, see Stein (2002).
3. For a similar framework on Bronze Age Europe's socioeconomic and cultural transmissions, see, e.g., Kristiansen (2014, 2011).
4. The formation of Funan, according to Coedes (1966), was a result of a marriage between an Indian Brahman and the daughter of the local king. Coedes' (1966, 1967) account was shaped deeply by his overall view of how Southeast Asia's developmental trajectory was conduced by the Indianization process, with Southeast Asia seen as Greater India.
5. This measure of distance of one li is equivalent to one quarter of a mile, or around half a kilometer.
6. Recent excavations have also revealed the remains of five ships at the site where port facilities have been unearthed. The ancient river located at the site has been estimated to have a width of one hundred meters and a depth of thirty meters (Arnold Loh, "Ancient Shipwrecks Find May Force a Rewrite of SEA History," *The Star*, 2 September 2015).
7. By no means is this accounting of what transpired in early Southeast Asian atypical of Southeast Asian historical reporting; such time-period delays in documenting the past have also occurred for accounts of Mycenaean Greece, the Trojan Wars, etc.
8. For a summary of the Indianization process debate, see Mabbett (1977a, 1977b).
9. For an interesting interpretation of cultural hybridization in relation to globalization and hybridization, see Friedman (2002).
10. Such Indocentricity is even reflected in the attribution of the natural resources used in commodity production. In an earlier study, Bellina (2007) states that the tin used in the manufacturing process was imported from India, but in a recent study, Bellina (2014) states that tin was sourced locally in Thailand. Thailand and Malaya, historically, have been known to have large deposits of tin.
11. I have borrowed parts of this sentence from the late Eric Wolf's (1982) book *Europe and the People without History*. In our context, the apt title would be *India and the People without History*.

Methodological Reprise

This book has offered an interpretation of Southeast Asia in world history by framing the region within a broader structure of a world economy. It is an exercise in doing "theory-informed history." Our understanding of Southeast Asia's place in this world history is therefore shaped by the trends and dynamics of the global processes of this world economy, of which trade is one of the key elements, and especially in determining the social evolutionary trends of the Southeast Asian polities in this world system. Such a point of departure assumes that the economic and political structures of a region or country have been shaped by these global processes. However, by no means should we assume that this tendency occurs exclusively in one direction. Regional dynamics and local economic and political trends also emerge to determine the trends and tendencies of these global processes. This development we have seen in various narratives in the previous chapters, especially chapters 3 and 4, which have focused on the economic and political transformations.

Our tracing of Southeast Asian economic and political transformations offers another interpretation of "what happened in history," in this case in Southeast Asia. This account is based on a number of literary, linguistic, historical, anthropological, and archaeological sources. No doubt the veracity of these sources is less clear-cut in terms of "truth criteria," for they belong to the humanities rather than the natural sciences. In this respect, there will be questions and debates about what this book has presented on what happened in history for Southeast Asia. There is no doubt that as more archaeological and anthropological studies are undertaken and their results reported there should be more challenges and corrections to the place of Southeast Asia in world history. In this book, I have presented some of the recent archaeological findings pertaining to Southeast Asian socioeconomic changes, such as the various archaeobotanical analyses of food crops and animals reported by Dorian Fuller and Nicole Boivin et al., and the ongoing investigations of prehistoric urban complexes with metallurgical works at Sungai Batu in Malaysia, and in Southern Thailand, that, in my view, provide material evidence that support my interpretation of the place of Southeast Asia in world history. What archaeological studies such as those by Fuller and Boivin et al. have also shown with their analyses of the material evidences are the global trade connections and the trade exchanges that have encompassed Eurasia, including Southeast Asia, for more than five thousand years. They move us to consider the deep structural relationships that have long existed between different regions of the Eurasian world economy. The maritime and land silk routes that have long existed in the prehistoric era have connected the regions of the world from Europe, Africa, South Asia, Southeast Asia, and East Asia. In this respect, no longer should studies of Southeast Asia be comfortable in considering what happened in the past by restricting the analysis to the local and regional. To continue to do that, I fear, will miss too much of the "action" that occurred in Southeast Asia from 200 BC to AD 500.

In this book, a theory-informed history approach provided me with a motif to inform my interpretation of what happened in the past for Southeast Asia. This motif emphasizes a reconstruction that is historical and materially based. I have no doubt that comments with respect to this book's interpretation of Southeast Asian history will continue as new archaeological studies produce material evidences of socioeconomic structures of Southeast Asia's long-term past. If the resolution of what happened in Southeast Asia's past is deliberated and decided based on the rules of existence of materialistic evidences, agreement is much easier to attain. However, if the historical accounting is based mainly on a worldview or mentalité, agreement can be more elusive. Perhaps resolution of this can be reached when circumstances have changed, such as when hegemonic ideological shifts start to occur in world history—for example, in this context, the critique of Eurocentrism following the recent rise of the East and the questioning of the findings of Eurocentric-inspired studies of our understanding of world transformations (Frank 1998; Goody 2004, 2006).

In this book, I have tried to address this issue of interpretations of world history influenced mainly by a worldview or mentalité in my analysis of the Indianization process propounded by some archaeologists, anthropologists, and historians to explain socioeconomic and political transformations of Southeast Asia. As I have stated in the previous chapter, a position taken by some scholars then, and even now, to explain Southeast Asia's socioeconomic and political transformations between 200 BC–AD 500 assumes an Indocentric mentalité. This, I believe, has shaped some of our impressions of Southeast Asia in world history, thereby underscoring its peripheral status, and continues to do so, for the period between 200 BC–AD 500. Whether we continue to be comfortable with this Indocentric manner of explaining socioeconomic and political changes in Southeast Asia needs to be deliberated further. This book's interpretation of the early history of Southeast Asia will, I hope, add to this consideration and encourage others to further question the received history of Southeast Asia. It is only by rubbing Southeast Asian history against its grain can we ever realize what happened in Southeast Asia!

Bibliography

Abbott, F. F., and A. H. Johnson. 1968. *Municipal Administration in the Roman Empire.* New York: Russell and Russell.

Abu-Lughod, J. 1989. *Before European Hegemony: The World System AD 1250–1350.* New York: Oxford University Press.

———. 1990. "Restructuring the Premodern World-System." *Review* 13: 273–286.

Adams, Robert McCormick, Jr. 1981. *Heartland of the Cities: Surveys of Ancient Settlement and Land Use on the Central Floodplain of the Euphrates.* Chicago: University of Chicago Press.

Agrawal, D. P., and R. K. Sood. 1982. "Ecological Factors and the Harappan Civilization." In *Harappan Civilization: Contemporary Perspective,* ed. G. Possehl, 223–231. New Delhi: Oxford University Press.

Algaze, Guillermo. 1989. "The Uruk Expansion: Cross-Cultural Exchange in Early Mesopotamia." *Current Anthropology* 30 (5): 571–608.

———. 1993a. *The Uruk World System.* Chicago: University of Chicago Press.

———. 1993b. "Expansionary Dynamics of Some Early Pristine States." *American Anthropologist* 95 (2): 304–333.

Allard, Francis. 1998. "Stirrings at the Periphery: History, Archaeology and the Study of Dian." *International Journal of Historical Archaeology* 2 (4): 321–341.

Allchin, Bridget. 1982. *The Rise of Civilization in India and Pakistan.* New York: Cambridge University Press.

Allen, S. Jane. 1998. "History, Archaeology and the Question of Foreign Control in Early Historic Period Peninsular Malaysia." *International Journal of Historical Archaeology* 2 (4): 261–289.

Alpers, Edward A. 2013. *The Indian Ocean in World History.* New York: Oxford University Press.

Alpert, Pinhas, et al. 2006. "Relations between Climate Variability in the Mediterranean Region and the Tropics: ENSO South Asian, and African Monsoons, Hurricanes, and Saharan Dust Developments." *Earth and Earth Sciences* 4: 149–177.

Amin, Samir. 1974. *Accumulation on the World Scale.* New York: Monthly Review Press.

———. 1991. "The Ancient World-System vs. the Modern Capitalist World-System." *Review* 14 (3): 349–385.

———. 1999. "History Conceived as an Eternal Cycle." *Review* 22 (3): 291–326.

———, et al. 1982. *Dynamics of Global Crisis.* New York: Monthly Review Press.

An, Jiayao. 1996. "Ancient Glass Trade in Southeast Asia." In *Ancient Trades and Cultural Contacts in Southeast Asia,* ed. Nandana Chutiwongs et al., 127–138. Bangkok: Office of National Cultural Commission.

Andaya, Barbara W. 1997. "The Unity of Southeast Asia: Historical Approaches and Questions. A Review Article." *Journal of Southeast Asian Studies* 28 (1): 161–171.

Anderson, A. 2005. "Crossing the Luzon Straits: Archaeological Chronology in the Batanes Islands: Philippines and the Regional Sequence of Neolithic Dispersal." *Journal of Austronesian Studies* 1 (2): 27–48.

Arrighi, Giovanni. 1994. *The Long Twentieth Century: Money, Power and the Origins of Our Times.* London: Verso.

———. 1999. "The World According to Andre Gunder Frank." *Review* 22 (3): 327–354.

———. 2007. *Adam Smith in Beijing.* London: Verso.

Asthana, Shashi. 1982. "Harappan Trade in Metals and Minerals: A Regional Approach." In *Harrapan Civilization,* ed. G. Possehl, 23–54. New Delhi: Oxford University Press.

Aung-Thwin, et al., eds. 2011. *New Perspective on History and Historiography of Southeast Asia.* London: Routledge.

Bacus, Elizabeth A. 2006. "Social Identities in Bronze Age Northeast Thailand: Intersections of Gender, Status, and Ranking at Non Nok Tha." In *Uncovering Southeast Asia's Past: Selected Papers from the 10th International Conference of the European Association of Southeast Asian Archaeology,* ed. Elizabeth A. Bacus et al., 105–115. Singapore: National University of Singapore Press.

Bacus, Elizabeth A., et al., eds. 2006. *Uncovering Southeast Asia's Past: Selected Papers from the 10th International Conference of the European Association of Southeast Asian Archaeology.* Singapore: National University of Singapore Press.

Barnard, N. 1993. "Thoughts on the Emergence of Metallurgy in Pre Shang and Early Shang China and a Technical Appraisal of Relevant Bronze Artifacts of the Time." *Bulletin of Metals Museum* 19: 3–48.

Badian, E. 1968. *Roman Imperialism in the Late Republic.* Oxford: Oxford University Press.

Barnes, Ruth, and David Parkin, eds. 2002. *Ships and the Development of Maritime Technology on the Indian Ocean.* New York: Routledge.

Barnett, R. D. 1975. "The Sea Peoples." In *Cambridge Ancient History,* vol. 2, part 2, 359–378. Cambridge: Cambridge University Press.

Bayard, D. T. 1984. "A Tentative Regional Phase Chronology for Northeast Thailand." In *Southeast Asian Archaeology at the XV Pacific Science Congress,* ed. D. T. Bayard, 161–168. Dunedin: Otago University Studies in Prehistoric Anthropology #16.

Baynes, N. H. 1943. "The Decline of the Roman Empire in Western Europe: Some Modern Explanations." *Journal of Roman Studies* 33: 29–35.

Beaujard, Philippe. 2005. "The Indian Ocean in Eurasian and African World-Systems before the Sixteenth Century." *Journal of World History* 16 (4): 411–465.

———. 2007. "East Africa, The Comoros Islands and Madagascar Before the 16th Century: On a Neglected Part of the World System." *Azania* 42: 15–35.

———. 2010. "From Three Possible Iron-Age World-Systems to a Single Afro-Eurasian World-System." *Journal of World History* 21 (1): 1–43.

———. 2011. "Evolution and Temporal Delimitations of Possible Bronze Age World-Systems in Western Asia, Africa and the Mediterranean." In *Interweaving Worlds: Systemic Interactions in Eurasia 7th to 1st Millennia BC,* ed. T. Wilkinson et al. Oxford: Oxbow Press.

————. 2012a. *Les Mondes de L'Océan Indien.* Vol. 1, *De la Formation de L'État Au Premier Système-Monde Afro-Eurasien.* Paris: Armand Colin.

————. 2012b. *Les Mondes de L'Océan Indien.* Vol. 2, *L'Océan Indien, Au Coeur Des Globalisations de L'Ancien Monde.* Paris: Armand Colin.

Begley, Vimala, and Richard Daniel De Puma, eds. 1991. *Rome and India: The Ancient Sea Trade.* Madison: University of Wisconsin Press.

Bell, Barbara. 1971. "The Dark Ages in Ancient History I: The First Dark Age in Egypt." *American Journal of Archaeology* 75: 1–20.

————. 1975. "Climate and History of Egypt." *American Journal of Archaeology* 79: 223–279.

Behre, Karl Ernst. 1990. "Some Reflections on Anthropogenic Indicators and the Record of Prehistoric Occupation Phases in Pollen Diagrams." In *Man's Role in the Shaping of the Eastern Mediterranean Landscape,* ed. S. Bottema, G. Entjesbieburg, and W. Van Zeist, 219–230. Rotterdam: Balkema.

Bellina, B. 2003. "Beads, Social Change and Interaction between India and Southeast Asia." *Antiquity* 77 (296): 285–297.

————. 2007. *Cultural Exchange between India and Southeast Asia: Production and Distribution of Hard Stone Ornaments Vic. BC–Vic. AD.* Paris: Editions de la Maison des Sciences de l'Homme.

————. 2014. "Maritime Silk Roads Ornament Industries: Socio-Political Practices and Cultural Transfers in the South China Sea." *Cambridge Archaeological Journal* 24 (3): 345–377.

Bellina, B., and P. Silapanth. 2006a. "Weaving Cultural Identities on Trans Asiatic Networks: Upper Thai-Malay Peninsula An Early Social-Political Landscape." *Bulletin de l' Ecòle française d'Extrême-Orient* 93: 257–293.

————. 2006b. "Khao Sam Kaeo and the Upper Thai Peninsula: Understanding the Mechanisms of Early Trans-Asiatic Trade and Cultural Exchange." In *Uncovering Southeast Asia's Past,* ed. E. A. Bacus et al., 379–392. Singapore: National University of Singapore Press.

Bellina, B., P. Silapanth, B. Chaisuwan, C. Thongcharoenchaikit, J. Allen, V. Berard, B. Borrel, P. Bouvet, C. Castillo, L. Dussubieux, J. Malakie Laclair, S. Peronnet, and T. O. Pryce. 2014. "The Development of Coastal Polities in the Upper Thai Malay Peninsula in the Late First Millennium BCE and the Inception of Long Lasting Economic and Social Exchange between Polities on the East Side of the Indian Ocean and the South China Sea." In *Before Siam was Born: New Insights on the Art and Archaeology of Pre-Modern Thailand and Its Neighbouring Regions,* ed. Nicolas Revire and Stephen A. Murphy, 69–89. Bangkok: River Books.

Bellwood, Peter. 1979. *Man's Conquest of Southeast Asia and Oceania.* Oxford: Oxford University Press.

————. 1997. *Prehistory of the IndoMalayan Archipelago.* Honolulu: University of Hawaii Press.

————. 2004. "The Origins and Dispersal of Agricultural Communities in Southeast Asia." In *Southeast Asia: From Prehistory to History,* ed. I. Glover and P. Bellwood, 21–40. London: Routledge.

————. 2005. *First Farmers: The Origins of Agricultural Societies.* London: Blackwell.

————, et al. 2007. "Ancient Boats, Boat Timbers, and Locked Mortise-and-Tenon Joints from the Bronze/Iron Age Northern Vietnam." *International Journal of Nautical Archaeology* 36 (1): 2–20.

———. 2013. *First Migrants*. New York: Wiley-Blackwell.

Benda, Harry J. 1962. "The Structure of Southeast Asia History: Some Preliminary Observations." *Journal of Southeast Asian History* 3 (1): 106–138.

Benjamin, J. 2006. "The World and Africa: World System Theories and the Erasure of East Africa from World History." *World History Bulletin* 22 (1): 20–27.

Bentaleb, I. et al. 1997. "Monsoon Regime Variations during the Late Holocene in Southwestern India." In *Third Millennium BC Climate Change and Old World Collapse*, ed. H. Dalfes et al., 193–144. Heidelberg: Springer-Verlag.

Bentley, Jerry. 1993. *Old World Encounters*. Oxford: Oxford University Press.

———. 2003. "World History and Grand Narratives." In *Writing World History 1800–2000*, ed. Benedikt Struchtey and Eckhardt Fuchs, 47–65. Oxford: Oxford University Press.

———. 2006. "Beyond Modernocentrism: Toward Fresh Visions of the Global Past." In *Contact and Exchange in the Ancient World*, ed. Victor H. Mair, 17–29. Honolulu: University of Hawaii Press.

———. 2007. *Traditions and Encounters: A Global Perspective on the Past*. Vol. 1, *From the Beginning to 1500*. New York: McGraw Hill.

Blench, Roger. 2010. "Evidence for the Austronesian Voyages in the Indian Ocean." In *The Global Origins and Development of Seafaring*, ed. Anderson Atholl et al., 239–249. Cambridge: McDonald Institute for Archaeological Research.

Blintiff, J. 1992. "Erosion in the Mediterranean Lands: Reconsideration of Pattern, Process, and Methodology." In *Past and Present Soil Erosion*, ed. M. Bell and J. Boardman. Oxford: Oxbow.

Boivin, Nicole, Roger Blench, and Dorian Q. Fuller. 2009. "Archaeological, Linguistic and Historical Sources on Ancient Seafaring: A Multidisciplinary Approach to the Study of Early Maritime Contact and Exchange in the Arabian Peninsula." In *The Evolution of Human Populations in Arabia*, ed. M. D. Petraglia and J. I. Rose, 251–278. Berlin: Springer.

Boivin, Nicole, Alison Crowther, Richard Helm, and Dorian Q. Fuller. 2013. "East Africa and Madagascar in the Indian Ocean World." *Journal of World Prehistory* 26 (3): 213–281.

Boivin, Nicole, and Dorian Q. Fuller. 2009. "Shell Middens, Ships and Seeds: Exploring Coastal Subsistence, Maritime Trade and the Dispersal of Domesticates in and around the Ancient Arabian Peninsula." *Journal of World Prehistory* 22: 113–180.

Boivin, Nicole, Dorian Q. Fuller, and Alison Crowther. 2015. "Old World Globalization and Food Exchanges." In *Archaeology of Food: An Encyclopedia*, ed. M. C. Beaudry and K. B. Metheny, 350–356. Lanham: Rowman and Littlefield.

Boomgard, Peter, and Mark R. Stoll. 2006. *Southeast Asia: An Environmental History*. London: ABC-Clio.

Booth, B. 1984. "A Handlist of Maritime Radiocarbon Dates." *International Journal of Nautical Archaeology* 12 (3): 189–204.

Bopearachchi, Osmund. 2011. "Sea Faring in the Indian Ocean: Archaeological Evidence from Sri Lanka." In *Tradition and Archaeology*, ed. H. P. Ray and J. F. Salles, 60–77. New Delhi: Manohar.

Borell, Brigitte. 2013. "The Glass Vessels from Guangxi and the Maritime Silk Road in the Han Period 206BCE–220CE." In *Unearthing Southeast Asia's Past*, ed. Marijke J. Klokke and Véronique Degroot, 141–154. Singapore: National University of Singapore Press.

———, et al. 2014. "Contacts between Upper Thai-Malay Peninsula and the Mediterranean World." In *Before Siam was Born: New Insights on the Art and Archaeology of Pre-Modern Thailand and Its Neighbouring Regions,* ed. Nicholas Revire and A. Stephen, 99–117. Bangkok: River Books.

Bose, Sugata. 2006. *A Hundred Horizons: The Indian Ocean in the Age of the Global Empire.* Cambridge, MA: Harvard University Press.

Bottema, S. 1994. "The Prehistoric Environment of Greece: A Review of Palynological Record." In *Beyond the Site,* ed. Nick Kardulias, 45–68. Lanham, MD: University Press of America.

———. 1997. "Third Millennium Climate in the Near East Based upon Pollen Evidence." In *Third Millennium BC Climate Change and Old World Collapse,* ed. H. Dalfes et al., 488–515. Heidelberg: Springer-Verlag.

Bovarski, Edward. 1998. "First Intermediate Period Private Tombs." In *Encyclopedia of Ancient Egypt,* ed. K. Bard, 316–319. New York: Routledge.

Bowen, Richard Le Baron. 1952. "Primitive Watercraft of Arabia." *The American Neptune* 12 (3): 186–221.

Boyd, W., and N. Chang. 2010. "Integrating Social and Environmental Change in Prehistory: A Discussion of the Role of Landscape as a Heuristic in Defining Prehistoric Possibilities in N. E. Thailand." In *Terra Australis: Altered Ecologies—Fire, Climate, and Human Influence on Terrestrial Landscapes,* ed. S. Haberle, J. Stevenson, and M. Prebble, 273–297. Canberra: ANU E Press.

Boyd, W., and R. J. McGrath. 2001. "Iron Age Vegetation Dynamics and Human Impacts on the Vegetation of Upper Mun River Floodplain N. E. Thailand." *New Zealand Geographer* 57 (2): 21–32.

Braudel, Fernand. 1972. *The Mediterranean and the Mediterranean World in the Age of Philip II,* vol. 1. London: Fontana.

———. 1981. *The Structure of Everyday Life.* Vol. 1 of *Civilization and Capitalism 15th to 18th Century.* New York: Harper and Row.

———. 1982. *The Wheels of Commerce.* Vol. 2 of *Civilization and Capitalism 15th to 18th Century.* New York: Harper and Row.

———. 1984. *The Perspective of the World.* Vol. 3 of *Civilization and Capitalism 15th to 18th Century.* New York: Harper and Row.

———. 1989, 1991. *The Identity of France.* Vol. 1, *History and Environment,* and Vol. 2, *People and Production.* New York: Harper and Row.

———. 2001. *Memory and the Mediterranean.* New York: Alfred Knopf.

Brinkman, J. A. 1968. "Ur: The Kassite Period and the Period of Assyrian Kings." *Orientalis* 38: 310–348.

Bronson, Bennet. 1978. "Exchange at the Upstream and Downstream Ends: Notes Toward a Functional Model of the Coastal State in Southeast Asia." In *Economic Exchange and Social Interaction in Southeast Asia: Perspectives from Prehistory, History and Ethnographies,* ed. Karl L. Hutterer, 39–52. Ann Arbor: University of Michigan Press.

Bronson, Bennet, and J. White. 1992. "Southeast Asia." In *Chronologies in Old World Archaeology,* ed. R. W. Ehrich, 475–515. Chicago: University of Chicago Press.

Bryce, Trevor. 2002. *Life and Society in the Hittite World.* Oxford: Oxford University Press.

Bryson, R. A., H. H. Lamb, and David L. Donley. 1974. "Drought and the Decline of Mycenae." *Antiquity* 48 (189): 46–50.

Bryson, R. A., and C. Padoch. 1980. "On Climates of History." *Journal of Interdisciplinary History* 10 (4): 583–597.

Butzer, K. W. 1997. "Socio Political Discontinuity in the Near East c. 2200 BCE: Scenarios from Palestine and Egypt." In *Third Millennium BC Climate Change and Old World Collapse*, ed. H. Dalfes et al., 245–296. Heidelberg: Springer-Verlag.

Calo, Ambra. 2009. *The Distribution of Bronze Drums in Early Southeast Asia: Trade Routes and Cultural Spheres.* London: BAR Series.

Cappers, R. T. S. 2006. *Roman Footprints at Berenike: Archaeobotanical Evidence of Subsistence and Trade in the Eastern Desert of Egypt.* Cotsen Institute of Archaeology Monograph #65. Los Angeles: UCLA.

Carpenter, Rhys. 1968. *Discontinuity in Greek Civilization.* Cambridge: Cambridge University Press.

Carter, Alison Kyra. 2015. "Beads, Exchange Networks and Emerging Complexity: A Case Study from Cambodia and Thailand (500 BCE—CE 500)." *Cambridge Archaeological Journal* 25 (4): 733–757.

Carter, Vernon, and Tom Dale. 1974. *Topsoil and Civilization.* Norman: University of Oklahoma Press.

Casson, Lionel. 1954. "Trade in the Ancient World." *Scientific American* 191 (5): 98–104.

———. 1991. *The Ancient Mariners.* Princeton: Princeton University Press.

———. 1994. *Ships and Sea Faring.* Texas: University of Texas Press.

———. 1995. *Ships and Seamanship in the Ancient World.* Baltimore: John Hopkins University Press.

———, trans. 1989. *The Periplus Maris Erythraei.* Princeton: Princeton University Press.

Castillo, Cristina Cobo, Katsunori Tanaka, Yo-Ichiro Sato, Ryuji Ishikawa, Bérénice Bellina, Charles Higham, Nigel Chang, Rabi Mohanty, Mukund Kajale, and Dorian Q. Fuller. 2016. "Archaeogenetic Study of Prehistoric Rice Remains from Thailand and India: Evidence of Early Japonica in South and Southeast Asia." *Archaeological Anthropological Sciences* 8, (3): 523–543. doi: 10.1007/s12520-015-0236-5.

Catton, William, and R. Dunlap. 1978. "Environmental Sociology: A New Paradigm." *American Sociologist* 13: 41–49.

Chadwick, J. 1976. *The Mycenaean World.* New York: Cambridge University Press.

Chandler, Tertius. 1974. *Three Thousand Years of Urban Growth.* New York: Academic Press.

Chandra, Satish, and Himanshu Prabha Ray. 2013. *The Sea, Identity and History: From the Bay of Bengal to the South China Sea.* New Delhi: Manohar.

Chang, Kuang-Jen. 2013. "Foreign Trade, Local Taste: A Consumption-Based Study of Trade Ceramics in Late Proto-Historic Island Southeast Asia." In *Unearthing Southeast Asia's Past*, ed. Marijke J. Klokke and Véronique Degroot, 170–185. Singapore: National University of Singapore Press.

Chapell, J., and B. G. Thom. 1979. "Sea Levels and Coasts." In *Sunda and Sahul*, ed. J. Allen, J. Golson, and R. Jones, 275–292. London: Academic.

Charlesworth, M. P. (1926) 1970. *Trade Routes and Commerce of the Roman Empire.* New York: Cooper Square Publishers and Cambridge University Press.

Chase-Dunn, C., and T. Hall. 1997. *Rise and Demise: Comparing World-Systems.* Boulder: Westview Press.

Chaudhuri, K. N. 1978. *Asia before Europe.* Cambridge: Cambridge University Press.

———. 1985. *Trade and Civilization in the Indian Ocean.* Cambridge: Cambridge University Press.

Chen, Yunzhen, James Syvitski, Shu Gao, Irina Overeem, and Albert Kettner. 2012. "Socio-Economic Impacts on Flooding: A 4000-Year History of the Yellow River, China." *AMBIO—A Journal of the Human Environment* 41 (7): 682–698.

Chernykh, E. N. 1992. *Ancient Metallurgy in the U.S.S.R.: The Early Metal Age*. Cambridge: Cambridge University Press.

Chew, Sing C. 1997. "For Nature: Deep Greening World Systems Analysis for the Twenty-First Century." *Journal of World-Systems Research* 3 (3): 381–402.

———. 1999. "Ecological Relations and the Decline of Civilizations in the Bronze Age World System: Mesopotamia and Harrapa 2500 BC–1700 BC." In *Ecology and the World System*, ed. W. Goldfrank et al., 87–106. Westport, CT: Greenwood Press.

———. 2001. *World Ecological Degradation: Accumulation, Urbanization, and Deforestation*. Lanham, MD: AltaMira Press, Rowman and Littlefield Publishers.

———. 2007. *The Recurring Dark Ages: Ecological Stress, Climate Changes and System Transformation*. Lanham, MD: AltaMira Press, Rowman and Littlefield Publishers.

———. 2008. *Ecological Futures: What History Can Teach Us*. Lanham, MD: AltaMira Press, Rowman and Littlefield Publishers.

———. 2015. "The Southeast Asian Connection in the First Eurasian World Economy." In *Trade, Circulation, and Flow in the Indian Ocean World*, ed. Michael Pearson, 27–54. London: Palgrave.

Chia, Stephen, and Barbara Andaya. 2011. *Bujang Valley and Early Civilizations in Southeast Asia*. Kuala Lumpur: Department of National Heritage.

Chia, Stephen, and A. Naizatul. 2011. "Evidence of Iron Production at Sungai Batu, Kedah." In *Bujang Valley and Early Civilizations in South East Asia*, ed. Stephen Chia and Barbara Andaya, 350–364. Kuala Lumpur: Department of National Heritage.

Childe, Gordon. 1942. *What Happened in History*. Harmondsworth: Penguin.

———. 1950. "The Urban Revolution." *Town Planning Review* 21: 3–17.

———. 1952. *New Light on the Most Ancient East*. London: Routledge.

Christie, Jan W. 1990. "Trade and State Formation in the Malay Peninsula and Sumatra 300 BC–AD 700." In *The Southeast Asian Port and Polity*, ed. Jaya Kathirithamby-Wells and John Villiers, 39–60. Singapore: Singapore University Press.

Chutiwongs, Nandana, et al. 1996. *Ancient Trades and Cultural Contacts in Southeast Asia*. Bangkok: The Office of the Natural Culture Commission.

Cicero, Marcus Tullius. 1942. *Rhetorical Treatises: On the Orator, Books 1–2*. Translated by Edward William Sutton and Harris Rackham. Cambridge, MA: Harvard University Press.

Clark, Graheme. 1977. *World Prehistory*. Cambridge: Cambridge University Press.

Clift, Peter D., and R. Alan Plumb. 2008. *The Asian Monsoon. Causes, History and Effects*. Cambridge: Cambridge University Press.

Cline, E. H. 1994. *Sailing the Wine-Dark Sea. International Trade and the Late Bronze Age Aegean*. Oxford: Oxford University Press.

Coedes, G. 1966. *The Making of Southeast Asia*. Berkeley: University of California Press.

———. 1968. *The Indianised States of Southeast Asia*. Honolulu: East West Center Press.

Colani, M. 1927. "L'Âge de la pierre dans la province de Hoa Binh." *Mémoires du Service Géologique de l'Indochine* 13: 1.

———. 1930. "Recherches sur le Préhistorique Indochinoise." *Bulletin de l'École française d'Extrême Orient* 30: 299–422.

Crawford, G. W., and C. Shen. 1998. "The Origin of Rice Agriculture: Recent Progress in East Asia." *Antiquity* 72: 858–866.

Crowther, Alison, M.-A. Veall, N. Boivin, M. Horton, A. Kotarba-Morley, D. Q. Fuller, T. Fenn, O. Haji, and C. D. Matheson. 2015. "Use of Zanzibar Copal (Hymenaea verrucosa Gaertn) as Incense at Unguja Ukuu in the 7th–8th Century CE: Insights into Trade and Indian Ocean Interactions." *Journal of Archaeological Science* 53: 374–390.

Cunliffe, Barry. 2008. *Europe between the Oceans 9000 BC–AD 1000.* New Haven: Yale University Press.

Dalby, Andrew. 2000. *Dangerous Taste: The Story of Spices.* London: British Museum Press.

Dales, G. F. 1977. "Shifting Trade Patterns between Iranian Plateau and the Indus Valley." In *Le Plateau Iranien et l'Asie Centrale,* ed. J. Deshayes, 67–78. Paris: CNRS.

———. 1979. "The Decline of the Harrapans." In *Ancient Cities of the Indus,* ed. G. Possehl, 307–312. New Delhi: Vikas.

Davidson, Jeremy H. C. S. 1979. "Urban Genesis in Vietnam." In *Early Southeast Asia: Essays in Archaeology, History, and Historical Geography,* ed. R. B. Smith and W. Watson, 304–314. Oxford: Oxford University Press.

Davis, Richard. 1980. *Global India Circa 100CE: South Asia in Early World History.* New York: Association for South Asian Studies.

Deng, Gang. 1997. *Chinese Maritime Activities and Socio-Economic Development c. 2100 BC–AD 1900.* Westport, CT: Greenwood Press.

De Bary, Theodore W., and Peter H. Lee, eds. 1997. *Sources of Korean Tradition.* New York: Columbia University Press.

De Romanis, F., and A. Techernia, eds. 1997. *Crossing: Early Mediterranean Contacts with India.* New Delhi: Manohar.

Deger-Jalkotzy, S. 1998. "The Last Mycenaeans and Their Successors Updated." In *Mediterranean Peoples in Transition: Thirteenth to Early Tenth Centuries BCE. In Honor of Professor Trude Dothan,* ed. S. Gitin, A. Mazar, and E. Stern, 114–128. Jerusalem: Israel Exploration Society.

Denemark, R., et al., eds. 2000. *World System History: The Social Science of Long-Term Change.* London: Routledge.

Deo, S. B. 1991. "Roman Trade: Recent Archaeological Discoveries in Western India." In *Rome and India: The Ancient Sea Trade,* ed. Vimala Begley and Richard Daniel DePuma, 39–45. Madison: University of Wisconsin Press.

Desborough, V. R. 1972. *The Greek Dark Ages.* London: Ernest Benn.

Dien, Albert E. 2007. *Six Dynasties Civilization.* New Have: Yale University Press.

Domett, K. M. 1999. "Health in Late Prehistoric Thailand." Ph.D. dissertation, University of Otago, Dunedin, New Zealand.

Dos Santos, Theotonio. 1970. "The Structure of Dependence." *American Economic Review* 60: 231–236.

Drews, R. 1993. *The End of the Bronze Age.* Princeton: Princeton University Press.

Drummond, Steven, and Lynn H. Nelson. 1994. *The Western Frontiers of Imperial Rome.* Armonk, NY: M. E. Sharpe.

Dubowski, Y. J., and M. Stiller. 2003. "Isotopic Paleolimnology of Lake Kineret." *Liminology and Oceanography* 48 (1): 68–78.

Duncan-Jones, Richard. 1990. *Structure and Scale in the Roman Economy.* Cambridge: Cambridge University Press.

Dunn, F. L. 1975. *Rainforest Collectors and Traders: A Study of Resource Utilization in Modern and Ancient Malaya.* Kuala Lumpur: Malayan Branch of the Royal Asiatic Society #5.

Dzung, Lam Thi My. 2011. "Central Vietnam During the Period from 500 BCE to CE 500." In *Early Interactions between South and Southeast Asia,* ed. Pierre-Yves Manguin et al. 3–16. Singapore: Institute of Southeast Asian Studies.

Earle, Timothy, and Kristian Kristiansen. 2010. *Organizing Bronze Age Societies.* Cambridge: Cambridge University Press.

Eckert, Carter J., Ki-baik Lee, Young Lew, Michael Robinson, and Edward Wagner. 1990. *Korea, Old and New: A History.* Seoul: Korea Institute.

Edens, Christopher. 1992. "The Dynamics of Trade in Ancient Mesopotamian World System." *American Anthropologist* 94: 118–139.

Ekholm, Kajsa, and Jonathan Friedman. 1982. "Capital, Imperialism and Exploitation in the Ancient World Systems." *Review* 6: 87–110.

Ellen, R. F. 1977. "The Trade in Spices." *Journal of the Indonesian Circle* 12: 21–25.

Enzel, Y., et al. 1999. "High Resolution Holocene Environmental Changes in the Thar Desert, Northwest India." *Science* 284 (5411): 125–128.

Evans, Arthur. 1992. *The Palace of Minos.* London: MacMillan.

Fagan, Brian. 2004. *The Long Summer.* New York: Basic Books.

Fa-Hsien. 1965. *A Record of Buddhistic Kingdoms.* Translated by James Legge. New York: Paragon Books.

Fairbridge, R. O., et al. 1997. "Background to Mid-Holocene Climate Change in Anatolia and Adjacent Regions." In *Third Millennium BC Climate Change and Old World Collapse,* ed. H. Dalfes et al., 34–56. Heidelberg: Springer-Verlag.

Flecker, Michael. 2005. "Tang Treasures from the Sea: An Arab Shipwreck in Indonesian Waters." *Heritage Asia* 2 (4): 7–11.

Flotz, Richard C. 2003. "Does Nature Have Historical Agency? World History and Environmental History and How Histories Can Help to Save the Planet." *The History Teacher* 37 (1): 9–28.

Francis, Peter. 1996. "Bead, the Bead Trade, and State Development in Southeast Asia." In *Ancient Trades and Cultural Contacts in Southeast Asia,* ed. Nandana Chutiwongs et al., 139–152. Bangkok: The Office of the Natural Culture Commission.

———. 2002. *Asia's Maritime Bead Trade 300 BC to the Present.* Honolulu: University of Hawaii Press.

Frank, Andre Gunder. 1966. "The Development of Underdevelopment." *Monthly Review* 18 (4): 1–20.

———. 1991. "Transitional Ideological Modes: Feudalism, Capitalism, and Socialism." *Critique of Anthropology* 11 (2): 171–188.

Frank, Andre Gunder, and B. K. Gills. 1992. "World System Cycles, Crises, and Hegemonial Shifts." *Review* 15 (4): 621–688.

———. 1993. "Bronze Age World System Cycles." *Current Anthropology* 34 (4): 383–429.

———. 1998. *ReOrient: Global Economy in the Asian Age.* Berkeley: University of California Press.

———. 2002. "A Structural Theory of the Five Thousand Year Old System." In *Structure, Culture, and History,* ed. Sing C. Chew and David Knottnerus, 151–176. Lanham: Rowman and Littlefield.

———, eds. 1996. *The World System: 500 or 5,000 years.* London: Routledge.

Friedman, H. 2000. "What on Earth is the Modern World-System? Food Getting and Territory in the Modern Era and Beyond." *Journal of World-Systems Research* 6 (2): 480–515.

Friedman, Jonathan. 2002. "Situating Hybridity: The Positional Logics of Discourse." In *Structure, Culture, and History,* ed. Sing C. Chew and David Knottnerus, 125–150. Lanham: Rowman and Littlefield.

Friedman, Kajsa. 2003. "Structure, Dynamics, and the Final Collapse of Bronze Age Civilizations in the Second Millennium." Paper presented at Political Economy of the World-Systems Conference, University of California Riverside, 23–25 March 2002.

Fuller, Dorian Q. 2006. "Silence before Sedentism and the Advent of Cash Crops: A Status Report on Early Agriculture in South Asia from Plant Domestications to the Development of Political Economies (with an Excursus on the Problem of Semantic Shift among Millets and Rice)." In *Proceedings of the PreSymposium of RIHN and 7th ESCA Harvard-Kyoto Roundtable*, ed. T. Osada, 175–213. Kyoto: Research Institute for Humanity and Nature.

Fuller, Dorian Q., Nicole Boivin, Cristina Cobo Catillo, Tom Hoogervorst, and Robin G. Allaby. 2010. "The Archaeobiology of Indian Ocean Translocation: Cultural Outlines of Cultural Exchange by ProtoHistoric Seafarers." In *Maritime Contacts of the Past: Deciphering Connection Amongst Communities*, ed. Sila Tripati, 1–23. New Delhi: Delta Book.

Fuller, Dorian Q., Ling Qin, Yunfei Zheng, Zhijun Zhao, Xugao Chen, Leo Aoi Hosoya, and Guo-Ping Sun. 2009. "The Domestication Process and Domestication Rate: Spikelet Basis from the Lower Yangtze." *Science* 323 (5921): 1607–1610.

Fuller, Dorian Q., Y.-I. Sato, C. Castillo, L. Qin, A. R. Weisskopf, E. J. Kingwell-Banham, J. Song, S.-M. Ahn, and J. van Etten. 2010. "Consilience of Genetics and Archaeobotany in the Entangled History of Rice." *Archaeological and Anthropological Science* 2 (2): 115–131.

Fuller, Dorian Q., N. Boivin, T. Hoogervorst, and R. Allaby. 2011. "Across the Indian Ocean: Prehistoric Movement of Plants and Animals." *Antiquity* 85: 544–558.

Furtado, Celso. 1971. *Development and Underdevelopment*. Berkeley: University of California Press.

Gallon, Matt. 2013. "Ideology, Identity and the Construction of Urban Communities." Ph.D. dissertation, University of Michigan, Ann Arbor.

Garnsey, Peter, and Richard Saller. 1987. *The Roman Empire*. Berkeley: University of California Press.

Gettens, Rutherford J., Roy S. Clarke, and W. T. Chase. 1971. *Two Early Chinese Bronze Weapons with Meteoritic Iron Blades*. Freer Gallery of Art Occasional Papers vol. 4, no. 1. Washington, DC: Freer Gallery of Art.

Geyh, M. A., H. R. Kudrass, and H. Streif. 1979. "Sea Level Changes during the Late Pleistocene and Holocene in the Straits of Malacca." *Nature* 278: 441–443.

Gills, Barry K., and A. G. Frank. 1990. "The Cumulation of Accumulation: Theses and Research Agenda for Five Thousand Years of World System History." *Dialectical Anthropology* 15: 19–42.

———. 1991. "Five Thousand Years of World System History: The Cumulation of Accumulation." In *Core-Periphery Relations in the Pre-Capitalist World*, ed. C. Chase-Dunn and T. Hall, 34–59. Boulder, Colorado: Westview Press.

Glover, Ian. 1977. "Prehistoric Plant Remains from Southeast Asia." In *South Asian Archaeology*, ed. M. Taddei, 7–37. Naples: Instituto Universitario Orientale.

———. 1979. "The Late Prehistoric Period in Indonesia." In *Early Southeast Asia*, ed. R. B. Smith and W. Watson, 24–42. Oxford: Oxford University Press.

———. 1989–1990. *Early Trade between India and Southeast Asia: A Link in the Development of a World Trading System*. Hull: University of Hull Centre for Southeast Asian Studies.

———. 1991. *Early Trade between India and Southeast Asia: A Link in the Development of a World Trading System.* 2nd revised edition. Hull: University of Hull Centre for Southeast Asian Studies.

———. 1996a. "Recent Archaeological Evidence for Early Maritime Contacts between India and Southeast Asia." In *Tradition and Archaeology: Early Maritime Contacts in the Indian Ocean*, ed. H. P. Ray and J. F. Salles, 129–158. New Delhi: Manohar.

———. 1996b. "The Archaeological Evidence for Early Trade between South and Southeast Asia." In *The Indian Ocean in Antiquity*, ed. J. Reade, 23–43. London: Routledge.

———. 2000. "The Southern Silk Road: Archaeological Evidence of Early Trade between India and Southeast Asia." In *The Silk Roads: Highways of Culture ad Commerce*, ed. Vadime Elisseeff, 93–121. New York: Berghahn Books.

———, ed. 1992. *Early Metallurgy, Trade, and Urban Centers in Thailand and Southeast Asia.* Bangkok: White Lotus Press.

Glover, Ian, and B. Bellina. 2011. "Ban Don Ta Phet and Khao Sam Kaeo: The Earliest Indian Contacts Re-Assessed." In *Early Interactions between South and Southeast Asia*, ed. P.-Y. Manguin, A. Mani, and G. Wade, 17–45. Singapore: Institute of Southeast Asian Studies.

Glover, Ian, and B. Syme. 1993. "The Bronze Age in Southeast Asia: Its Recognition, Dating and Recent Research." *Man and Environment* 18 (2): 41–74.

Glover, Ian, and Peter Bellwood, eds. 2006. *Southeast Asia: From Prehistory to History.* London: Routledge.

Golden, Peter B. 2011. *Central Asia in World History.* Oxford: Oxford University Press.

Goldstone, J. 2008. *Why Europe? The Rise of the West in World History.* New York: McGraw Hill.

Goody, Jack. 2004. *Capitalism and Modernity.* London: Polity Press.

———. 2006. *The Theft of History.* London: Cambridge University Press.

———. 2009. *The Eurasian Miracle.* Oxford: Polity Press.

Gorman, C. F. 1972. "Excavations at Spirit Cave, Northern Thailand: Some Interim Impressions." *Asian Perspectives* 13: 79–107.

———. 1977. "A Priori Models and Thai Prehistory: A Reconsideration of the Beginnings of Agriculture in Southeast Asia." In *Origins of Agriculture*, ed. C. A. Reed, 322–355. The Hague: Mouton.

Gorman, C. F., and P. Charoenwongsa. 1976. "Ban Chiang: A Mosaic of Impressions from the First Two Years." *Expedition* 8 (4): 14–26.

Graf, D. F. 1996. "The Roman East from the Chinese Perspective." *International Colloquium on Palmyra and the Silk Road* 42: 199–216.

Guangqi, Sun. 2000. "The Development of China's Navigation Technology and of the Maritime Silk Route." In *The Silk Roads: Highway of Culture and Commerce*, ed. Vadime Elisseeff, 288–303. New York: Berghahn Books.

Guo, Yuanyuan, Duowen Mo, Longjiang Mao, Yuxiang Jin, Weimin Guo, and Peta J. Mudie. 2014. "Settlement Distribution and its Relationship with Environmental Changes from the Paleolithic to Shang–Zhou Period in Liyang Plain, China." *Quaternary International* 321: 29–36.

Guo, Yuanyuan, Duowen Mo, Longjiang Mao, Shougong Wang, and Shuicheng Li. 2013. "Settlement Distribution and Its Relationship with Environmental Changes from the Neolithic to Shang-Zhou Dynasties in Northern Shandong, China." *Journal of Geographical Sciences* 23 (4): 679.

Gutman, Pamela, and Bob Hudson. 2004. "The Archaeology of Burma (Myanmar): From the Neolithic to Pagan." In *Southeast Asia: From Prehistory to History*, ed. Ian Glover and Peter Bellwood, 149–176. London: Routledge.

Habermas, Jurgen. 1970. *Toward a Rational Society: Student Protest, Science and Politics*. Boston: Beacon Press.

———. 1981. *Communication and Evolution of Society*. Boston: Beacon Press.

———. 1989. *The Theory of Communicative Action*. 2 vols. Boston: Beacon Press.

Habu, J., and M. E. Hall. 2012. "Climate Change, Human Impacts on the Landscape, and Subsistence Specialization: Historical Ecology and Changes in Jomon Hunter-Gatherer Lifeways." In *The Historical Ecology of Small Scale Economies*, ed. Victor D. Thompson and James Waggoner, 34–56. Gainesville: University of Florida Press.

Hall, D. M. 1993. "Aspects of the Pottery Decoration." In *The Excavation of Khok Phanom Di*, vol. 3, ed. C. F. W. Higham and R. Thossarat, 239–274. London: Society of Antiquaries of London.

Hall, John W. 1970. *Japan from Prehistory to Modern Times*. New York: Delacorte Press.

Hall, Kenneth R. 1982. "The Indianization of Funan: An Economic History of Southeast Asia's First State." *Journal of Southeast Asian Studies*. 13 (1): 81–106.

———. 1985. *Maritime Trade and State Development in Early Southeast Asia*. Honolulu: University of Hawaii Press.

———. 2011. *A History of Early Southeast Asia*. Walnut Creek, CA: Altamira Press.

Hall, Kenneth R., and John K. Whitmore, eds. 1976. *Explorations in Early Southeast Asian History: The Origins of Southeast Asian Statecraft*. Ann Arbor, MI: Center for South and Southeast Asian Studies.

Hansen, Mogens Herman, ed. 2000. *A Comparative Study of Thirty City-State Cultures: An Investigation*. Copenhagen: The Royal Danish Academy of Sciences and Letters.

Hansen, Valerie. 2012. *The Silk Roads*. Oxford: Oxford University Press.

Harding, A., ed. 1982. *Climatic Change in Later Prehistory*. Edinburgh: Edinburgh University Press.

Harrison, Anne B., and Nigel Spencer. 1998. "After the Palace: The Early History of Messinia." In *Sandy Pylos*, ed. Jack Davis, 147–166. Austin: University of Texas Press.

Harrison, Terry. 1996. "The Paleoecological Context at Niah Cave, Sarawak: Evidence from the Primate Fauna." *Bulletin of the Indo-Pacific Prehistory Association* 14: 90–100.

Harrison, Timothy. 1997. "Shifting Patterns of Settlement in the Highlands of Central Jordan during the Early Bronze Age." *Bulletin of the American School of Oriental Research* 306: 1–38.

Haselgrove, Colin. 1980. "Culture Process on the Periphery: Belgic Gaul and Rome during the Late Republic and Early Empire." In *Centre and Periphery in the Ancient World*, ed. M. Rowlands et al., 104–124. Cambridge: Cambridge University Press.

Hassan, Fekri. 1997. "Nile Floods and Political Disorder in Early Egypt." In *Third Millennium BC Climate Change and Old World Collapse*, ed. H. Dalfes et al., 1–23. Heidelberg: Springer-Verlag.

Headland, Thomas, and Lawrence Reid. 1989. "Hunter-Gatherers and Their Neighbors from Prehistory to the Present." *Current Anthropology* 30: 43–51.

Heaney, L. R. 1991. "Climate and Vegetational Change in Southeast Asia." *Climate Change* 19: 53–60.

Heather, P. J. 2010. *Empires and Barbarians*. Oxford: Oxford University Press.

Hedeager, Lotte. 1980. In *Centre and Periphery in the Ancient World*, ed. M. Rowlands et al., 125–140. Cambridge: Cambridge University Press.

Heichelheim, Fritz M. 1968. *An Ancient Economic History*, vol 1. Leiden: A. W. Sijthoff.

Heng, Derek Thiam. 2008. "Structures, Networks, and Commercial Practices of Private Chinese Maritime Traders in Island Southeast Asia in the Earl Second Millennium AD." *International Journal of Maritime History* 20 (2): 27–54.

———. 2013. "State Formation and the Evolution of Naval Strategies in the Melaka Straits c 500–1500 CE." *Journal of Southeast Asian Studies* 44 (3): 380–399.

Hiebert, Fredrik. 2000. "Bronze Age Central Eurasian Cultures in their Steppe and Desert Environments." In *Environmental Disaster and the Archaeology of Human Response*, ed. G. Bawden and R. Reycraft, 51–62. Albuquerque: University of New Mexico Press.

Higham, C. F. W. 1989. *The Archaeology of Mainland Southeast Asia*. Cambridge: Cambridge University Press.

———. 1996. *The Bronze Age of Southeast Asia*. Cambridge: Cambridge University Press.

———. 1998. "The Transition from Prehistory to Historic Period in the Upper Mun Valley." *International Journal of Historical Archaeology* 2 (3): 235–260.

———. 2002. *Early Cultures of Mainland Southeast Asia*. Bangkok: River Books.

———. 2004. "Mainland Southeast Asia from the Neolithic to the Iron Age." In *Southeast Asia: From Prehistory to History*, ed. Ian Glover and Peter Bellwood, 41–67. London: Routledge.

———. 2006. "Crossing National Boundaries: Southern China and Southeast Asia in Prehistory." In *Uncovering Southeast Asia's Past*, ed. Elizabeth Bacus et al., 13–21. Singapore: National University of Singapore Press.

———. 2011. "The Bronze Age of Southeast Asia: New Insight on Social Change from Ban Non Wat." *Cambridge Archaeological Journal* 21 (3): 365–389.

———. 2012. "The Long and Winding Road that Leads to Angkor." *Cambridge Archaeological Journal* 22 (2): 265–289.

———. 2013. "Dating the Bronze Age of Southeast Asia: The Cultural Implications." In *Unearthing Southeast Asia's Past*, ed. Marijke J. Klokke and Véronique Degroot, 55–63. Singapore: National University of Singapore Press.

———. 2014. *Early Mainland Southeast Asia: From First Humans to Angkor*. Bangkok: River Books.

———. 2015. "Debating a Great Site: Ban Non Wat and the Wider Prehistory of Southeast Asia." *Antiquity* 89 (347): 1211–1220.

Higham, C. F. W., Katerina Douka, and Thomas Higham. 2015. "A New Chronology for the Bronze Age of Northeastern Thailand and Its Implications for Southeast Asian Prehistory." PLOS ONE 10 (9). doi: 10.1371/journal.pone.0137542.

Higham, C. F. W., and T. Higham. 2009. "A New Chronological Framework for Prehistoric Southeast Asia, Based on a Bayesian Model from Ban Non Wat." *Antiquity* 83: 125–144.

Higham, C. F. W., T. Higham, R. Ciarla, K. Douka, Amphan Kijngam, and Fiorella Rispoli. 2011. "The Origins of the Bronze Age of Southeast Asia." *Journal of World Prehistory* 24: 227–274.

Higham, C. F. W., T. Higham, and A. Kijngam. 2010. "Cutting a Gordian Knot: The Bronze Age of Southeast Asia: Origins, Timing and Impact." *Antiquity* 85: 583–598.

Higham, C. F. W., and T. Lu. 1998. "The Origins and Dispersal of Rice Cultivation." *Antiquity* 72: 867–877.

Higham, C. F. W., and R. Thosarat. 2006. "Ban Non Wat: The First Three Seasons." In *Uncovering Southeast Asia's Past*, ed. Elizabeth Bacus et al., 98–115. Singapore: National University of Singapore Press.

Higham, C. F. W., and R. Thosarat. 2012. *Early Thailand: From Prehistory to Sukhothai.* Bangkok: River Books.

Higham, C. F. W., Guangmao Xie, and Qiang Lin. 2011. "The Prehistory of a Friction Zone: First Farmers and Hunters-Gatherers in Southeast Asia." *Antiquity* 85: 529–543.

Higham, C. F. W., and R. Thosarat, eds. 1998. *The Excavation of Nong Nor, A Prehistoric Site in Central Thailand.* New Zealand: Otago University Studies in Prehistoric Archaeology #18.

Hilgers, Lauren. 2016. "Vietnam's First City." *Archaeology* 69 (4): 48–53.

Hirth, Friedrich. 1885. *China and the Roman Orient: Researches into Their Ancient and Medieval Relations as Represented in Old Chinese Records.* Chicago: Ares Publishers.

Hla, U. K. 1979. "Ancient Cities in Burma." *Journal of the Society of Architectural Historians* 38 (2): 95–102.

Hole, Frank. 1997. "Evidence for Mid-Holocene Environmental Change in the Western Khabur Drainage, Northeastern Syria." In *Third Millennium BC Climate Change,* ed. H. Dalfes et al., 41–45. Berlin: Springer-Verlag.

Hoogervorst, Tom. 2012. "Southeast Asia in the Ancient Indian Ocean World: Combining Historical Linguistic and Archaeological Approaches." Ph.D. dissertation, University of Oxford, Oxford, UK.

———. 2013. *Southeast Asia in the Indian Ocean World.* Oxford: British Archaeological Reports.

Hopkins, Keith. 1978. "Economic Growth and Towns in Classical Antiquity." In *Towns in Societies,* ed. Peter Abrams and E. Wrigley, 35–77. London: Cambridge University Press.

———. 1980. "Taxes and Trade in the Roman Empire 200 BC–AD 400." *Journal of Roman Studies* 70: 101–125.

———. 1988. "Roman Trade, Industry and Labor." In *Civilization of the Ancient Mediterranean: Greece and Rome,* ed. P. Kitzinger, 753–778. New York: Charles Scribner.

Hopkins, T., and I. Wallerstein. 1996. *The Age of Transition.* London: Zed Books.

Horton, H., and J. Middleton. 2000. *The Swahili: The Social Landscape of a Mercantile Society.* Cambridge: Blackwell.

Hoselitz, Bert. 1960. *Sociological Aspects in Economic Growth.* New York: Free Press.

Hourani, George F., and John Carswell. 1995. *Arab Seafaring: In the Indian Ocean in Ancient and Early Medieval Time.* Princeton, NJ: Princeton University Press.

Huang, Chun Chang, Zhao Shichao, Pang Jiangli, Zhou Qunying, Chen Shue, Pinghua Li, Longjia Mao, and Min Ding. 2003. "Climatic Aridity and the Relocations of the Zhou Culture in the Southern Loess Plateau of China." *Climatic Change* 61 (3): 361–378.

Huang, Chun Chang, and Hongxia Su. 2009. "Climate Change and Zhou Relocations in Early Chinese History." *Journal of Historical Geography* 35 (2): 297–310.

Hubert, M., et al. 2014. "Pleistocene Cave Art from Sulawesi, Indonesia." *Nature* 514: 223–227.

Hudson, R. 2004. *The Origins of Bagan: The Archaeological Landscape of Upper Burma.* Sydney: University of Sydney.

Hughes, Donald. 1994. *Pan's Travail.* Baltimore: Johns Hopkins University Press.

———. 2001. *Environmental History of the World.* London: Routledge.

Hung, Hsiao-chun, and Peter Bellwood. 2010. "Movement of Raw Materials and Manufactured Goods across the South China Sea after 500 BCE: From Taiwan to Thailand and Back." In *50 Years of Archaeology in Southeast Asia,* ed. B. Bellina et al., 235–245. Bangkok: River Books.

Hung, Hsiao-chun, Yoshiyuki Lizuka, et al. 2007. "Ancient Jades Map: 3,000 Years of Pre-historic Exchange in Southeast Asia." *Proceedings of the National Academy of Sciences* 104 (50): 19745–19750.

Hung, Hsiao-chun, and C. Y. Chao. 2016. "Taiwan's Early Metal Age and Southeast Asian Trading Systems." *Antiquity* 90 (354): 1537–1551.

Hunter, Thomas M., Jr. 2016. *Exploring the Role of Language in Early State Formation of Southeast Asia.* Nalanda-Sriwijaya Centre Working Paper Series no. 7. Singapore: Institute of Southeast Asian Studies.

Hutterer, Karl L. 1982. "Early Southeast Asia: Old Wine in New Skins." *Journal of Southeast Asian Studies* 41: 559–570.

Imamura, Keiji. 1996. *Prehistoric Japan: New Perspectives on Insular East Asia.* Honolulu: University of Hawaii Press.

Ikeda, Satoshi. 1996. "The History of the World System vs. the History of East-Southeast Asia." *Review* 19 (1): 49–77.

Immerwahr, Sara A. 1960. "Mycenaean Trade and Colonization." *Archaeology* 3 (1): 4–13.

Inoue, H., et al. 2012. "Polity Scale Shifts in World Systems since the Bronze Age: A Comparative Inventory of Upsweeps and Collapses." *International Journal of Comparative Sociology* 53 (3): 210–229.

———. 2015. "Urban Scale Shifts since the Bronze Age: Upsweeps, Collapse, and Semi-peripheral Development." *Social Science History* 39 (2): 175–200.

Ishizawa, Y. 1995. "Chinese Chronicles of the 1st–5th Century AD. Funan, Southern Cambodia." In *South East Asia and China: Art, Interaction, and Commerce,* ed. R. Scott and J. Guy, 11–31. London: Percival David Foundation of Chinese Art, University of London.

Issar, Arie. 1998. "Climate Change and History during the Holocene in the Eastern Mediterranean Region." In *Water, Environment, and Society in Times of Climatic Change,* ed. A Issar and N. Brown, 113–128. Hague: Kluwer.

Jacq-Hergoualc'h, M. 2002. *The Malay Peninsula: Crossroads of the Maritime Silk Road (100 BC–AD 1300).* Leiden: Brill.

Jameson, Michael, et al. 1994. *A Greek Countryside: The Southern Argolid from Prehistory to the Present Day.* Palo Alto: Stanford University Press.

Jennings, Justin. 2011. *Globalization and the Ancient World.* Cambridge: Cambridge University Press.

Ji, Shen, Richard Jones, et al. 2006. "The Holocene Vegetation History of Lake Erhai, Yunnan Province: The Role of Climate and Human Forcings." *The Holocene* 16 (2): 265–276.

Junker, Laura Lee. 1998. "Integrating History and Archaeology in the Study of Contact Period Philippine Chiefdoms." *International Journal of Historical Archaeology* 2 (4): 291–320.

———. 2004. "Political Economy in the Historic Period Chiefdoms and States of Southeast Asia." In *Archaeological Perspectives on Political Economies,* ed. Gary Freeman and Linda Nicholas, 23–43. Salt Lake City: University of Utah Press.

———. 2006. "Population Dynamics and Urbanization in Premodern Island Southeast Asia." In *Urbanism in the Preindustrial World: Cross Cultural Approaches,* ed. Glenn Storey, 211–214. Tuscaloosa: University of Alabama Press.

Kameyama, Yasuko, A. Sari, and M. Soejachmoeh. 2008. *Climate Change in Asia: Perspective on Future Climatic Regime.* Tokyo: UN University Press.

Kennedy, J. 1898. "The Early Commerce of Babylon with India." *Journal of the Royal Asiatic Society of Great Britain and Ireland* (April): 241–288.

Kim, Nam C. 2013. "Lasting Monuments and Durable Institutions: Labor, Urbanism and Statehood in Northern Vietnam and Beyond." *Journal of Archaeological Research* 21 (3): 217–267.

Klokke, Marijke, and Véronique Degroot, eds. 2013. *Unearthing Southeast Asia's Past*, vols. 1–2 Singapore: National University of Singapore Press.

Knapp, A. Bernard. 1993. "Thalassocracies in the Bronze Age Eastern Mediterranean Trade: Making and Breaking a Myth World." *World Archaeology* 24 (3): 332–347.

Kohl, Philip. 1987. "The Ancient Economy, Transferable Technologies, and the Bronze Age World System: A View from the Northeastern Frontiers of the Ancient Near East." In *Centre and Periphery in the Ancient World*, ed. M. Rowlands, Mogens Larsen, and Kristian Kristiansen. Cambridge: Cambridge University Press.

———. 2008. "Shared Social Fields: Evolutionary Convergence in Prehistory and Contemporary Practice." *American Anthropologist* 110 (4): 495–506.

Kohl, Philip, and E. N. Chernykh. 2003. "Different Hemisphere, Different Worlds." In *Post Classic MesoAmerican World*, ed. M. E. Smith and F. E. Berdan, 307–312. Salt Lake City: University of Utah Press.

Krementski, Constantin. 1997. "The Late Holocene Environmental and Climate Shift in Russia and Surrounding Lands." In *Third Millennium BC Climate Change and Old World Collapse*, ed. H. Dalfes et al., 351–370. Heidelberg: Springer-Verlag.

Kristiansen, Kristian. 1993. "The Emergence of the European World System in the Bronze Age: Divergence, Convergence, and Social Evolution during the First and Second Millennia BC in Europe." Sheffield Archaeological Monographs, no. 6.

———. 1998. *Europe before History*. Cambridge: Cambridge University Press.

———. 2011. "Constructing Social and Cultural Identities in the Bronze Age." In *Investigating Archaeological Cultures: Material Culture, Variability, and Transmission*, ed. B. W. Roberts and M. Vander Linden, 201–210. New York: Springer.

———. 2014. "The Decline of the Neolithic and the Rise of Bronze Age Society." In *The Oxford Handbook of Neolithic Europe*, ed. Chris Fowler, Jan Harding, and Daniela Hoffman, 1–19. Oxford: Oxford Handbooks.

Kristiansen, Kristian, and Thomas Larsson. 2005. *The Rise of Bronze Age Society Travels, Transmission, and Transformation*. Cambridge: Cambridge University Press.

Kulke, H. 1990. "Indian Colonies, Indianization or Cultural Convergence? Reflections on the Changing Image of India's Role in Southeast Asia." In *Onderzoekin Zuidoost-Azië: Agenda's voor de Jaren Negentig*, ed. H. Schulte Nordholt, 8–32. Leiden: Rijksuniversiteit te Leiden.

Lal, B. B. 1997. *The Earliest Civilization of South Asia: Rise, Maturity, and Decline*. New Delhi: Aryan Books International.

Lamberg-Karlovsky, C. C. 1975. "Third Millennium Exchange and Production." In *Ancient Civilization and Trade*, ed. Jeremy Sabloff and C. C. Lamberg-Karlovsky, 120–145. Albuquerque: University of New Mexico Press.

Lambrick, H. T. 1967. "The Indus Food Plain and the 'Indus' Civilization." *The Geographical Journal* 133 (4): 483–489.

Lamb, H. 1967. "R. Carpenter's Discontinuity in Greek Civilization." *Antiquity* 41: 33–34.

Lankton, J., and L. Dussubieux. 2006. "Early Glass in Asian Maritime Trade: A Review and Interpretation of Compositional Analysis." *Journal of Glass Studies* 48: 121–144.

Larsen, Mogens Trolle. 1976. *The Old Assyrian City-State and Its Colonies*. Copenhagen: Akademisk Forlag.

———. 1987. "Commercial Network in the Ancient Near East." In *Centre and Periphery in the Ancient World*, ed. Michael Rowlands et al., 47–56. Cambridge: Cambridge University Press.

Lattimore, Owen. 1940. *Inner Asian Frontiers of China*. Boston: Beacon Press.

———. 1943. "Yunnan: Pivot of Southeast Asia." *Foreign Affairs* 21 (3): 476–493.

Lechtmann, H. 1979. "Issues in Andean Metallurgy." In *Pre Columbian Metallurgy of South America*, ed. E. P. Benson, 1–40. Washington: Dumbarton Books.

———. 1980. "The Central Andes: Metallurgy without Iron." In *The Coming of the Age of Iron*, ed. T. A. Wertime and J. D. Muhly, 267–334. New Haven: Yale University Press.

Lerner, David. 1965. *The Passing of Traditional Society*. New York: Free Press.

Leong, S. H. 1990. "Collecting Centres, Feeder Points and Entrepots in the Malay Peninsula 1000 BC–AD 1400." In *The Southeast Asian Port and Polity*, ed. Jaya Kathirithamby-Wells and John Viliers, 17–38. Singapore: Singapore University Press.

Leslie, D. D., and K. H. J. Gardiner. 1996. *The Roman Empire in Chinese Sources*. Rome: Bardi.

Li, Liu, and Chen Xing. 2012. *The Archaeology of China. From the Late Paleolithic to the Early Bronze Age*. Cambridge: Cambridge University Press.

Li, Tana. 2016. "A Historical Sketch of the Landscape of the Red River Delta." TRANS (June): 1–13.

Li, Zhong (pseud.). 1975. "The Development of Iron and Steel Technology in Ancient China." *Kaogu Xue Bao* 1975 (2): 1–22.

———. 1976. "Studies on the Iron Blade of a Shang Dynasty Bronze Yüeh-Axe Unearthed at Kao-ch'eng, Hupei, China." *Kaogu Xue Bao* 1976 (2): 17–34.

Liu, Tsui Jung. 2001. *Asia's Population History*. Oxford: Oxford University Press.

Liu, Xinru. 2010. *The Silk Road in World History*. Oxford: Oxford University Press.

Lieberman, Victor. 1993. "Local Integration and Eurasian Analogies: Structuring Southeast Asian History." *Modern Asian Studies* 27 (3): 475–572.

———. 1995. "An Age of Commerce in Southeast Asia? Problems of Regional Coherence. A Review Article." *Journal of Asian Studies* 54 (3): 796–807.

———, ed. 1999. *Beyond Binary Histories: Re-imagining Eurasia to 1830*. Ann Arbor: University of Michigan Press.

———. 2003, 2009. *Strange Parallels*. Vol. 1, *Integration on the Mainland: Southeast Asia in Global Context c. 800–1830*, and Vol. 2, *Mainland Mirrors: Europe, Japan, China, South Asia, and the Islands*. Cambridge: Cambridge University Press.

Linduff, K., H. Rubin, and S. Shuyun. 2000. *The Beginnings of Metallurgy in China*. New York: Edwin Mellen Press.

Liverani, Mario. 1987. "The Collapse of the Near Eastern Regional System at the End of the Bronze Age: The Case of Syria." In *Centre and Periphery in the Ancient World*, ed. Michael Rowlands et al., 60–73. Cambridge: Cambridge University Press.

Lockard, Craig. 2009. *Southeast Asia in World History*. Oxford: Oxford University Press.

Lombard, Denys. 1995. "Networks and Synchronisms in Southeast Asian History." *Journal of Southeast Asian Studies* 26 (1): 10–16.

Lombard, Denys, and Jean Aubin, eds. 2000. *Asian Merchants and Businessmen in the Indian Ocean and the China Sea*. Oxford: Oxford University Press.

Lombard, Maurice. 1975. *The Golden Age of Islam*. Amsterdam: North Holland.

Loofs-Wissowa, Helmut H. E. 1983. "The Distribution of Dong Son Drums: Some Thoughts." In *Ethnologie und Geschichte: Festschrift für Karl Jettmar*, ed. P. Snoy, 410–418. Wiesbaden: Steiner.

Mabbett, I. W. 1977a. "The Indianization of Southeast Asia: Reflections on the Prehistoric Sources." *Journal of Southeast Asian Studies* 8 (1): 1–14.

———.1977b. "The Indianization of Southeast Asia." *Journal of Southeast Asian Studies* 8 (2): 143–161.

MacDowall, David W. 2011. "The Evidence of the Gazetteer of Roman Artifacts in India." In *Tradition and Archaeology*, ed. H. Ray and J. F. Salles, 79–95. New Delhi: Manohar.

Majumdar, R. C. 1952. *Greater India*. New Delhi: Motilal Banavarsides.

Mallaret, L. 1959–1963. *L'archéologie du Delta du Mékong*. Paris: École française d'Extrême Orient.

———. 1962. "L'Archéologie du Delta du Mékong: La Culture du Fou-nan." *École française d' Extrême Orient* 43 (3).

Mango, M. M. 1996. "Byzantine Maritime Trade with the East (4–7th centuries)." *Aram* 8: 139–163.

Manguin, P. I. 1980. "The Southeast Asian Ship: An Historical Approach." *Journal of Southeast Asian Studies* 11 (2): 266–276.

———. 1985a. "Sewn-Plank Craft of Southeast Asia: A Preliminary Survey." In *Sewn Plank Boats*, ed. Sean McGrail and Eric Kentley, 319–343. Oxford: BAR International.

———. 1985b. "Late Medieval Asian Shipbuilding in the Indian Ocean: A Reappraisal." *Moyen Orient and Océan Indien* 2 (2): 1–30.

———. 1991. "The Merchant and the King: Political Myths of Southeast Asia Coastal Polities." *Indonesia* 52: 41–54.

———. 1993a. "Trading Ships of the South China Sea: Shipping Techniques and their Role in the History of the Development of Asian Trade Networks." *Journal of the Economic and Social History of the Orient* 36 (3): 253–280.

———. 1993b. "Southeast Asian Shipping in the Indian Ocean during the First Millennium AD." In *Tradition and Archaeology: Early Maritime Contact in the Indian Ocean*, ed. H. Ray and J. Salles, 36–65. New Delhi: Manohar.

———. 2000. "City-States and City-State Culture in the Pre-15th-Century Southeast Asia." In *A Comparative Study of City-State Cultures*, ed. Mogen Hermand Hansen, 409–416. Copenhagen: C. A. Reitzels Forlag.

———. 2004. "The Archaeology of Early Maritime Polities of Southeast Asia." In *Southeast Asia: From Prehistory to History*, ed. Ian Glover and Peter Bellwood, 282–313. London: Routledge.

———. 2009. "The Archaeology of Funan in the Mekong River Delta: The Oc Eo Culture of Vietnam." In *Arts of Ancient Vietnam: From River Plain to Open Sea*, ed. Nancy Tingley, 100–118. Houston: Asian Society Museum of Fine Arts.

Mann, Michael. 2016. "Have Human Societies Evolved? Evidence from History and Prehistory." *Theory and Society* 45 (3): 203–237.

Manning, Patrick. 2013. "Africa and World Historiography." *Journal of African History* 54 (3): 319–330.

Mao, L. J., D. W. Mo, K. S. Zhou, W. M. Guo, Y. F. Jia, J. H. Yang, H. Deng, C. X. Shi, and J. Y. Jia. 2009. "Rare Earth Elements and the Environmental Significance of the Dark Brown Soil in Liyang Plain, Hunan Province, China." *Acta Scientiae Circumstantiae* 29 (7): 1561–1568.

Marinatos, S. 1939. "The Volcanic Eruption of Minoan Crete." *Antiquity* 13: 425–39.

Marshall, Wolfgang. 1980. "Indonesia in Indian Ocean Culture History." *Indonesian Circle* 21: 15–23.

Marx, Karl. 1963. *Early Writings*. New York: Vintage Books.

Matthews, R. 2002. "Zebu: Harbinger of Doom in Bronze Age Western Asia." *Antiquity* 76: 438–446.

Matsumura, Y. 1991. "Temporal Distribution of Cereal Remains of Asian Neolithic." *Ki-kan Koukogaku* 37: 33–35.

McClelland, David. 1967. *The Achieving Society*. New York: Free Press.

McCune, Shannon. 1956. *Korea's Heritage: A Regional and Social Geography*. Tokyo, Japan: C. E. Tuttle.

McGovern, P. 1987. "Central TransJordan in Late Bronze Age and Early Iron Ages: An Alternative Hypothesis of Socioeconomic Collapse." In *Studies in the History and Archaeology of Jordan 3*, ed. A. Hadidi, 267–273. London: Routledge and Kegan Paul.

McLaughlin, Raoul. 2010. *Rome and the Distant East: Trade Route to the Ancient Lands of Arabia, India, and China*. London: Continuum.

———. 2014. *The Roman Empire and the Indian Ocean*. Barnsley: Pen and Sword.

McNeill, J. R., and W. McNeill. 2003. *The Human Web*. New York: Norton.

McPherson, K. 1995. *The Indian Ocean: A History of People and the Sea*. New Delhi: Oxford University Press.

Medway, Lord. 1977. "The Niah Excavation: An Assessment of the Impact of Early Man on Mammals in Borneo." *Asian Perspectives* 20: 51–69.

Meiyuan, Mozi. 1971. *Ancient Jade in Japan*. Xingzhou: ShiJie.

Mellink, Machfeld. 1986. "The Early Bronze Age in Western Anatolia: Aegean and Asiatic Correlations." In *End of the Early Bronze Age in the Aegean*, ed. G. Cadogan, 139–152. Leiden: Brill.

Meyer, J. C. 2007. "Roman Coins as a Source for Roman Trading Activities in the Indian Ocean." In *The Indian Ocean in the Ancient Period: Definite Places and Translocal Exchange*, ed. E. H. Seland, 59–67. Oxford: BAR International Series 1593.

Miksic, John. 2000. "Heterogenetic Cities in Premodern Southeast Asia." *World Archaeology* 32 (1): 106–120.

———. 2003. "Introduction: The Beginning of Trade in Ancient Southeast Asia: The Role of Oc-Eo and the Lower Mekong Delta." In *Art and Archaeology of Funan: Pre-Khmer Kingdom of the Lower Mekong Valley*, ed. J. Khoo, 1–33. Bangkok: Orchid Press.

———. 2013. *Singapore and the Silk Road of the Sea 1300–1800*. Singapore: National University of Singapore Press.

Millar, F. 1981. *The Roman Empire and its Neighbors*. New York: Holmes and Meier.

Miller, Innes. 1969. *The Spice Trade of the Roman Empire*. Oxford: Oxford University Press.

Mitchell, P. 2005. *African Connections: Archaeological Perspectives on Africa and the Wider World*. Walnut Creek, CA: AltaMira Press.

Modelski, George. 2003. *World Cities*. Washington, DC: Faros

Modelski, George, and W. Thompson. 2000. "The Evolutionary Pulse of the World System: Hinterland Incursion and Migrations 4000 BC to AD 1500." In *World System Theory in Practice*, ed. Nick Kardulias, 241–274. Lanham, MD: Rowman and Littlefield.

Mookerji, R. K. (1912) 1957. *Indian Shipping: A History of the Sea-Borne Trade and Maritime Activities of the Indians from the Earliest Times*. London: Longmans.

Moore, E. H. 1988. *Moated Sites in Early Northeast Thailand*. Oxford: BAR International Series.

———. 2007. *Early Landscapes of Myanmar*. Bangkok: River Books.

Moore, M. 1993. *The Burnishing Stones: The Excavation of Khok Phanom Di*. London: Society of Antiquaries of London.

Moorey, P. R. S. 1994. "Early Metallurgy in Mesopotamia." In *The Beginning of the Use of Metals and Alloys*, ed. R. Maddin, 28–33. Cambridge, MA: MIT Press.

Mormina, M., and C. F. W. Higham. 2010. "Climate and Population History of Southeast Asia." In *Climate Crises and Human History*, ed. A. B. Mainwaring, 197–212. Philadelphia: American Philosophical Society.

Morris, Ian. 1987. *Burial and Ancient Society: The Rise of the Greek City-State*. Cambridge: Cambridge University Press.

———. 1988. "Tomb Cult and the Greek Renaissance: The Past in the Present 8th Century BC." *Antiquity* 62 (237): 750–761.

———. 2000. *Archaeology as Cultural History: Words and Things in Iron Age Greece*. Malden, MA: Blackwell.

Mudar, K. M. 1999. "How Many Dvaravati Kingdoms? Locational Analysis of First Millennium AD Moated Settlements in Central Thailand." *Journal of Anthropological Archaeology* 18 (1): 1–28.

Muhly, J. D. 1984. "The Role of the Sea People of Cyprus during the LC III Period." In *Cyprus at the Close of the Late Bronze Age*, ed. V. Karageorghis and J. Muhly, 39–56. Nicosia, Cyprus: Zavallis.

———. 1988. "The Beginnings of Metallurgy in the Old World." In *The Beginnings of the Use of Metals and Alloys*, ed. R. Maddin, 2–20. Cambridge, MA: MIT Press.

Murray, G. 1907. *The Rise of the Greek Epic*. Oxford: Oxford University Press.

Murillo-Barroso, M., et al. 2010. "Khao Sam Kaeo: An Archaeometallurgical Crossroad from Trans-Asiatic Technological Traditions." *Journal of Archaeological Science* 37 (1): 1761–1772.

Nash, Daphne. 1987. "Imperial Exchange under the Roman Republic." In *Centre and Periphery in the Ancient World*, ed. Michael Rowlands et al., 87–103. Cambridge: Cambridge University Press.

Neelis, Jason. 2012. "Central Asian Silk Routes and Early South Asian Trade Networks." In *Great Trade Routes*, ed. Philip Parker, 71–79. London: Anova.

Neumann, J., and S. Parpola. 1987. "Climate Change and 11–10th Century Eclipse of Assyria and Babylonia." *Journal of Near Eastern Studies* 46: 161–182.

O'Connor, James. 1988. "Capitalism, Nature, Socialism: A Theoretical Introduction." *Capitalism, Nature, Socialism* 1: 11–38.

———. 1998. "The Conditions of Production and the Production of Conditions." In *Natural Causes: Essays in Ecological Marxism*, 135–178. New York: Guilford.

O'Connor, Richard. 1983. *A Theory of Indigenous Southeast Asian Urbanism*. Singapore: Institute of Southeast Asian Studies.

Ooi, Kee Beng. 2011. *The Eurasian Core and Its Edges: Dialogues with Wang Gungwu on the History of the World*. Singapore: Institute of Southeast Asian Studies.

Oppenheimer, Stephen. 1998. *Eden in the East: The Drowned Continent of Southeast Asia*. London: Weidenfeld and Nicola.

O'Reilly, Dougald. 2000. "From the Bronze Age to the Iron Age in Thailand: Applying the Heterarchical Approach." *Asian Perspectives* 39 (1/2): 1–19.

———. 2003. "Further Evidence of Heterarchy in Bronze Age Thailand." *Current Anthropology* 44 (2): 300–306.

———. 2007. *Early Civilizations of Southeast Asia*. Walnut Creek, CA: AltaMira Press.

———. 2008. "Multivallate Sites and Socio-Economic Change: Thailand and Britain in Their Iron Ages." *Antiquity* 82 (316): 377–389.

———. 2014. "Increasing Complexity and the Political Economy Model: A Consideration of Iron Age Moated Sites in Thailand." *Journal of Anthropological Archaeology* 35: 297–309.

Ouyang, Xiu, and Richard L. Davis. 2004. *Historical Records of the Five Dynasties.* New York: Columbia University Press.

Oxenham, Marc, and Nancy Tayles. 2009. *Bioarchaeology of Southeast Asia.* Cambridge: Cambridge University Press.

Pare, C., ed. 2000. *Metals Make the World Go Round: The Supply and Circulation of Metals in Bronze Age Europe.* Oxford: Oxbow Books.

Park, Hyunhee. 2012. *Mapping the Chinese and Islamic Worlds: Cross Cultural Exchange in Premodern Asia.* Cambridge: Cambridge University Press.

Parker, Grant. 2002. "Ex Oriente Luxuria: Indian Commodities and Roman Experience." *Journal of the Economic and Social History of the Orient* 45: 40–95.

———. 2008. *The Making of Roman India.* Cambridge: Cambridge University Press.

Parkin, David, and Ruth Barnes. 2002. *Ships and the Development of Maritime Technology in the Indian Ocean.* London: Routledge.

Parsons, Talcott. 1964. "Evolutionary Universals in Society." *American Sociological Review* (June): 339–357.

Paz, V. 2002. "Island Southeast Asia: Spread or Friction Zone?" In *Examining the Farming/Language Dispersal Hypothesis,* ed. P. Bellwood and C. Renfrew, 275–285. Cambridge: McDonald Institute for Archaeological Research.

———. 2004. "Of Nuts and Tubers: The Archaeobotanical Evidence from Leung Burung 1." In *Quarternary Research in Indonesia,* ed. S. G. Keates and J. M. Pasveer, 191–220. Leiden: A. A. Balkema Publishers.

Pearson, M. N. 2003. *The Indian Ocean.* London: Routledge.

Perlin, John. 1989. *A Forest Journey.* Cambridge: Harvard University Press.

Péronnet, Sophié. 2013. "Overview of Han Artifacts in Southeast Asia with Special Reference to the Recently Excavated Material from Khao Sam Kaeo in Southern Thailand." In *Unearthing Southeast Asia's Past,* vol. 1, ed. Marijke J. Klokke and Véronique Degroot, 155–169. Singapore: National University of Singapore Press.

Pigott, V. C. 1999. "Reconstructing the Copper Production Process as Practised among Prehistoric Mining Metallurgical Communities in the Khao Wong Prachan Valley of Central Thailand." In *Metals in Antiquity,* ed. S. M. M. Young et al., 10–21. Oxford: BAR International Series #792.

Pigott, V. C., and R. Ciarla. 2007. "On the Origins of Metallurgy in Prehistoric Southeast Asia: The View from Thailand." In *Metals and Mines: Studies in Archaeometallurgy,* ed. S. La Niece, D. Hook, and P. Craddock, 76–88. London: Archetype Press.

Pigott, V. C., and S. Natapintu. 1988. "Archaeological Investigation into Prehistoric Copper Production: The Thailand Archaeometallurgy Project 1984–1986." In *The Beginning of the Use of Metals and Alloys,* ed. R. Maddin, 156–162. Cambridge: MIT Press.

Pigott, V. C., and G. Weisgerber. 1998. "Mining Archaeology in Geological Context: The Prehistoric Mining Complex at Phu Lon, Nong Khai Province, Northeast Thailand." *Der Anschitt Beiheft* 8: 135–162.

Pliny the Elder. (AD 77–79) 1961–1968. *Natural History,* vols. 1, 2, 4. Translated by H. Rackham. Loeb Classical Library. London: Heinemann.

Polanyi, Karl. 1977. *The Livelihood of Man.* New York: Academic Press.

Pollock, Sheldon. 2000. *The Language of the Gods in the World of Men*. Berkeley: University of California Press.

Ponton, Camilio, et al. 2012. "Holocene Aridification of India." *Geophysical Research Letters* 39 (3): 23–36.

Possehl, G. 1979. *Ancient Cities of the Indus*. New Delhi: Vikas.

———, ed. 1982. "The Harappan Civilization: A Contemporary Perspective." In *Harappan Civilization*. New Delhi: Oxford University Press.

———. 2002. *The Indus Civilization*. Walnut Creek, CA: AltaMira Press.

Prebisch, Raul. 1959. "Commercial Policy in the Underdeveloped Countries." *American Economic Review* 44: 251–273.

Pryce, Thomas, et al. 2006. "The Development of Metal Technologies in the Upper Thai-Maly Peninsula: Initial Interpretation of the Archaeometallurgical Evidence from Khao Sam Kaeo." *Bulletin de L'Ecole Francaise d'Extrême Orient* 93: 295–315.

———. 2011. "Isotopic and Technological Variation in Prehistoric Primary Southeast Asian Copper Production." *Journal of Archaeological Science* 38: 3309–3322.

Ptolemy, Claudius. (150 AD) 1991. *The Geography*. Translated by E. L. Stevenson. New York: Dover.

Pye, Lucien. 1962. *Personality, Politics, and Nation Building*. New Haven: Yale University Press.

Raikes, Robert. 1964. "The End of the Ancient Cities of the Indus." *American Anthropologist* 66 (2): 284–299.

Raikes, Robert, and G. F. Dales. 1977. "The Mohenjo-Daro Floods Reconsidered." *Journal of the Palaeontological Society of India* 20: 251–260.

Rajan, K. 2011. "Emergence of Early Historic Trade in Peninsular India." In *Early Interactions between South and Southeast Asia*, ed. P. Manguin et al., 197–220. Singapore: Institute of Southeast Asian Studies.

Raman, K. V. 1991. "Further Evidence of Roman Trade from Coastal Sites in Tamil Nadu." In *Rome and India: The Ancient Sea Trade*, ed. Vimala Begley and Richard Daniel DePuma, 125–133. Madison: University of Wisconsin Press.

Ratnagar, Shereen. 1981. *Encounters: The Westerly Trade of the Harappan Civilization*. New Delhi: Oxford University Press.

———. 2002. "The Bronze Age: Unique Island of a Preindustrial World System?" *Current Anthropology* 42 (3): 351–379.

———. 2004. *Trading Encounters: From the Euphrates to the Indus in the Bronze Age*. Oxford: Oxford University Press.

Ray, Himanshu P. 1989. "Early Maritime Contacts between South and Southeast Asia." *Journal of Southeast Asian Studies* 20 (1): 42–54.

———. 1997. "The Emergence of Urban Centres in Bengal: Implications for the Late Prehistory of Southeast Asia." *Bulletin of the Indo-Pacific Prehistory Association* (The Chiang Mai Papers vol. 3) 16: 43–48.

———. 2003. *The Archaeology of Seafaring in Ancient Southeast Asia*. Cambridge: Cambridge University Press.

Reid, Anthony. 1988. *Southeast Asia in the Age of Commerce 1450–1680*. Vol. 1, *The Lands below the Winds*. New Haven: Yale University Press.

———. 1993. *Southeast Asia in the Age of Commerce 1450–1680*. Vol. 2, *Expansion and Crisis*. New Haven: Yale University Press.

Renfrew, Colin. 1969. "The Autonomy of South Eastern Europe Copper Age." *Proceedings of the Prehistoric Society* 35: 12–47.

———. 1973. *Before Civilization.* London: Penguin.

———. 1986. "Varna and the Emergence of Wealth in Prehistoric Europe." In *The Social Life of Things,* ed. A. Appadurai, 141–168. Cambridge: Cambridge University Press.

———. 1993. "Trade as Action at a Distance: Questions of Integration and Communication." In *Ancient Civilization and Trade,* ed. J. A. Sabloff and C. C. Lamberg-Karlovsky, 3–60. Albuquerque: University of New Mexico Press.

Rispoli, F. 2008. "The Incised and Impressed Pottery Style of Mainland Southeast Asia: Following the Paths of Neolithization." *East and West* 57 (1–4): 235–304.

Rispoli, F., et al. 2013. "Establishing the Prehistoric Cultural Sequence for the Lopburi Region, Central Thailand." *Journal of World Prehistory* 26: 101–171.

Roberts, J. Timmons, and Peter Grimes. 2002. "World-Systems Theory and the Environment: A New Synthesis." In *Sociological Theory and the Environment.* Lanham, ed. Riley Dunlap et al., 167–196. Rowman and Littlefield.

Rostow, W. W. 1960. *The Stages of Economic Growth: A Non-Communist Manifesto.* Cambridge: Cambridge University Press.

Rowlands, Michael, et al., eds. 1987. *Centre and Periphery in the Ancient World.* Cambridge: Cambridge University Press.

Rowton, M. B. 1967. "The Woodlands of Ancient Western Asia." *Journal of Near Eastern Studies* 26: 261–77.

Ruddiman, William F. 2008. *Earth's Climate: Past and Future.* New York: W. H. Freeman.

———. 2013. "The Anthropocene." *Annual Review of Earth and Planetary Sciences* 41: 45–68.

Runnels, Curtis N. 1995. "Environmental Degradation in Ancient Greece." *Scientific American* 272 (3): 96–99.

Rutter, Jeremy. 1989. "Cultural Novelties in the Post Palatial Aegean World: Indices of Vitality or Decline." In *The Crisis Years: The 12th Century BC,* ed. W. Ward and M. Joukowsky, 61–78. Dubuque, IA: Kendall Hunt.

Sachsenmaier, Dominio. 2011. *Global Perspectives on Global History.* Cambridge: Cambridge University Press.

Sahni, M. R. 1956. "Biogeological Evidence Bearing on the Decline of the Indus Valley Civilization." *Journal of the Palaeontological Society of India* 1 (1): 101–107.

Saidin, M. 2012. *From Stone Age to Early Civilization in Malaysia.* Pulau Pinang: Universiti Sains Malaysia Press.

Saidin, M., et al. 2011. "Issues and Problems of Previous Studies in the Bujang Valley and the Discovery of Sungai Batu." In *Bujang Valley and Early Civilization in Southeast Asia,* ed. Dalam S. Chia and B. W. Andaya, 15–36. Kuala Lumpur: Department of National Heritage.

Salles, J. F. 1998. "Antique Maritime Channels from the Mediterranean to the Indian Ocean." In *From the Mediterranean to the China Sea: Miscellaneous Notes,* ed. C. Guillot, D. Lombard, and R. Ptak, 45–68. Wiesbaden: Harrassowitz.

———. 2011. "Hellenistic Seafaring in the Indian Ocean: A Perspective from Arabia." In *Tradition and Archaeology: Early Maritime Contacts in the Indian Ocean,* ed. H. P. Ray and J. F. Salles, 293–309. New Delhi: Manohar.

Salles, J. F., and H. P. Ray, eds. 2011. *Tradition and Archaeology: Early Maritime Contacts in the Indian Ocean.* New Delhi: Manohar.

Sarabia, Daniel. 2004. "Dark Age Phases as Periods of Ecological Crisis: An Analysis of the Interplay between Economy, Nature, and Culture." Ph.D dissertation, Oklahoma State University, Stillwater, OK.

Schäfer, Wolf. 2012. "World into Globe IV: History as a Tool of Foresight." *Globality Studies Journal* 28: 1–8.

Schiedel, Walter. 2014. "The Shape of the Roman World: Modeling Imperial Connectivity." *Journal of Roman Archaeology* 27: 7–32.

Schug, Gwen Robbins. 2011. *Bioarchaeology and Climate Change from South Asian Prehistory*. Gainesville: University of Florida Press.

Scott, Glen, and D. O'Reilly. 2015. "Rainfall and Circular Moated Sites in Northeast Thailand." *Antiquity* 89 (347): 1125–1138.

Sedov, A. V. 2007. "The Port of Qana and the Incense Trade." In *Food for the Gods: New Light on the Ancient Incense Trade*, ed. D. Peacock and D. F. Williams, 71–111. Oxford: Oxbow.

Seland, Eiviand Heldaas. 2007. *The Indian Ocean in the Ancient Period: Definite Places, Translocal Exchange*. British Archaeological Report International #1593. Oxford: Archaeopress.

———. 2010. *Ports and Power in the Periplus: Complex Societies and Maritime Trade on the Indian Ocean in the 1st Century AD*. Oxford: Archaeopress.

———. 2013. "Networks and Social Cohesion in Ancient Indian Ocean Trade: Geography, Ethnicity and Religion." *Journal of Global History* 8 (3): 373–390.

Sheratt, Andrew. 1981. "Plough and Pastoralism: Aspects of the Secondary Products Revolution." In *Pattern of the Past*, ed. Ian Hodder et al., 261–306. Cambridge: Cambridge University Press.

———. 1995. "Reviving the Grand Narrative: Archaeology and Long Term Change." *Journal of European Archaeology* 3 (1): 1–32.

———. 1997. *Economy and Society in Prehistoric Europe: Changing Perspectives*. Princeton, NJ: Princeton University Press.

———. 2006. "The Trans-Eurasian Exchange: The Prehistory of Chinese Relations with the West." In *Contact and Exchange in the Ancient World Perspectives on the Global Past*, ed. V. H. Mair, 30–61. Honolulu: University of Hawaii Press.

Sheratt, Susan 1998. "Sea Peoples and the Economic Structure of the late 2nd Millennium in the Eastern Mediterranean." In *Mediterranean Peoples in Transition: 13th to Early 10th Century BCE*, ed. S. Gitin, A. Mazar and E. Sternleds, 292–313. Jerusalem: Jerusalem Archaeological Society.

———. 2000. "Circulation of Metals and the End of the Bronze Age in the Eastern Mediterranean." In *Metals Make the World Go Round*, ed. C. Pare, 82–98. Oxford: Oxbow Books.

Sheratt, Susan, and Andrew Sheratt 1993. "The Growth of the Mediterranean Economy in the Early First Millennium BC." *World Archaeology* 24 (3): 361–378.

Sheriff, A. 2010. *Dhow Cultures of the Indian Ocean: Cosmopolitanism, Commerce, and Islam*. New York: Columbia University Press.

Shoocondej, R. 2006. "Late Pleistocene Activities at Tham Lod Rockshelter in Highland Bang Mapha, Mae Hongson Province, Northwest Thailand." In *Uncovering Southeast Asia's Past*, ed. E. Bacus, I. Glover, and V. Pigott, 22–37. Singapore: National University of Singapore Press.

Sidebotham, Steven E. 1986. *Roman Economic Policy in the Erythra Thalassa 30 BC–AD 217*. Leiden: Brill.

———. 2011. *Berenike and the Ancient Maritime Spice Route*. Berkeley: University of California Press.

Sinha, P., and Ian C. Glover. 1984. "Changes in Stone Tool Use in Southeast Asia 10,000 Years Ago." *Modern Quaternary Research in Southeast Asia* 8: 137–164.

Smail, John. 1961. "On The Possibility of an Autonomous History of Modern Southeast Asia." *Journal of Southeast Asian History* 2 (2): 72–102.

Small, D. 1990. "Handmade Burnished Ware and Prehistoric Aegean Economics." *Journal of Mediterranean Archaeology* 3: 3–25.

Smith, Frank E. 2003. "The Ancient World." Available online: http://www.fsmitha.com/index.html.

Smith, Michael. 2012. *The Comparative Archaeology of Complex Societies*. Cambridge: Cambridge University Press.

Smith, Monica L. 1999. "'Indianization' from the Indian Point of View: Trade and Cultural Contacts with Southeast Asia in the Early First Millennium CE." *Journal of Economic and Social History of the Orient* 42:1–26.

Snodgrass, A. M. 1971. *The Dark Age of Greece*. Edinburgh: University Press.

———. 1980. *Archaic Greece*. London: MacMillan.

———. 1989. "The Coming of the Iron Age in Greece: Europe's Earliest Bronze/Iron Transition." In *The Bronze-Iron Age Transition in Europe*, ed. M. L. Sorensen and R. Thomas, 34–67. BAR International Series no. 483. Oxford: Archeopress.

Snooks, G. D. 1991. *Exploring Southeast Asia's Economic Past*. Melbourne: Oxford University Press.

Solheim, W. G. 1968. "Early Bronze Age in Northeastern Thailand." *Current Anthropology* 9 (1): 59–62.

Sorensen, P. 1972. "The Neolithic Cultures of Thailand (and North Malaysia) and Their Lungshanoid Relationship." In *Early Chinese Art and Its Possible Influence in the Pacific Basin*, ed. N. Barnard, 459–506. New York: Intercultural Press.

Spriggs, M. 2003. "Chronology of the Neolithic Transition in Island Southeast Asia and the Western Pacific: A View from 2003." *Review of Archaeology* 24 (2): 52–74.

Srinivasan, S., and I. Glover. 1995. "Wrought and Quenched and Cast High-Tin Bronzes in Kerala State, India." *Journal of Historical Metallurgy Society* 29 (2): 69–88.

Stanislawski, D. 1973. "Dark Age Contributions to the Mediterranean Way of Life." *Annals of the Association of American Geographers* 63 (4): 397–410.

Stargardt, J. 1990. *The Ancient Pyu of Burma*. Cambridge: Cambridge University Press.

———. 1994. "Urbanization before Indianization at Beikthano, Central Burma c. 1st Century BC–3rd Century AD." In *Southeast Asian Archaeology*, vol. 1, ed. Pierre-Yves Manguin, 125–138. Hull: Centre for Southeast Asian Studies.

Stark, Miriam. 1998. The Transition to History in the Mekong Delta: A View from Cambodia. *International Journal of Historical Archaeology* 2 (3): 175–203.

———. 2001a. "Some Preliminary Results of the 1999–2000 Archaeological Field Investigations at Angkor Borei, Takeo Province." *Journal of Khmer Studies* 2: 19–35.

———. 2001b. "Mainland Southeast Asia Late Prehistoric." In *Encyclopedia of Prehistory*, vol. 3, ed. Peter N. Peregrine and Melvin Ember, 160–205. New York: Kluwer Academic.

———. 2004. "PreAngkorian and Angkorian Cambodia." In *Southeast Asia: From Prehistory to History*, ed. Ian Glover and Peter Bellwood, 89–119. London: Routledge.

———. 2005. *Archaeology of Asia*. Oxford: Blackwell.

———. 2006. "Early Mainland Southeast Asia Landscapes in the 1st Millennium AD." *Annual Review of Anthropology* 35: 407–432.

———. 2015. "Southeast Asian Urbanism: From Early City to Classical State." In *Early Cities in Comparative Perspective 4000 BCE–1200 CE*, ed. Norman Yoffee, 74–91. Cambridge: Cambridge University Press.

Stark, Miriam, and J. Allen. 1998. "The Transition to History in Southeast Asia: An Introduction." *International Journal of Historical Archaeology* 2 (3): 163–174.

Stark, Miriam, P. Bion Griffin, Chuch Phoeurn, Judy Ledgerwood, Michael Dega, Carol Mortland, Nancy Dowling, James M. Bayman, Bong Sovath, Tea Van, Schhan Chamroeun, and Kyle Latinis. 1999. "Results of the 1995–1996 Archaeological Field Investigations at Angkor Borei, Cambodia." *Asian Perspectives* 38 (1): 7–36.

Stark, Miriam, and Bong Sovath. 2001. "Recent Research on Emergent Complexity in Cambodia's Mekong." *Indo Pacific Prehistory Bulletin* 5 (21): 85–98.

Staubwasser, Michael, and Harvey Weiss. 2006. "Holocene Climate and Cultural Evolution in Late Prehistoric–Early Historic West Asia." *Quaternary Research* 66 (3): 372–387.

Stein, Gil. 2002. "From Passive Periphery to Active Agents: Emerging Perspectives in the Archaeology of Interregional Interaction." *American Anthropologist* 104: 903–916.

Steinberg, Ted, 2002. "Down to Earth: Nature, Agency, and Power in History." *American Historical Review* 107 (3): 798–820.

Storey, A. A., et al. 2012. "Investigating the Global Dispersal of Chickens in Prehistory Using Ancient Mitochondrial DNA Signature." *PlusONE* 7: 1–11.

Strabo. (7 BC–AD 23) 1917–1935. *Geography*, vols. 2, 7, 8. Translated by H. L. Jones. London: Loeb Classical Library.

Sunkel, Osvaldo. 1973. "Transnational Capitalism and National Disintegration in Latin America." *Social and Economic Studies* 22: 133–177.

Sutherland, Heather. 2003. "Southeast Asian History and the Mediterranean Analogy." *Journal of Southeast Asian Studies* 34 (1): 1–20.

Tan, Ha Va. 1980. "Nouvelles recherches préhistoriques au Viêt Nam." *Bulletin de l'École française d'Extrême-Orient, Paris* 68.

———. 1997. "The Hoabinhian and Before." *Bulletin of the Indo-Pacific Prehistory Association* 16: 35–41.

Tan, Noel Hidalgo. 2014. "The Global Implications of Early Surviving Rock Art of Greater Southeast Asia." *Antiquity* 88 (342): 1050–1064.

Tarling, Nicholas. 1999. *The Cambridge History of Southeast Asia*, vol. 1 Cambridge: Cambridge University Press.

Tayles, N. G. 1999. *The Excavation of Khok Phanom Di: A Prehistoric Site in Central Thailand*, vol. 5. London: Society of Antiquarians of London.

Taylor, Keith W. 1976. "Madagascar in the Ancient Malayo-Polynesian Myths." In *Explorations in Early Southeast Asian History: The Origins of Southeast Asia Statecraft*, ed. K. W. Hall and John K. Whitmore, 25–60. Ann Arbor: University of Michigan Centre for Southeast Asian Studies.

Takakura, M. 1991. "The Route of the Arrival of Rice." *Kikan Koukogaku* 37: 40–45.

Tchernia, André. 1997. "Winds and Coins: From Supposed Discovery of the Monsoon to the Denarii of Tiberius." In *Crossings: Early Mediterranean Contacts with India*, ed. F. De Romanis and A. Techernia, 250–276. New Delhi: Manohar.

Thapar, Romila. 1997. "Early Mediterranean Contacts with India: An Overview." In *Crossings: Early Mediterranean Contacts with India*, ed. F. De Romanis and A. Techernia, 11–40. New Delhi: Manohar.

Theunisson, R., P. Grave, and G. Bailey. 2000. "Doubts on Diffusion: Challenging the Assumed Indian Origin of Iron Age Agate and Carnelian Beads in Southeast Asia." *World Archaeology* 32 (1): 84–105.

Tierney, Brian, and Sidney Painter. 1992. *Western Europe in the Middle Ages 300–1475*. New York: McGraw Hill.

Tjia, H. D. 1980. "The Sunda Shelf, Southeast Asia." *Zeitschrift für Geomorphologie*. N.F. 24 (4): 408–427.

Tjoa-Bonatz, Mai Lin, Andreas Reinecke, and Dominik Bonatz, eds. 2012a. *Connecting Empires and States: Selected Papers from the 13th International Conference of the European Association of Southeast Asian Archaeologists*, vol. 2. Singapore: National University of Singapore Press.

———. 2012b. *Crossing Borders: Selected Papers from the 13th International Conference of the European Association of Southeast Asian Archaeologists*, vol. 1. Singapore: National University of Singapore Press.

Thompson, William. 2000. "C-Waves, Center-Hinterland Contact and Regime Change in the Ancient Near East: Early Impacts of Globalization." Paper presented at the International Studies Association Annual Meetings, Los Angeles, 23–26 March.

———. 2001. "Trade Pulsations, Collapse, and Reorientation in the Ancient World." Paper presented at the International Studies Association Annual Meetings, Chicago, 24–27 March.

Tibbetts, G. R. 1956. "PreIslamic Arabia and Southeast Asia." *Journal of the Malayan Branch of the Royal Asiatic Society* 29 (3): 182–208.

Tomber, Roberta. 2007. "Rome and Mesopotamia: Importers into India in the First Millennium AD." *Antiquity* 81: 972–988.

———. 2008. *Indo-Roman Trade: From Pots to Pepper*. London: Duckworth.

———. 2014. "The Periplus of the Erythraean Sea and the World of the Indian Ocean." *Journal of Roman Archaeology* 127: 883–886.

Tongko, Luokong. 1971. "Study on Eastern Movement of Japanese." *Kaogu* 5: 439–558.

Tosi, Maurizio. 1982. "The Harappan Civilization beyond the Indian Subcontinent." In *Harappan Civilization*, ed. Gregory Possehl, 14–35. New Delhi: Oxford University Press.

Toynbee, A. J. 1939. *A Study of History*, vols. 4 and 5. Oxford: Oxford University Press.

Treerayapeewat, C. 2005. "Pattern of Habitation and Burial Activity in the Ban Rai Rockshelter Northwest Thailand." *Asian Perspectives* 44: 231–245.

Trigger, B. G. 1969. "The Myth of Meroe and the African Iron Age." *African Historical Studies* 2 (1): 23–50.

Turnbull, Stephen. 2000. *Fighting Ships of the Far East*. Vol. 1, *China and Southeast Asia 202 BC–AD 1419*. New York: Osprey.

Turner, Paula. 1989. *Roman Coins from India*. London: Royal Numismatic Society.

Van Andel, T., C. Runnels, and O. Pope. 1986. "Five Thousand Years of Land Use and Abuse in the Southern Argolid Greece." *Hesperia* 55 (1): 103–128.

Van Leur, Jacob. 1967. *Indonesian Trade and Society*. The Hague: W. van Hoeve.

Vermeule, Emily. 1960. "The Fall of the Mycenaean Empire." *Archaeology* 13 (1): 66–75.

Vickery, M. 2003. "Funan Reviewed: Deconstructing the Ancients." *Bulletin de l'École française d'Extrême-Orient* 90–91: 101–143.

Wade, Geoff. 2015. *Asian Expansions*. London: Routledge.

Wagner, Donald B. 1987. "The Dating of the Chu Graves of Changsha: The Earliest Iron Artifacts in China?" *Acta Orientalia* 48: 111–156.

———. 1993. *Iron and Steel in Ancient China*. New York: E. J. Brill.

———. 2001. *The State and Iron Industry in Han China*. Copenhagen: NIAS.

Wallerstein, I. 1974, 1980, 1988, 2011. *The Modern World-System*, vols. 1–4. New York: Academic Press.

———. 1979. "Kondratieff Up or Down." *Review* 2 (4, Spring): 663–673.

———. 1991. "World System versus World-Systems: A Critique." *Critique of Anthropology* 11 (2): 47–82.

———. 1992. "The West, Capitalism, and the Modern World System." *Review* 15 (4): 561–620.

———. 1999a. *The End of the World as We Know It.* Minnesota: The University of Minnesota Press.

———. 1999b. "Frank Proves the European Miracle." *Review* 22 (3): 355–71.

Warmington, E. H. 1928. *The Commerce between Roman Empire and India.* Cambridge: Cambridge University Press.

Wang, Gungwu. 1958. "The Nanhai Trade: A Study of the Early History of Chinese Trade in Southeast Asia." *Journal of the Malayan Branch of the Royal Asiatic Society* 31 (2): 1–135.

———. 2008. "The China Seas: Becoming an Enlarged Mediterranean." In *The East Asia "Mediterranean" Maritime Cross Roads of Culture, Commerce and Human Migration,* ed. Angela Schoftenhammer, 7–22. Weisbaden: Harrassowitz Verlag.

———. n.d. "Semiterranean Southeast Asia: Between the Ocean." Unpublished Paper.

———. 2015. "Global History: Continental and Maritime." *Asian Review of World Historians* 3 (2): 231–248.

Wang, Kuan-wen, and Caroline Jackson. 2014. "A Review of Glass Compositions around the South China Sea Region (The late 1st Millennium BC to the 1st Millennium AD): Placing Iron Age Glass Beads from Taiwan in Context." *Journal of Indo-Pacific Archaeology* 34: 51–60.

Warmington, E. H. 1928. *The Commerce Between the Roman Empire and India.* Cambridge: Cambridge University Press.

Warren, Peter M. 1985. "Minoan Palaces." *Scientific American* 253 (1): 94–103.

Watrous, L. Vance. 1994. "Review of the Aegean Prehistory III: Crete from Earliest Prehistory through the Protopalatial Period." *American Journal of Archaeology* 98: 695–753.

Weber, Max. 1987. *Economy and Society.* Berkeley: University of California Press.

Weiss, H., and R. Bradley. 2001. "Archaeology: What Drives Societal Collapse?" *Science* 291 (5504): 609–610.

Welch, David. J. 1998. "Archaeology of Northeast Thailand in Relation to Prekhmer and Khmer Historical Records." *International Journal of Historical Archaeology* 2 (3): 205–233.

Wertime, T. A. 1964. "Man's Encounters with Metallurgy." *Science* 146 (3649): 1251–1267.

Wheatley, Paul 1955a. "Tun-Sun." *Journal of the Royal Asiatic Society of Great Britain and Ireland* 1955: 17–30.

———. 1955b. "The Maly Peninsula as Known to the Chinese of the Third Century AD." *Journal of the Malayan Branch of the Royal Asiatic Society* 28 (1): 1–23.

———. 1956. "Langkasuka." *T'oung Pao* 44: 387–412.

———. 1959. "Geographical Notes on Some Commodities Involved in the Sung Maritime Trade." *Journal of the Malayan Branch of the Royal Asiatic Society* 32 (2): 1–40.

———. 1961. *The Golden Khersonese.* Singapore: University of Malaya Press.

———. 1964a. *Desultory Remarks on the Ancient History of the Malayan Peninsula.* Berkeley: University of California Press.

———. 1964b. *Impressions of the Malay Peninsula in Ancient Times.* Singapore: Eastern University Press.

———. 1979. "Urban Genesis in Mainland Southeast Asia." In *Early Southeast Asia,* ed. R. B. Smith and W. Watson, 288–303. Oxford: Oxford University Press.

———. 1982. "Presidential Address: India Beyond the Ganges. Desultory Reflections on the Origin of Civilization in Southeast Asia." *Journal of Asian Studies* 42: 13–28.

———. 1983. *Negara and Commandery. Origins of the Southeast Asian Urban Traditions.* University of Chicago Department of Geography Research Paper #207–208. Chicago: U. of Chicago Committee on Geographical Studies.

Wheeler, Robert Eric Mortimer. 1954. *Rome Beyond the Imperial Frontiers.* London: Bell.

Whitley, James. 1991. *Style and Society in Dark Age Greece: The Changing Face of Pre-Literate Society 1100–700 BC.* Cambridge: Cambridge University Press.

White, Joyce C. 1995. "Incorporating Heterarchy into Theory on Socio-Political Development: The Case from Southeast Asia." In *Heterarchy and the Analysis of Complex Societies*, ed. C. Crumley et al., 101–123. Washington: American Anthropology Association.

White, Joyce C., and E. Hamilton. 2009. "The Transmission of Early Bronze Age Technology to Thailand: New Perspectives." *Journal of World Prehistory* 22 (4): 357–397.

White, Joyce C., Helen Lewis, Bounheuang Bouasisengpaseuth, Ben Marwick, and Katherine Arrell. 2009. "Archaeological Investigations in Northern Laos: New Contributions to Southeast Asian Prehistory." *Antiquity* 83 (319): 145–176.

Whitmore, J. K. 1977. "The Opening of Southeast Asian Trading Patterns through the Centuries." In *Economic Exchange and Social Interaction in Southeast Asia*, ed. Karl L. Hutterer, 139–154. Ann Arbor: Center for South and Southeast Asian Studies.

Wicks, R. S. 1992. *Money, Markets and Trade in Early Southeast Asia. The Development of Indigenous Monetary System to AD 1400.* Ithaca: Cornell University Press.

Wilcox, G. H. 1992. "Timber and Trees: Ancient Exploitation in the Middle East." In *Trees and Timber in Mesopotamia*, ed. J. N. Postgate and M. A. Powell. Bulletin on Sumerian Agriculture 6. Cambridge: Cambridge University.

Wilkinson, David. 2000. "Civilizations, World Systems and Hegemonies." In *World System History: The Social Science of Long-Term Change*, ed. Robert Denemark et al., 54–84. London: Routledge.

Wilkinson, T. J. 1990. *Town and Country in Southeastern Anatolia.* Chicago: Oriental Institute.

Will, Elizabeth. 1991. "The Mediterranean Shipping Amphoras from Arikamedu." In *Rome and India: The Ancient Sea Trade*, ed. Vimala Begley and Richard Daniel DePuma, 151–156. New Delhi: Oxford University Press.

Williams, Michael. 2003. *Deforesting the Earth: From Prehistory to Global Crisis.* Chicago: University of Chicago Press.

Wink, Andre. 1996, 1997. *Al Hind: The Making of the Indo Islamic World*, vols. 1–2. Leiden: Koln.

———. 1988. "'Al Hind' India and Indonesia in the Islamic World Economy c. 700–1800 AD." *Itinerario* 12 (1): 33–72.

Wisserman, Christie, J. 1990. "Trade and State Formation in the Malay Peninsula and Sumatra 300 BC–AD 700." In *The Southeast Asia Port and Polity: Rise and Demise*, ed. J. Kathirilhamby-Wells and J. Villiers. Singapore: Singapore University Press.

———. 1995. "State Formation in Early Maritime Southeast Asia. Bijdragen tot de Taal-Lard en Volkenkunde." 151 (2): 235–288.

Wittfogel, Karl. 1957. *Oriental Despotism.* New Haven: Yale University Press.

Wolf, Eric. 1982. *Europe and the People without History.* Berkeley: University of California Press.

Wolters, O.W. 1967. *Early Indonesian Commerce.* Ithaca, NY: Cornell University Press.

———. 1999. *History, Culture and Region in Southeast Asian Perspective.* Ithaca: Cornell Southeast Asia Publications.

Wood, Frances. 2004. *The Silk Road: 2000 Years in the Heart of Asia*. Berkeley: University of California Press.

Wright, Henry T. 1998. "Developing Complex Societies in Southeast Asia: Using Archaeological and Historical Evidence." *International Journal of Historical Archaeology* 2 (4): 343–348.

Wright, Rita. 2010. *The Ancient Indus*. Cambridge: Cambridge University Press.

Wu, W., and T. Liu. 2004. "Possible Role of the Holocene Event 3 on the Collapse of Neolithic Cultures around the Central Plain of China." *Quaternary International* 117: 153–166.

Xunming, Wang, Chen Fahu, Zhang Jiawu, Yang Yi, Li Jijun, Hasi Eerdun, Zhang Caixia, and Xia Dunsheng. 2010. "Climate, Desertification, and the Rise and Collapse of China's Historical Dynasties." *Human Ecology: An Interdisciplinary Journal* 38 (1): 157–172.

Yamagata, M. 1998. "Formation of Lin-yi Internal and External Factors." *Journal of Southeast Asian Archaeology* 18: 51–89.

Yasuda, Yoshinori. 2008. "Climate Change and the Origin and Development of Rice Cultivation in the Yangtze River Basin, China." *Ambio* 14: 502–506.

Yang, Bin. 2009. *Between Winds and Clouds: The Making of Yunnan*. New York: Columbia University Press.

Yen, D. E. 1977. "Hoabinhian Horticulture: The Evidence and the Question from Northwest Thailand." In *Sunda and Sahal: Prehistoric Studies in Southeast Asia, Melanesia and Australia*, ed. J. Allen et al., 567–599. London: Academic Press.

———. 1982. "Ban Chiang Pottery and Rice." *Expedition* 24 (1) 51–64.

Yian, Goh Geok. 2012. "A Look at Settlement Patterns of 5th–16th Century Sites in Myanmar." In *Connecting Empires and States*, ed. Mai Lin Tjoa-Bonatz et al., 349–361. Singapore: National University of Singapore Press.

Young, Gary K. 2001. *Rome's Eastern Trade*. New York: Routledge.

Yuan, Jinjing, and Xiande Zhang. 1977. "Shang-Period Tombs Excavated in Pinggu County, Beijing." *Beijing Municipal Cultural Relics Office* 11: 1–8.

Zangger, E. 1998. "The Environmental Setting." In *Sandy Pylos*, ed. Jack Davis, 1–9. Austin: University of Texas Press.

Zhang, C., and H. C. Hung. 2010. "The Emergence of Agriculture in Southern China." *Antiquity* 84: 11–25.

Zhanyue, Huang. 1976. "On the Problem of the First Smelting of Iron and Use of Iron Implements in China." *Wen Wu* 8: 62–70.

Zhimin, An. 1984. "Effect of Prehistoric Cultures of the Lower Yangtze River on Ancient Japan." Translated by W. Tsao. *Kaogu* 5: 439–558.

———. 1990. "Ancient Culture of the Lower Yangtze River and Ancient Japan." Translated by W. Tsao. *Kaogu* 4: 375–384.

Zou, Houben. 1984. "Stone-Chamber Tumulus Sites at Wufengshan in Wuxian County, Jiangsu." *Nianjian* 1: 105–106.

Zuraina, Majid. 1990. "The Tapanian Problem Resolved." *Modern Quaternary Research in Southeast Asia* 11: 71–96.

———. 1991. *Prasejarah Malaysia: Sudahkah Zaman Gelap Menjadi Cerah?* Penang: Universiti Sains Malaysia.

Zuraina, Majid, and H. D. Tjia. 1988. "Kota Tampan, Perak: The Geological and Archaeological Evidence for a Late Pleistocene Site." *Journal of the Malayan Branch of the Royal Asiatic Society* 61: 123–134.

Index